DEEP MAP COUNTRY

DEEP MAP COUNTRY

LITERARY CARTOGRAPHY

OF THE GREAT PLAINS

Susan Naramore Maher

UNIVERSITY OF NEBRASKA PRESS

LINCOLN AND LONDON

Acknowledgments for the use of copyrighted
material appear on pages xxiii–xxiv, which
constitute an extension of the copyright page.

Library of Congress Cataloging-
in-Publication Data

Maher, Susan Naramore, author.
Deep Map Country: Literary Cartography of
the Great Plains / Susan Naramore Maher.
pages   cm
Includes bibliographical references and index.
ISBN 978-0-8032-4502-0 (hardback: alk. paper)—
ISBN 978-0-8032-5502-9 (pdf) —
ISBN 978-0-8032-5503-6 (epub)—
ISBN 978-0-8032-5504-3 (mobi)
1. American prose literature—Great
Plains—History and criticism. 2. Great
Plains—In literature. I. Title.
PS274.M34 2014
810.9'97648—dc23
2013041973

Set in Minion by L. Auten.
Designed by Nathan Putens.

CONTENTS

> An effort to understand the historical influence of the Great Plains
> on American civilization would be futile without a clear com-
> prehension of the physical forces that have worked and continue
> to work in that region. These forces, historically speaking, are
> constant and eternal; therefore they make a permanent factor
> in the interpretation of history—one that must be understood.
> Walter Prescott Webb, *The Great Plains*

For twenty-seven years I called the Great Plains home and took
many journeys on national, state, and county roads to explore its
many regions and cultures. I have criss-crossed from east to west
as well as all the way up and down this grand expanse of North
America, from Canada to the southern reaches of the Plains. David
J. Wishart, geographer and editor of the definitive *Encyclopedia of
the Great Plains*, describes the Great Plains in this way: the "distinctive southern boundary of the Great Plains . . . is pinched out
at the Rio Grande by the convergence of the Coastal Plain and the
Mexican Highland section of the Basin and Range province."[1] The
eastern boundary is less clarified. For his volume, Wishart states,
"Our boundary follows the eastern border of the states of North
Dakota, South Dakota, Nebraska, and Kansas, including these
entire units in the region."[2] The Rocky Mountains "from Alberta
to New Mexico" mark "the least ambiguous limit of the Great
Plains" and shape the long western reaches of the grasslands.[3]
In the north, in Canada, "the Parkland Belt of mixed woodland
and grassland and the boreal forest" demarcate the final border
of this immense landscape.[4] Within this physical geography are

natural and cultural dimensions unique to the Plains.[5] It is a space I continue to love with all the ardency of topophilia.[6] When I have reasons to return, by air or land, I feel a reconnection to horizon and sky that delights me to the cellular level.

One of my favorite stops over the years has been to a rest area just east of Grand Island, Nebraska, where artist John Raimondi's sculpture *Erma's Desire* grabs the attention of passers-by. I have written a few essays in which Erma plays a role, but I first became interested in Erma from reading, not traveling, after I had encountered an essay by biologist John Janovy Jr. Opening his second collection, *Back in Keith County*, the essay "Erma's Desire" gives Janovy the opportunity to wax eloquently on the American West, American mobility, and the joys of working west of the hundredth meridian on the high plains of Nebraska. Erma signifies many things to Janovy: "the totality of freedom of uninhibited intellectual exchange, no jockeying for positions of power, the flow of unhindered thoughts open to all interpretations."[7] In looking at Erma's geography—steel points that jut in all directions, vertically and horizontally—Janovy sees "assumed positions of relative importance that depended on their angle of view, a shifting, changing, intellectual experience."[8] The indeterminate nature of Erma is one of her pleasures, and Janovy knows that he is offering just one reading, his, for his readers' consideration. This essay was published in 1981, and in three decades I would imagine Janovy rereading Erma, casting new light on her spires, interpreting her steel body in wholly different ways. The best art inspires variable self-reflection, and I know that my own encounters with Erma on the Plains have altered my readings of her over the years.

I am a map-lover and a mapmaker by nature. As a young girl, I was often my father's navigator when my brother wasn't along, folding and unfolding the maps of states as we traveled through them. Even though I now have cartographic apps on my cell phone to help me navigate places, I still prefer the fanning of air, crinkling of paper, and scanning by finger that published maps, not Google maps, induce. By mapmaker, I don't mean in any conventional sense. I am not a trained geographer. I have always had a good head for directions, creating idiosyncratic maps in my head filled with landmarks and road names to get around places. If dropped in New Providence, New Jersey, today, a town I have not lived in since the 1960s, I could still find my way home from the elementary school that I attended. I could find my way to Indian Lake in the Adirondacks, where my family summered for years, from many directions. Maps, movement, and itinerancy fascinate me.

Erma signifies cartography to me. She points in directions and forces me to consider what her gestures mean in terms of place. Installed at a Grand Island, Nebraska, interstate rest stop, close by one of the great migratory paths in North America for humans and nonhumans alike—most recently for sojourners on Interstate 80— Erma embodies movement. The Platte River valley is famous for its role in the early nineteenth-century fur trade and mid-nineteenth-century Oregon Trail migration to California that swelled after the discovery of gold in the Sierra Nevada. Erma stands in alliance with ways west. But her pointing limbs reach in other directions as well, making her body a complex crossroads that aligns well with the actual movements of people and animals over many millennia. Indigenous trails move multidirectionally. Sandhill cranes fly through here, congregating by the tens of thousands each spring along the Platte, one of the great northward migrations that predates human habitation on the Plains.[9] Northward movement also signifies modern immigration, much of it from Mexico and Central America, which has changed the demographics of the grasslands. More abstractly, Erma presents horizontal and vertical planes, the most basic geometry of this enveloping landscape. The dominant horizontal vista of the river valley makes anything vertical literally stand out. Erma sits resplendently on waving grasses and forbs, unmoved since her installation. She is rooted to this particular part of the Nebraska Plains. Though controversial at first as a piece of abstract art some felt impractical and wasteful, Erma now seems at home among all the other human relics of this place.

Erma is suggestively poststructural in her cartography and for me a powerful trope of this book's focus: deep map country. Her way is many ways, her meaning is many meanings, her essence is paradox. She refutes linearity, digs complexity, and voices many truths. Her spirit reflects that of the last two generations of writers of the Plains who seek a new understanding of the American West and the Canadian prairies, of what it means to be from this singular yet complicated landscape, and of the intersections of nature and humanity, of time and space, and of region and planet.

I have worked in studied collaboration with many other scholars and writers to find my way into deep map country, and I would have been lost without them. The deep map owes its existence to William Least Heat-Moon, who subtitled his masterwork *PrairyErth*: *(a deep map)*. His concept is the starting point of my cartographical exploration of Great Plains spaces, but a number of related concepts wend their way through my chapters as well. Any cartographical reality is a rendering of space. Gaston Bachelard's *La poétique de l'espace*, published in 1958 and translated into English in 1964, remains a classic text on spatial meaning, or, as the subtitle in the English translation puts it, "how we experience intimate places." Bachelard's poetics examines a spectrum of spaces, from small, human-made spaces like cellars, attics, wardrobes, or dresser drawers, to enormous natural spaces. It isn't the size of the space that matters, but how individuals remember these spaces, imagine them, and feel them. Humans grasp the poetic truths of spaces in dreams; this poetic, symbolic configuration of space is particularly important to the group of writers I present. The material matrix of the Plains is the portal into interior, lyrical musings, which drift in many directions, including the ineffable and spiritual. Bachelard intimates other dimensions of space as well that matter to deep map writers: dialectics of inside and outside, movement and stasis, sacred and profane, imminent and transcendent.

Geographer Yi-Fu Tuan, in such groundbreaking works as *Topophilia: A Study of Environmental Perception, Attitudes, and Values* (1974) and *Space and Place: The Perspective of Experience* (1977), also examines the experiential nature of space, how one feels about one's surroundings. He writes, in *Space and Place*, that

> human beings require both space and place. Human lives are a dialectical movement between shelter and venture, attachment and freedom. In open space one can become intensely aware of place; and in the solitude of a sheltered place the vastness of space beyond acquires a haunting presence. A healthy being welcomes constraint and freedom, the boundedness of place and the exposure of space.[10]

Again, this dialectical perspective on space connects to deep map writing, which is multivalent and complex. Tuan's interest in the intersection of vertical and horizontal planes has helped me discern the axes at play in deep map narrative from the Plains, and his argument that "space and time coexist, intermesh, and define each other in personal experience" is confirmed repeatedly in the stories that deep map writers present.[11]

Topophilia has proved highly influential in environmental writing. Tuan mentions the Great Plains in this study, examining the experiences of farmers during times of environmental stresses. "Attachment to place," he argues, "can also emerge, paradoxically, from the experience of nature's intransigence."[12] Those individuals who chose to endure the hardships of dryland conditions on the Plains do so, he says, out of a love "for the soil and the challenge of making a go of it."[13] Increasingly, those who are making a go of it are learning to read the land that they love more carefully, revising their attitudes toward agriculture and husbandry. Deep map writers present the accumulated knowledge of loved places to assist in the living and survival of place and people. Topophiles understand that forces of topocide coexist with their efforts. Deep map writers of the Plains see themselves in a struggle against culture's intransigence.

Bachelard and Tuan both address the contradictory impulses of homing in and moving out, what Susan Stanford Friedman, in her impressive study *Mappings: Feminism and the Cultural Geographies of Encounter* (1999), calls the "symbiosis" of "roots/routes."[14] Friedman discerns that the body is itself a place of encounter, a cartographical embodiment of contexts and axes. "I am struck by the centrality of space," she admits, "to the locations of identity within the mappings and re-mappings of ever-changing cultural formations."[15] To understand any one individual, we must realize that "as a historically embedded site, a positionality, a location, a standpoint, a terrain, an intersection, a network, a crossroads of multiply situated knowledges," identity is no simple matter.[16] To imagine such a layered narrative of self, one must turn to methodologies of hybridity, complexity, and depth.

In this "geographics," Friedman's term for "locational feminism," a dialectic of roots and routes develops.[17] These homonymic words exist in relationship, a creative dynamic. One longs for the knowledge of both. This textual and visual mapping of self requires "greater fluidity" and discernment.[18] It also insists that individuals are sites of contact and separation, borders and commons, and oppression and resistance. An understanding of place emerges from an understanding of the corporeal map. All of my deep map writers underscore bodily negotiation in play with cultural and natural forces. These bodies are gendered as well, an important facet of Stanford Friedman's mappings. They are intensely aware that the axes of productive and oppressive power, of social construction and systemic nature, define them and the places that they study and love.

The importance of this bodily negotiation is underscored in the work of Kristie S. Fleckenstein, who first articulated her theory of somatics in "Writing Bodies," a 1999 article in *College English*. "Using the work of cultural anthropologist Gregory Bateson," she writes, "I define the somatic mind as a 'being-in-a-material-place,' whose fluid and permeable boundaries are (re)constituted through the mutual play of discursive and corporeal coding."[19] Somatic experience requires "immersion and emergence, of pleasure and commitment."[20] To give a view from somewhere—say the Great Plains—a writer must be located "within concrete spatiotemporal contexts."[21] One must also "[recognize] the cultural, historical, and ecological systems that penetrate and reconstitute these material places."[22] Deep mappers from the Plains become adept at this sort of reconstitution, this negotiation of place through other ways of knowing. The body of the land and the body of the writer merge in creative textual fusion in deep map writing.

The concept of literary cartography crystallized in two important studies of American landscape writing, Kent C. Ryden's *Mapping the Invisible Landscape: Folklore, Writing, and the Sense of Place* (1993) and Rick Van Noy's *Surveying the Interior: Literary Cartographers and the Sense of Place* (2003). Ryden's chapter, "Of Maps and Minds," examines cartography as more than a literal, mimetic mapping of a landscape. Honoring the art and science of mapmaking, he explains that "through the precise graphic shorthand of modern cartography, [mapmakers] have been able to summarize in a very small space a wealth of topographical and cultural information that would otherwise have taken pages and pages of verbal description and mathematical figures to contain."[23] What such a map cannot contain is the feel of legs on an incline, a memory of a fall drive, the nuances of a river. "Maps," Ryden concludes, "have their limitations."[24] Writing at the time of Heat-Moon's publication of *PrairyErth*, Ryden shares this work's gestalt: "Where the map fails, however, the imagination takes over."[25] The reality of maps is that "they can inspire imagination, emotion, and words."[26]

Ryden's interest in folklore has given him another perspective on maps: folk narrative is alive in any place, "dwelling in the invisible landscape."[27] Deepness and depth become operative words in Ryden's analysis. The surface experiences of landscape are only a port of entry for literary cartographers. These artists limn a matrix of communal and personal memory, competing histories, and polyvocal narrative, "a world of deep and subtle meaning."[28] With an explosion of deep map writing in the 1990s and beyond, Ryden's study helped many scholars understand how landscapes take on meaning, how literary mapmaking expands over and beneath the surface reality.

Rick Van Noy's work on nineteenth- and twentieth-century nonfiction writers of place provides a working definition of literary cartography. "A literary cartographer not only examines how maps function in literary texts," he comments, "or how maps in themselves can tell a story, but also how literature can be used for cartographic means: to control, order, or limn a place."[29] Van Noy, writing after Heat-Moon and Ryden, discusses both writers and extends their metaphors of deepness and invisibility in new directions. The interior that he reads is not only the American landscape; it is the idiosyncratic method of distinctive authors, the idiolect of personal literary mapmaking that absorbs his attention. Looking at such diverse texts as Thoreau's *Walden* (1854) and *The Maine Woods* (1864), Clarence King's *Mountaineering in the Sierra Nevada* (1872), John Wesley Powell's *The Explorations of the Colorado River of the West and Its Tributaries* (1875), and Wallace Stegner's *Wolf Willow* (1962), Van Noy provides a comprehensive examination of important American literary mapmakers. His readings of a number of texts in my own study have been formative for me. While Van Noy does not focus on the deep map per se, his insights into the literary mapping of America are indispensable. His conclusion—"what maps may tell us about places, if we pause long enough to look at them, is how much we don't know"—is crucial to the deep map.[30] Literary cartographers enter complex space that often leaves them in inconclusive, illegible territory.

In the first decade of the twenty-first century, a number of scholars, including myself, began to discuss the emergence of the deep map as a significant environmental genre.[31] Most significant was Randall Roorda's proclamation, in a 2001 special issue of *Michigan Quarterly Review*, entitled "Reimagining Place," that the deep map is "an incipient genre of environmental writing."[32] Roorda notes that "[w]here maps and ordinary experience of place were once equally personalized and scarcely separable, a rift between subjective familiarity and objectified cartography has widened in modern times, and nonfiction writers on nature have sought to dramatize this antinomy."[33] Citing Kent Ryden's memorable 1993 study as a powerful influence, Roorda continues, "This 'depth,' this sedimentation of impressions and, especially, texts (since history is textual) underlying a sense of place, is what Heat-Moon sets out to 'map' in *PrairyErth*, in the process exhausting nearly every resource of observation, record, reminiscence, myth, and impression Chase County can afford him."[34] In the same year, I published "Deep Mapping the Great Plains" in *Western American Literature*, declaring that deep mapping is a signature intergenerational effort of Plains writers. My original argument is embedded into chapter 1. More recently, in 2011, the remix ejournal *Journal of the Imaginary and Fantastic* brought together a number of previously published essays on the deep map. The issue, entitled "Deep Maps: Liminal Histories and the Located Imagination," marks a crystallization of scholarship on the deep map.[35]

Neil Campbell, who studies the American West from his academic post in Derby in the United Kingdom, has written two studies that have guided some of my thinking on the deep map genre: *The Cultures of the American New West* (2000) and *The Rhizomatic West: Representing the American West in a Transnational, Global, Media Age* (2008). In his first book, Campbell examines a plethora of "New West" writers and notes "its heterogeneity and its hybrid, relational texture."[36] Moreover, "to achieve this requires a new mapping: simultaneous, dialogical, sensitive to diverse histories and voices, and to the relations that exist between them."[37] Noting such theorists of space as M. M. Bakhtin, Edward Soja, Henri Lefebvre, Michel Foucault, among others, as well as New Western historians like Patricia Nelson Limerick, Donald Worster, William Cronin, and Richard White, Campbell argues for the necessity of a "new spatial, cultural geohistory of the American West" that gives way to "*Wests*—plural, multidimensional, imbricated, and contradictory."[38] He could be describing the textual domain of the deep map.

In his examination of the "rhizomatic" West, Campbell furthers his adaptation of geospatial theory, focusing on Gilles Deleuze's and Félix Guattari's metaphor of the rhizome.[39] Again, examining contemporary writers who "deframe" the West, Campbell articulates a poststructural cartography of folded, relational, "transmotional" space where an "interplay of roots and routes" disrupts any monological representation of this region.[40] Campbell speaks directly to the grid of cartography, what Heat-Moon connects to Thomas Jefferson and the great surveys of western American territories, noting that "the gridlike literal and metaphoric patterns of mapping, perceiving, and representing are in need of constant rearrangement and dismantling" if a complex, rhizomatic, deep version of Western stories is to supplant a powerful, static, and mythic view of a won West.[41] Citing Arjun Appadurai, Campbell argues for a new architecture of American regional studies that dismantles "seeing the West as a fixed, permanent geographical and ideological fact."[42] Again, deep map writing seeks just such a new reading of the West, on both sides of the forty-ninth parallel.

While the sources and influences of much of my conceptualizing go beyond the distillation of scholars that I present in this preface, I want to highlight three other significant scholars of the

Great Plains: Robert Thacker, Diana Dufva Quantic, and John T. Price. Thacker's *The Great Prairie Fact and Literary Imagination* (1989) sets the coordinates of all future studies of the Plains with his focus on the land itself, his considerable literary history of the Plains going back to the first days of contact, his cross-border, biome-centric view of Plains literary production, and his careful, persuasive readings of nonfiction and fiction writers as diverse as Pedro de Castañeda, John Palliser, Washington Irving, Hamlin Garland, Willa Cather, and Robert Kroetsch. In Thacker's assessment, "prairie writing reveals that whether a person is traveling through, settling on, or living on the prairie, 'the great fact' has always been and is still 'the land itself.'"[43] Thacker studies many more writers than this list, providing a comprehensive view of Plains literary imaginers over many centuries and an elegant model of border-crossing analysis. His comments on Wallace Stegner, Canadian history, and literary geographers, travelers, surveyors, and adventurers have been invaluable for me.

Following Thacker's study, Quantic's *The Nature of the Place: A Study of Great Plains Fiction* (1995) examines the history, myths, and biological realities of Plains life as depicted in fiction. Like Thacker, she declares the primacy of the land itself over this literary history. She also discerns the cultural difference between American and Canadian Plains fiction, based more in myth than lived reality. Quantic's study is built upon themes; rather than give extended close readings of selected texts, she surveys writers through the many layers of myth that attempt to define this vast and varied space. Nonfiction writers do not claim her particular interest, though she does, like Thacker, discuss formative nonfiction works of travel, geography, and history. Her comprehensive, macrostudy of the Plains has deeply impressed me and convinced me that it needed a counterpart that examined nonfiction writing.

Thacker and Quantic write from the Plains because each is committed to this landscape through experience and scholarship.

Equally attuned to this region is John T. Price's *Not Just Any Land: A Personal and Literary Journey into the American Grassland* (2004), which begins with a personal quest to write from the landscape that he loves, the Trans-Mississippi West of Iowa, Missouri, and Kansas where much of his family history has played out. Price sees his work as memoir because much of his personal story is interwoven among the contexts of literary readings, interviews, and history. In turning to writers Linda Hasselstrom, Dan O'Brien, William Least Heat-Moon, and Mary Swander, he is attempting to discover why each has stayed close to the landscape that he or she writes about. Two of these writers, Hasselstrom and Heat-Moon, figure largely in my study of deep maps. Price's interviews with them and his careful reading of their works have provided me with a significant understanding of place-based writing. Price is adamant about the value and beauty of the North American grasslands, a passion that he shares with me. As such, his memoir is charged with environmental advocacy. He and the writers he studies believe that the Great Plains are threatened by misuse of its resources, by disregard for its subtleties, and by cultural neglect of its peoples.

I could not have furthered my own study of nonfiction writers of the Great Plains without the models embodied by these three scholars. Scholarship from New West historians, cultural geographers, ecocritics, and a new generation of literary readings on both sides of the border also persuaded me that a focus on the literary deep map was timely and a corresponding part of the ongoing conversation on western spaces.

Which brings me back to Erma and her desire. When she was brought from Raimondi's studio to the rest area near Grand Island, Erma was part of a bicentennial celebration, one of a number of art works placed along Interstate 80 across Nebraska. Perhaps part of her controversy, apart from Erma's abstract construction, which will always garner its share of critics, was the nature of the bicentennial itself. Following the unsettling, divisive years of the Vietnam War, the bicentennial released considerable cultural bombast, the kind of flag-waving and myth-pronouncing theater that inspires political factions to this day. Over several centuries, the Great Plains has witnessed the efforts to win and settle the West in the nineteenth century and loomed large in ideas of a receding frontier, Manifest Destiny, American exceptionalism, and pioneer heroics. Interstate 80 itself follows one of the primary trails across this frontier, this space of westering movement and national destiny.

But Erma is a muse to ambiguity, contradiction, and contrariness. In my view, she stands in resistance to any one way to read the West. Her desire is for many stories, not a master story, many viewpoints and dimensions. Reclining in grasslands, she apparently looks up to the sky and opens her limbs to the landscape. Her figure desires the landscape, what looks to be "original" landscape of grasses and forbs (despite the nearby rest area and farms). So little remains of this ancient biome that Erma could be the muse of restitution as well. When I encounter Erma, I have the impulse to walk around her, lie down next to her, lean against her, point with her. An object that suggests both routes and roots, she projects restlessness and placed-ness. One must negotiate Erma, just as one must negotiate the landscape surrounding her. An emblem of the deep map, Erma expounds navigation, engagement, and complexity. Her desire leads to openness and exploration, not to closure. Erma inspirits beginnings. What follows is an exploration of the deep map, and my hope is that many others will investigate this form of writing and discern even more than I have been able to articulate in this study.

ACKNOWLEDGMENTS

In charting this study of literary cartography, I have been fortunate to have many generous colleagues serve as sounding boards, early readers, and enthusiastic cheerleaders. Their critique, commentary, and reading suggestions motivated me to stay the course and complete this project. Many of the essential navigators of this study are peers and colleagues in the Western Literature Association. In particular, I would like to thank Drs. Alan Weltzien, David Mogen, Neil Campbell, David Peterson, Bob Thacker, and Melody Graulich for their formative help and astute advice. Melody, as editor of *Western American Literature*, gave me important feedback on an early version of chapter 1 that appeared in the journal. The annual WLA meeting allowed me to share work in progress, to have scholarly conversations with colleagues working in parallel with me, and to hear from other scholars and writers who informed my thinking. What a rich matrix of people and ideas!

From many corners of North America and abroad, annual WLA meetings bring together exceptional scholars and people, all passionate about the literature and culture of the North American West. I want to thank former WLA president Dr. Diane Quantic for her support, especially for allowing me to use Cabin Q in the Rockies for a few weeks of undisturbed writing. The May snowfall kept me in the cabin, where I hunkered down for days of productive drafting.

Poets Eamonn Wall and Drucilla Mims Wall have been along on this deep mapping journey from the start. We have shared many trips to western places, including a memorable ride across the Sand Hills of Nebraska, and a shimmering summer in western Ireland.

Over teacups and wine glasses, we have discussed literature, life, and families—conversations that leave imprints and shape ideas. Their art and intellectual work has been an inspiration to me.

Colleagues at the University of Nebraska at Omaha have also been central in this decade-long scholarly exploration. Dr. John J. McKenna has given me wise counsel and unwavering support. Photographer and nonfiction writer Dr. Phil Smith listened to my work and gave me instructive feedback. Dr. Mike Skau has been a model scholar and a generous mentor. Dr. Christina Dando, a cultural geographer with a passion for the Plains, kept feeding me books and articles from her discipline and in the process reshaped my thinking. Especially important for me has been Dr. John Price, a formidable scholar of the Plains and one of the region's most significant creative nonfiction writers. John always believed in my book project, giving me encouragement, feedback, and timely nudges when necessary. Reading his work has been revelatory for me.

The University of Nebraska at Omaha awarded me two sabbaticals that were essential for drafting this book, and I am grateful for the support I received from two deans, the late Dr. John Flocken and Dr. Shelton Hendricks. When I moved to an administrative position as dean of the College of Liberal Arts at the University of Minnesota Duluth, I received outstanding financial support from Vice Chancellor Vince Magnuson. He insisted that I maintain my identity as a scholar and gave me the resources to do so. I want to especially thank Dean Gregory Sadlek at Cleveland State University for his collegial support and friendship. I have been very fortunate in the academic leadership that has supported me over the years.

I have been equally fortunate with the academic press I am working with. The staff at the University of Nebraska Press has been exceptionally helpful. In particular, I want to thank Kristen Elias Rowley, humanities acquisitions editor, for her support of my work. Wesley N. Piper assisted me along the way with my questions and concerns. The anonymous readers of my submitted manuscript provided me with invaluable revision advice. I also want to thank them for their confidence in the value of this study. Their positive and enthusiastic support of publication has given me that final boost of energy I needed to complete this book. This finished book is a stronger articulation of the deep map genre as a result of their careful reading of my manuscript.

I grew up in a family that read and enjoyed long car trips. What great preparation for studying literary cartography and deep maps. Those many miles on the road instilled in me a love of long distance, which served me well when I left the East Coast and took up residence on the Plains. My children, Dana Craig and Anna-Turi Maher, have shared in many of the journeys at home and on vacations that led to this book's inception. They have been wonderful companions along the way, and I thank them for their patience during those years when I was juggling the many tasks of an academic career. With my husband, Al Kammerer, I have traveled thousands of miles across the American and Canadian West and spent indelible time in many landscapes: grasslands, mountains, desert, and Pacific coastal. He also bought me my first Stetson hat and pair of cowgirl boots. If I have any right to claim some connection to the grasslands, as an adoptive Plains daughter, it is because of Al. Nebraska born, he has been a true guide into the many Plains landscapes of the deep map.

Portions of this book were previously published and appear here with permission of the original publishers. An early version of chapter 1 first appeared as "Deep Mapping the Great Plains: Surveying the Literary Cartography of Place," *Western American Literature* 36, no. 1 (2001): 4–24. An earlier, much abbreviated version of chapter 2 originally appeared as "Deep Mapping History: Wallace Stegner's *Wolf Willow* and William Least Heat-Moon's *PrairyErth: A Deep Map*," *Heritage of the Great Plains* 38, no. 1 (Spring/Summer 2005): 39–54. An early version of chapter 3, without Wes Jackson, appeared as "Deep Mapping the Biome: The Biology of Place in Don Gayton's *The Wheatgrass Mechanism* and John Janovy Jr.'s *Dunwoody Pond*," *Great Plains Quarterly* 25, no. 1 (2005): 7–27. Material in chapters 2, 3, and 5 was adapted with permission from "Deep Map Country: Proposing a *Dinnseanchas* Cycle of the Northern Plains," *Studies in Canadian Literature/Études en literature canadienne* 34, no. 1 (2009): 160–81. Portions of chapter 4 were previously published in *Artifacts and Illuminations: Critical Essays on Loren Eiseley*, ed. Tom Lynch and Susan N. Maher (Lincoln: University of Nebraska Press, 2013), 55–76. Used by permission of the University of Nebraska Press. Copyright 2012 by the Board of Regents of the University of Nebraska.

DEEP MAP COUNTRY

CHAPTER ONE

DEEP MAPPING THE GREAT PLAINS

Surveying the Literary Cartography of Place

> Since the first settlers arrived on the Great Plains, we have been
> trying to come to terms with the physical reality and the psycho-
> logical significance of open space. Our concept of the region is
> encapsulated in a tangle of phrases and images—the Garden of
> the World, the Great American Desert, the closed frontier, Mani-
> fest Destiny, the safety valve, democratic utopia. . . . Continuing
> efforts to define the region—the prairies as the ultimate ecological
> system, the romance or the reality of the plains frontier, the Great
> Plains wheat acreage as the ideal family farm—provide a kind of
> litmus test for the nation's state of mind.
>
> Diane Dufva Quantic, *The Nature of the Place*

In *The Way to Rainy Mountain*, N. Scott Momaday proclaims,
"[o]nce in his life a man ought to concentrate his mind upon the
remembered earth, I believe. He ought to give himself up to a
particular landscape in his experience, to look at it from as many
angles as he can, to wonder about it, to dwell upon it."[1] Momaday's
incantational passage speaks to memory that is tangible, that is
tied to a landscape that one can touch and hear, a landscape that
is shared through generations with other species and that imprints
its elemental forces upon the minds of dwellers. Like a painter,

each individual must also "recollect the glare of noon and all the colors of the dawn and the dusk."[2] Momaday's extended poetic essay presents a journey, what the author calls "a whole journey, intricate with motion and meaning."[3] What gives this journey urgency is aftermath: Momaday's grandmother came of age during the Indian Wars; she witnessed "the last Kiowa Sun Dance . . . held in 1887 on the Washita River above Rainy Mountain Creek."[4] Under orders from the United States government, U.S. Army soldiers in July 1890 forbad future ceremonies at the medicine tree, on which the Kiowas had "impale[d] the head of a buffalo bull" when bison were plentiful.[5] After the decimation of the bison herds, the Kiowas "had to hang an old hide from the sacred tree."[6] Then ceremonies stopped. Momaday soberly writes, "My grandmother was there. Without bitterness, and for as long as she lived, she bore a vision of deicide."[7] For a woman in whom "the immense landscape of the continental interior lay like memory in her blood," prayer gives expression for "suffering and hope."[8] "She began in a high and descending pitch," Momaday explains, "exhausting her breath to silence; then again and again—and always with the same intensity of effort, of something that is, and is not, like urgency in the human voice."[9] A lifetime of prayerful mourning defines her response to this history.

Momaday's task as writer is to counter that deicide, to re-present the landscape of the central Great Plains and to re-vision its role in sheltering the Kiowa people, providing for their subsistence, and embodying the narrative and sacred ceremonies of the ancestors.[10] In the trajectory of his journey, Momaday recovers history, particularly that of the nineteenth century, retells Kiowa stories, and bears witness to the changes that U.S. policies forced upon the Plains landscape and its Native peoples. The vanguard of white adventurers and military men prepared for the huge numbers of homesteaders, who aimed to settle on the Plains, vastly outnumbering the Kiowa and other tribes. The span of one woman's life lies within the larger story of the Kiowas and the even grander story of the Plains' biome.

Settlement on the Plains plowed open the biome, spurred on a dislocation of epic proportions for Native Americans, and restructured human cultures on the Plains. As William Least Heat-Moon explains in his tour de force, *PrairyErth*, the Jeffersonian grid platted the Plains, a remapping that served an economic system and an organization of towns and farms alien to the many tribes. The effects of this system have been far reaching. Donald Worster, in his biography of geologist John Wesley Powell, gives this description of "the federal land system, at once highly complex and deceivingly simple":

> The brainchild of Thomas Jefferson, who hoped to create a nation firmly secured in the hands of small, independent farmers, the land system began with passage of the Land Ordinance in 1785, which established a uniform survey of all land west of Pennsylvania into rectangles called townships, each six miles square. A single township contained, after completion of a map, thirty-six uniform sections of 640 acres each; the sections could be further broken down into half-sections, quarter-sections, or quarter-of-a-quarter sections. From the base point where the Ohio River crosses the Pennsylvania state line, a series of grid lines called ranges marched westward, establishing coordinates for the whole system and enabling anyone in Washington, D.C., Jackson, Ohio, or Chicago, Illinois, to put a finger precisely on the map location of a given piece of land. The simplicity of the system was appealing to a people who had experienced all the uncertainties and irregularities of using the land's own features as boundary markers. . . . On the other hand, the simplicity gained by ignoring the natural contours of the land levied a long-term cost on settlers, politicians, and later on land-use planners who had to wrestle with the manifold discrepancies between a simple, rational geometry and a messy, complicated terrain.[11]

Scholar Neil Campbell further emphasizes that the grid organizes space in "powerful checkerboard symmetries . . . seemingly cutting up and arranging nature into culture, ordering chaotic flows into a defined 'schedule.'"[12] The grid ignores the contours and variances of landscape, imposing an abstract geometry that serves to "control . . . [possess] . . . and [acculturate] . . . nature itself."[13] The grid desacralizes the landscape and subjects it to material desire, use, and exchange. Such reorganization of the Plains was anathema to the nomadic, seminomadic, and village cultures of Plains Native people.[14] For the many Indigenous peoples, the policies that promoted deicide also brought topocide and genocide to the land and its First People.

Momaday presents the desolating effects of this conquest in his narrative. The modern history of the Kiowa is "short-lived, ninety or a hundred years, say, from about 1740."[15] Its decline, hastened after 1875, left "very little material evidence that it had ever been."[16] Loss disturbs much of Momaday's recollection, but he also champions imagination, "a remarkably rich and living verbal tradition," and the enduring power of story and song.[17] Death in many forms darkens his chapters, but the light of "sacred earth," of ceremony and vision, acts as a pulling force against violence and tragedy. His grandmother's journey traces the paths of darkness and light, and her death places the author in a crossroads. He chooses the fullness of life's experience and sees his life folded into "a landscape that is incomparable, a time that is gone forever, and the human spirit, which endures."[18] Where paths or axes transit, Momaday finds meaning that requires the temporal and the spatial—domains of mortality—and yet grasps the subtle reverberations of the eternal. From his grandmother's stories, he embraces what Leanne Simpson has called the "strong and courageous" choices of ancestors. Her statement from Canada that the "reclamation of Indigenous lands, the revitalization of Indigenous traditions of governance and cultural teachings, and the revival of Indigenous environmental philosophies are a direct result of the strength of our Ancestors" speaks just as convincingly for Native people south of the forty-ninth parallel.[19] Colonization radically disturbed the relationship between Indigenous communities and their traditional lands. By reembracing the ancient narratives, Indigenous peoples have maps to guide them into renewed traditions.

The first wave of Great Plains settlement in the semiarid reaches of the United States and Canada—migrations that gained momentum after the Civil War and the great survey of the forty-ninth parallel—prefigured later diminishment. The challenging landscape and climate of the Plains, well-studied by Plains Native or First Nations people, were never suited for the small acreages and farming techniques of the eastern woodlands or northern and central Europe. Land rushes invariably led to exoduses, to failed or stressed communities and narratives of misery and marginal subsistence. Many communities on the Plains that survived west of the hundredth meridian are smaller than they were a century ago, and those settlements that have adapted their labors to the global economy understand their vulnerability in a way that early settlers and boosters could not. Mythologies have grown up around settlement, stories that celebrate rugged individualism, hardy, taciturn men and women who braved the elements and defeated all challenges, thus assisting in nation building, expanding cultural dominion, and closing the frontier. The Plains have loomed large as cultural iconography; the massive horizon and endless sky have provided an epic backdrop for fictional and cinematic representations of the winning of the West. But heroic scales are readily deflated by the losses, tragedies, and failures of real people. The Jeffersonian grid system, a national tool of colonization and yeoman ascendancy, proved less ideal and durable in practice. From an airplane, one still sees the outline of this grid in the road and crop layout; towns on the Plains are built around perpendicular crossings. Yet where crop circles articulate the requirements of central pivot irrigation, an efficient adaptation in semiarid land, and where human populations are now so low that millions of acres are reverting to wilderness (defined as two people per square mile), one can see a necessary rebalancing of efforts on the Plains, a reassessment of late nineteenth-century homesteading. In the twenty-first century, Momaday's vision of the Plains, grounded in longer history and respectful practice, resonates as a guide to place while the oeuvre of western expansion withers in its influence. The descendants of those earlier settlement migrations understand that they need new stories for living on the Plains. Stories that put front and center adaptation to a unique biome, that reassert the spiritual essence of place, and that look critically and creatively at human practices on the Plains are increasingly replacing narratives of winning, conquering, and mastering.

Historians like Elliott West have warned that simple, linear, triumphant narrative can no longer give us the understanding that we need of western North American emplacement. In both *The Way to the West* (1995) and *The Contested Plains* (1998), West considers the need for new stories and narrative structures. In *The Way to the West*, he remarks that "understanding the West is never by clean lines but by indirection and by webs of changing connections among people, plants, institutions, arrivals, politics, soil, weather, ambitions, and perceptions."[20] Additionally, he argues in *The Contested Plains*, we must "take into account the deep and the recent past, the interwoven choices of Indians and whites, and the inseparability of the environment from human society and action."[21] Parallel to Momaday's way, West's argument for a revised narrative foregrounds the biome, studies desire and human cognition, analyzes economic and social reality, and resists the pull of grandiose myth. His call for stories—"not those brought in but the ones built from the roots up"—mirrors the arguments of his contemporaries.[22]

Neil Campbell, in *The Cultures of the American New West*, has called this approach the "new spatial geo-history."[23] Rather than "totalizing" and "unifying," such histories seek narratives "in which many voices speak, many, often contradictory, histories are told, and many ideologies cross, coexist, and collide."[24] His most recent work, *The Rhizomatic West*, argues that the "metanarrative" of national identity belies "the West as a more complex text."[25] Campbell presents a "rhizomatic" rendering of the West—which includes the Great Plains—that scans for "connections, trails, traces, pathways, and echoes," that "[peels] back the layers of a complex, unending palimpsest," and that "[follows] glints and glances" to discern the multiple, dialogical dimensions of western spaces.[26] A decade separates West's and Campbell's work, reminding us that the work of new western narrative has taken some time, but these authors are part of an intergenerational argument to reexamine the multiple histories of the Plains and the West to help secure the future of this great expanse for the diverse people who call this landscape home.

For the last two generations, scholars and writers studying the effects of settlement on the Great Plains have been attempting intercalated narratives in an effort "to tell where and who they are."[27] Inspired by paradigm shifts across disciplines, these writers build stories using intricate, often paradoxical webs of cause and effect, loss and gain, natural and cultural forces, and of deep time and human time. The push and pull of dynamic influences has, in but two centuries, irrevocably altered the Great Plains biome, its human economies, and its store of natural resources. In the face of such massive upheaval and resettlement, many writers would agree with Donald Worster's assertion that "[we] need new kinds of heroes, a new appreciation of nature's powers of recovery, and a new sense of purpose in this region—all of which means we need a new past, one with the struggle for adaptation as its main narrative, one that regards successful adaptation as a kind of heroism too."[28] Whether one characterizes the old stories as paradigms, myths, or fighting words, Worster reminds us, narratives involving archetypes of human achievement and failure shape our sense of the past and our frame for the future.

In the aftermath of government-sponsored settlement, the need for new stories seems particularly urgent. The darker events of Plains history—genocide, species extermination, extractive farming practices, boom-and-bust cycles, Dust Bowl–proportion catastrophes—cast a long shadow over the present. "To many of us today," scientist Wes Jackson writes, "it seems tragic that our ancestors should have so totally blasphemed the grasslands with their moldboards . . . it was one of the two or three worst atrocities committed by Americans."[29] Candace Savage tells us that the "introduction of intensive agriculture" created a headlong momentum that seemed unstoppable: "Within less than half a human lifetime, between the 1870s and the 1920s, wildfire was brought under control by the settlers, the bison were killed off, and a mind-boggling expanse of grassland was brought under cultivation."[30] In the shadow of this past history, the future, demanding wiser human adaptation, appears uncertain. Writers comb the voices from the past for neglected wisdom while deliberating over current ideologies and practices for point. The assault upon place, meanwhile, continues to reflect what James Howard Kunstler has called "the geography of nowhere." In dystopian mood, Kunstler argues, "we have become accustomed to living in places where nothing relates to anything else, where disorder, unconsciousness, and the absence of respect reign unchecked."[31] Echoing Kunstler, William Bevis bemoans "the no-place of capitalist modernity" that affronts an appreciation of region and love of particular places.[32]

The Great Plains, whose ecosystem fell in quick order to the demands of Manifest Destiny, population growth, and, lately, industrial agriculture, has in recent historical memory served as a blank slate for human desire. As Richard Manning, Sharon Butala, and others have emphasized, when Euro-American settlers dismissed the accumulated knowledge of the many Plains tribes and métis cultures, to impose an agriculture evolved in wetter, forested regions and based on Jeffersonian yeoman mythology, they embraced "a century full of nonsense about the grassland."[33] Guided by misguided, deeply flawed maps and lore, settlers inevitably misread the land they claimed. A healthy respect for the Plains grasslands, Manning argues, "can only be taught by an unforgiving terrain."[34] The settlers' unwitting disrespect for place came with long-term costs that Plains inhabitants still tally.

From presettlement days forward, Plains writers and storytellers representing many literary and cultural traditions have addressed the changing face of the land. As Diane Quantic attests, "Great Plains writers share a conviction that one must first come to terms with this vast stretch of space that leaves no place to hide from the physical emptiness or psychological horrors that trick one with mirages of water or ghosts from the past."[35] Saskatchewan writer Sharon Butala speaks to the land's "elemental" power: "The landscape is so huge that our imaginations can't contain it or outstrip it, and the climate is concomitantly arbitrary and severe."[36] Great Plains writers, as a group, wrestle with the very "fact" of the land.[37]

Deserving particular notice is a dynamic, contemporary tradition of nonfiction writing focused on the environment and nature of the Plains. In the late twentieth and nascent twenty-first centuries, we find a renaissance of Plains nonfiction writers—essayists of place, to use Kim Stafford's term—grappling to understand and map the attempted or inadvertent erasure of rich natural and Indigenous histories and the subsequent effects on the Euro-American and Canadian cultures that gained dominion.[38] These writers come to their subject matter from various routes. They may follow geologists, like John McPhee. They may be ranchers on the northern Plains like Linda Hasselstrom and Sharon Butala, or farmers who have succeeded on the High Plains, like Julene Bair's family. They may be in quest of family and personal identity, like Wallace Stegner,

William Least Heat-Moon, and Kathleen Norris. They may be studying the paleohistory or natural history of place, like Loren Eiseley, Don Gayton, John Janovy, and Wes Jackson. Each of these writers chronicles a journey of sorts, a journey embedded in place, smelling of the land, bending to its topography, marked by its history. Their voices function as a chorus of literary cartographers, and the operative metaphor that connects their disparate studies is that of William Least Heat-Moon's *PrairyErth*: the deep map.

According to Randall Roorda, the deep map is an "incipient genre" that "impinge[s] upon genres more explicitly scholarly and research-oriented."[39] In its "sedimentation of impressions," the deep map presents the multiple histories of place, the cross-sectional stories of natural and human history as traced through eons and generations.[40] Such complex deep mapping demands innovative, layered storytelling. Despite groundbreaking work, the kind of linear thinking evident in Walter Prescott Webb's classic study *The Great Plains* (1931), carefully blocked around serial themes—human history, economy, literature, and mysteries—is not a precedent for deep map narrative. More recently, Ian Frazier, Richard Manning, Anne Matthews, and Jonathan Raban have published bestselling essays on the Great Plains, but their narrative forms do not engage in the artful braiding of deep past, scientific knowledge, cultural history, and personal participation in a spatial milieu. A book I particularly admire, Dan O'Brien's *Buffalo for the Broken Heart*, presents a compelling story of Plains restoration as the author switches from cattle to bison production on his Black Hills ranch. O'Brien gives the reader fascinating information about bison on the Plains, the economics of cattle ranching, and the persistent challenges of restoring the grasslands. His is an important book on reinhabiting and reimagining the Great Plains. He has not, however, written a deep map narrative.

What distinguishes the deep map form from other place-based essays is its insistence on capturing a plethora of interconnected stories from a particular location, a distinctive place, and framing the landscape within this indeterminate complexity. Deep maps present many kinds of tales in an effort to capture the quintessence of place, but the place itself remains elusive and incompletely limned. Writers who deeply map the Plains survey both the widest and smallest of spaces to elicit the most subtle and profound forms of knowledge. Christopher C. Gregory-Guider discerns that "landscapes, like texts, have multiple dimensions and depths, palimpsestically overlapping regions whose richness and variety produce an inexhaustible number of readings and experiences."[41] In following the many trails of text, these Plains essayists capture within their narrative structures a complex web of information, interpretation, and storytelling. Their cross-sections articulate scientific perspectives, national as well as personal history and mythology, dreamtime and vision, as well as layers of time both humanly brief and geologically deep. Steeped in the ironies of loss, these deep maps also serve to reestablish worlds that have been lost, to show us ways of honoring a diminished space, and to resist the larger culture's neglect of the rural center of America. As such, they are precisely the genre of storytelling Elliott West calls for at the end of *The Way to the West*: "rarely traced by clear distinctions, but by ambiguities and by blurred, evolving identities."[42]

The elusive interweaving that marks the deep map is closer to novelization, what M. M. Bakhtin calls dialogical narrative. Indeed, the Bakhtinian matrix, the "time space" narrative of chronotope, explains the efficacy of deep mapping the new story of the Plains. Defining his concept, Bakhtin says, "Time, as it were, thickens, takes on flesh, becomes artistically visible; likewise, space becomes charged and responsive to the movements of time, plot and history. This intersection of axes and fusion of indicators characterizes the artistic chronotope."[43] For writers who take experience of the land seriously, as Great Plains essayists of place are wont to do, such embodied narrative makes sense. Michael J. McDowell argues that

Bakhtinian webmaking is ideal for the environmental writer: "His literary theories [incorporate] much of the thinking about systems and relationships long ago embraced by the hard sciences . . . his work provides an ideal starting point for an ecological analysis of landscape writing."[44] Concurrently Kristie S. Fleckenstein has called such embodied discourse "somatic." In understanding the individual's response to space and time, writers must see "mind and body as permeable, intertextual territory that is continually made and remade."[45]

Such writing has an ethical import as well: in recognizing the complex nexus between the physical and symbolic, in heeding bodily experience over cultural mythology, somatic discourse can "have a material effect on the way we live."[46] In pondering "the environmental imagination," Lawrence Buell also touches upon the ethics of storytelling, upon the way narrative is structured: "Aesthetics can become a decisive force for or against environmental change."[47] In dialogics, the past presses against the present in lively interface, dramatizing human change on the cusp of the future. Deep map narrative engages in all of these strategies.

Deep map writers of the Plains, from Loren Eiseley and Wallace Stegner forward, have recognized the need for revisionary narratives that emerge from place, that are embodied in the writer's experience, that recognize the fluidity of interior and exterior boundaries, and that voice a place-based environmental ethic. As a group, Plains deep map essayists represent the kind of literary bioregionalism Buell and others celebrate as merging local color and natural history. In defining a bioregion, Robert L. Thayer emphasizes the word's etymology, "life-place," as

> a unique region definable by natural (rather than political) boundaries with a geographic, climatic, hydrological, and ecological character capable of supporting unique human communities. Bioregions can be variously defined by the geography

of watersheds, similar plant and animal ecosystems, and related, identifiable landforms . . . and by unique human cultures that grow from natural limits and potentials of the region. Most importantly, the bioregion is emerging as the most logical locus and scale for a sustainable, regenerative community to take root and to *take place*.[48]

Deep map narrative from the Plains celebrates the life place and promotes ways to sustain and advance the health of the spaces Plains people inhabit.

Yet what complicates Plains bioregional deep mapping is the reality of rapid, radical loss on the landscape urged on by a dominant historical view that the Plains landscape was desert, was useless land, was a space to pass through, or, conversely, was useful only when human effort transformed the grass to product, to garden. To this day, these contradictory images of the Plains persist, as Michael Martone's satirical version of the average American's journey to the prairies and plains makes clear: "I see them starting out, bighearted and romantic, from the density and the variety of the East to see just how big the country is. . . . And, in the dawn around Sandusky, they have had enough, and they hunker down and drive, looking for the mountains that they know are ahead somewhere. They cannot see what is around them now."[49] Heat-Moon attests that to many the Plains' surface appears "barren, desolate, monotonous, and land of more nothing than almost any other place you might name."[50] The local is an absence, a colorless flatness. Thus "local color" and the Great Plains appear oxymoronic, mutually exclusive. Compounding such limited perception, Don Gayton argues, is the fact that "[for] us, landscape is a construct, a fixed and enduring piece of literature. We assemble landscapes in our heads, from shreds of ancient mythology, half-remembered Disney movies, romantic yearnings, cultural assumptions, primal landscapes and genetic anachronisms. The final product of our mental assembling may not have much to do with the actual land-scape itself."[51] Too many citizens are programmed to dismiss the Plains. In the contemporary deep map from the Plains, however, the desire to reclaim and often to redeem a region runs strong. The editors of *The Bioregional Imagination* attest that bioregional writing emphasizes "most notably *dwelling, sustainability,* and *reinhabitation.*"[52] These concepts animate the Plains deep map.

"Aftermath," as Buell notes, "is an agricultural term for the second and inferior hay crop mown late in the season."[53] This sense of aftermath connects diverse Plains deep mappers. When the Plains biomass was plowed under, reseeded, or overgrazed, an epoch ended. The replacement culture, organized around various monocultures (agricultural and social), is akin to that second mowing. In a sense, Plains nonfiction writers use deep mapping to reinhabit a region lost over a century ago. Biologist Paul A. Johnsgard states that "[of] all of the grasslands types in North America, the tallgrass prairie has been the most ravaged. One estimate of its original extent . . . was 221,375 square miles. . . . At least 95 percent of the tallgrass prairie is now gone."[54] Mixed-grass and shortgrass prairies have also faced radical reduction.[55] What made it distinctive—grasslands—now represents a minor percentage of Plains acreage. Don Gayton has noted, "Much great literature has come from the simple desire to understand how things must have been, for a person or an era; it is time for ecologists to understand the value of this desire."[56] At the headwaters of contemporary Plains nature writing—Loren Eiseley and Wallace Stegner—this desire stands out and continues to find expression in the newest generation of writers. Examining a reduced place, these writers turn to multifaceted somatic narrative, to the deep map, in an attempt to repudiate "the geography of nowhere."

Following Prescott Webb, Plains essayists have sought ways to reframe and to reimagine regional history through cross-sectional narrative. The literary cartography of the Plains has been a multigenerational project, its striking possibilities first suggested in Loren Eiseley's early essays from the 1940s and 1950s and then embraced wholeheartedly in Wallace Stegner's *Wolf Willow* (1962). With William Least Heat-Moon's publication of *PrairyErth* in 1991, writers of dialogical, multilayered narrative exploded. In the hands of Stegner, Heat-Moon and others, deep mapping takes many forms. Like a literary survey team, these nonfiction writers map multiple measures. Inspired by geologists, Plains writers create cross-sectional narratives of natural history, illuminating the strata in which deep time and human time collide, scratching "the weathered surface of a very old layering."[57] Following cultural geographers, they mark the shifts and migrations, booms and busts, erasures and additions, always keeping an eye open for the palimpsests of former worlds. Palimpsest as metaphor "captures the history of the landscape as successive generations of human activity written on its surfaces."[58] Deep mappers develop keen eyes for such traces, such snatches of story. They are like Kent Ryden's folklorist, "a relief mapper, a cartographer of the invisible landscape, exploring and recording the local memory and ways of life, preserving them from erasure and decay, demonstrating how individual features on the map coalesce and form a unified whole rooted to a particular geographical location."[59]

Among the disciplines Plains nonfiction writers chart is biology. In a signature essay, Loren Eiseley climbs down into a slit secretly hidden in the prairie grass, a crack "only about a body-width" and reveals to us ten million years of history.[60] "Deep, deep below the time of man in a remote age near the beginning of the reign of mammals," he explains, he taps and chisels "the foundations of the world" (4–5, 6). The slit transforms into a deep map, presenting us with "many dimensions" that expand the narrow visions of our lifetimes, and which chart "an immense journey" (12). Like the vertical axis in one of Bakhtin's chronotopes, "[everything] that on earth is divided by time, here, in this verticality, coalesces into eternity, into pure simultaneous coexistence" (15). In this moment merging distant epochs, Eiseley's reach is intellectual, imaginative, and corporeal. The animal within, the vestigial rodent tied to him through evolution and genetics, gains voice as well. Similarly, the Platte River allows Eiseley, in "The Flow of the River," to "escape the actual confines of flesh."[61] Naked, he slips into the river. In the water, he converges with eons, slips through geological processes, and absorbs the instinctual nature of water creatures. In the Platte, of the Platte, in a magic moment of synthesis, Eiseley becomes "the meandering roots of a whole watershed" (16). Deep mappers of the Plains revel in such somatic experiences, when mind submits to body to reveal buried truths near at hand. Eiseley's lyrical somatic encounters suggest the potential of deep map writing that is scientifically focused, biocentric, and transcendently imaginative.

If a slit in the grass can take one on an immense journey, then so, too, can the study of a sample of contemporary flora and fauna. A new generation of scientist writers has taken up the challenge of mapping micro and macro life forms. Among them is John Janovy Jr., like Eiseley affiliated with the University of Nebraska. Janovy's work in Keith County, Nebraska, is central to contemporary Plains nonfiction writing. With an eye trained to the small scale, Janovy provides revelatory passages that speak to larger issues of adaptation, ecology, and loss. Janovy transforms a cliff swallow colony, for instance, into a micro-deep map: "It is a trip into a world one did not realize existed on earth. It is the strongest experience I have ever had in intruding into the territory of another creature."[62] The colony itself is only two hundred to three hundred feet long, built on the wall of a spillway. Yet this small space maps generations of birds, providing scientific information on local soils, insect populations, cycles of life and death, growth and limitation, coexistence and struggle.

Janovy's deep maps, like Eiseley's, track the mysteries of evolution and the wonder of adaptation. At the same time, Janovy's desire to go "very deep down" into the somatic experience of this place leaves him both elated and discomfited: "The closer one gets to the colony, however, the less comfortable one is, and to climb down on the divider between the spillway flumes with the colony swirling about one's head is to intrude deep within an organism" (65). "It is not a pleasant experience," he concludes about this "surreal" encounter, yet the struggle brings a sense of unexpected connection. Penetrated and reconstituted by his version of "the slit," Janovy writes, "[one] feels a sense of having been here before but perhaps on another planet, in a dream, in a previous life from which one has been incarnated"(66). The best deep maps inspire imagination and take us beyond the physical facts of place and the pressing contingencies of our own present history. Scientifically and physically alert in a bewildering matrix of place, the biologist writers in this study, Don Gayton, Wes Jackson, and John Janovy, guide readers through the intricacies of the Plains biome.

On the Great Plains, surfaces belie depth. The "so-called emptiness of the Plains" can blur one's sight, lull one into an unappreciative daze.[63] It takes attention to nuances, curiosity about deep-time realities, and an active imagination to appreciate such subtle land. Driving across I-80 on his way to Lincoln, Nebraska, John McPhee notes the discordancy between the seeming stability of rolling countryside—the solid stable core of a continent called the Stable Interior Craton—and the geologic history just beneath the soil of the Trans-Mississippi West. Rupture, rifting, and all the other components of geologic mayhem are etched in the rocks deep in the earth. The walls of this great rift, an event comparable to the rifting in Africa in the current era, are "three thousand feet sheer."[64] Over a billion years ago, the far side of this rift reached Lincoln. The Plains have witnessed radical changes in topography and climate through billions of years of earth history. In Candace Savage's assessment, "[the] great grasslands of central North America have been shaped over the past three or four billion years by the same forces that raised the Rockies and excavated the Grand Canyon. . . . They have experienced every shudder and wrench as continents have collided and torn away from each other, only to collide and tear away again."[65] They have been higher, they have been below sea level. They have hugged the arctic and dripped wet in the tropics. Currently, they harbor much of the eroded Rockies and have been lifted by hot spot activity in Yellowstone. In works like *Rising From the Plains* (1986) and *Crossing the Craton* (1998), McPhee's narrative cartography returns us to the earliest reaches of earth time and then shows us how human culture adapts to or resists the constraints of this history. As David Quammen discovers in his *New York Times Book Review* of McPhee's *Annals of the Former World*, "the great American Midwest . . . is not quite so flat and dull as it seems."[66] McPhee's narrative deep maps do not overtly chart the interior response to the world, nor do they bother themselves with dreamscapes, personal quest, or spiritual compass points. Yet his deep maps detail a complex web of history compelling in its own right.

At his home in New Jersey, pebbles from the flow of the Platte River fill petri dishes. The braids of the Platte are chock-full of such stones. Taken from a riverbank near the hundredth meridian in Nebraska, these pebbles "are without lustre when they are dry, but if you pour a little water on them," McPhee instructs, "their colors brighten and shine."[67] McPhee's pebbles, the pleasurable sight, smell, and touch of them, are not solely ornamental: they are reminders to him of complexity. Each of these pebbles has journeyed from a distinct origin, often many hundreds of miles away. McPhee's discernment of many landscapes pebbling the Platte River channels complements Eiseley's insights as he fluidly merges with the movement and natural processes of a continent.

Geologic and evolutionary history, recorded in the sweep of ecosystems that have emerged and disappeared in this region of North America, is rich; yet human use and abuse of the land rapidly alters what has taken millions of years to create. In Don Gayton's words, "over the span of 150 years, tallgrass has disappeared like a million grains of a precious sand running down an hourglass, but this was an hourglass with no bottom."[68] With the initial sodbusting, Wes Jackson adds, "a new way of life opened, which simultaneously closed, probably forever, a long line of ecosystems stretching back thirty million years."[69] Ironically, human history, as traced by Plains deep mappers, unravels at a faster pace. Deeply mapped natural histories, like those of Gayton, Janovy, and McPhee, are haunted by settlement-era vestiges: abandoned homesteads, ghost towns, dead businesses, empty schoolyards. Around these skeletal human institutions, nature has begun to assert its claim, slowly returning abandoned property to a natural state. Standing in Quitaque, Briscoe County, Texas, journalist Anne Matthews comments:

> Like the residents—the former residents—of other sections of the Plains, Quitaque's citizens appear to be voting with their feet. On a warm, clear Saturday afternoon, the silence in the central business district is absolute; no bird cries, no voices, no engines. Nothing. We wander the sidewalks and talk in whispers, like tourists at an archaeological site.[70]

Such silence communicates distress, communal erosion, and retreat.

These moments remind us that settlement contact with the Plains has been equivocal. After the grassland's ancient roots were ripped apart, many settlers put down shallow roots that could not adapt to the land's harsh dictates. Like the crops they imagined would enrich them, their hopes and spirits withered. Their dead remain, however, buried in forgotten cemeteries, where, ironically, prairie flora lost to the greater Plains survive. Such tenuous emplacement is complicated by species extinction: "Our society," Richard Manning argues, "ran through the landscape like a hot rod full of teenagers full of beer."[71] Plains deep mappers illustrate that an ecosystem's niches will be filled, but a history of loss hides behind the healing. Faced with such rapid transformation, individuals struggle within themselves and within their communities for significance and identity. As Sharon Butala illustrates in *The Perfection of the Morning*, altering the landscape brought "profound sorrow" to human communities: "North America, obsessed with the notion of progress and the technological means to achieve it, and increasingly urbanized, has failed to make a place for people on the land."[72] The devaluing of land and of people goes hand in hand, erasing generations of accumulated knowledge and practice. In response, many contemporary Plains writers offer protest, advocacy, and political engagement, arguing as Butala does that "[no] society can afford to wipe out the whole class of people in whom the practical knowledge laboriously passed down by generations remains alive."[73]

Illustrative of this engagement, Linda Hasselstrom, in *Going Over East*, maps a journey through twelve gates. Her movement through space also delimits movement through layers of history: personal, regional, national, and natural. Everywhere she sees the complicated network of this history. Hasselstrom, a proclaimed student of the prairies, digs up stories as part of her map: "The prairie is full of stories, though its civilized history is barely a hundred years old. And before that? Still other stories, written on the buffalo grass that breaks under our tires."[74] Deep mapping her section of Hermosa, South Dakota, in this and other volumes helps her retrieve wisdom that furthers responsibility toward the land. However, wisdom also gives troubling knowledge: so many have left in the century since settlement; public lands suffer from overuse; mini-mall culture destroys regional distinctiveness. In parts of the Plains where population growth has spurred new subdivisions, settlement history itself is disappearing under mown turf and concrete. Hasselstrom's deep map expresses a mournfulness common to much Plains writing, regardless of genre:

How far we have come from our origin as a part of the land; how far we are from truly mingling with and understanding our world. Our essential, primitive instincts have been switched off; our minds have been directed inward, analyzing our childhoods, fears, motives, needs. Probably all these things are important, but if we dive too deeply into our psyches and leave the natural world too far behind, we may never reach it again.[75]

When people ignore the intrinsic value of land, Hasselstrom argues, "They see the land as empty, unused, and thus a fit place for garbage or fun."[76] Deep mapping as protest challenges our assumptions about land use, about technology, about the efficient, "flavorless existences" many now accept as desirable.[77]

In scaling the intricate matrix of place, in fleshing out time and embodying space, deep mapping insists upon the spiritual claims of land. We must learn to love a land of limitations. In her essays, Hasselstrom's prose follows a quest to honor the land that has carried her family and that has given birth to the author's creative spirit. Writers Sharon Butala and Julene Bair, Plainsdaughters themselves, work in parallel from their own home places in Kansas and Saskatchewan.

From the beginning of Great Plains literature, as Robert Thacker reminds us, writers have sought to explain the uniqueness of this bioregion, to come to terms with its land: "From Castañeda's sixteenth-century exploration narrative to contemporary writers, prairie writing attests, that the land does, without question, speak louder than the people."[78] In his essays on the Great Plains, Ian Frazier has attempted to define the Plains "in terms of the many things they aren't."[79] They aren't woodlands. They aren't mountains. They aren't bespeckled by lakes. They aren't "standard farmland." They aren't a desert.[80] To the majority of Americans who do not live on the Plains, and merely drive through them, they aren't much of anything. Vacancy and absence define them. Kansas, in

PrairyErth, stands for all the Plains: "that place you have to get through, that purgatory of mileage."[81] Who would want to map such a place? Yet since the 1950s, Plains essayists of place have strenuously resisted this devaluing of a vast, complex, beautiful landscape. In 1948, Aldo Leopold called for "several national prairie reservations."[82] "No living man will see again the long-grass prairie, where a sea of prairie flowers lapped at the stirrups of the pioneer," he laments in *A Sand County Almanac*.[83] In response, two generations of Plains nonfiction writers have attempted to retrieve the raveled interconnections that prove the richness of this place. In their writings, these authors express multiple themes: to account for loss, to acknowledge mistakes, to preserve and celebrate what remains, and to retrace a long history's steps. To accomplish such layered cartography, nonfiction writers of the Plains cross boundaries of genre and discipline, region and country, time and space.

The defining metaphor for such dialogical narrative sojourning is Heat-Moon's articulation of the deep map. "Whatever else prairie is—grass, sky, wind—it is most of all a paradigm of infinity, a clearing full of many things except boundaries, and its power comes from its apparent limitlessness," he posits.[84] Deep mapping allows Plains essayists to chart multidimensional history, to "walk in the stories of this place," to extend our contemporary awareness of the region in order to "find the collective wisdom to truly heal a broken land."[85] Heat-Moon coined his subtitle for a 1991 publication, but its metaphoric resonance harmonizes over fifty years of nonfiction writing. "The land," Heat-Moon writes, "like a good library, lets a fellow extend himself, stretch time, rupture the constrictions of egocentrism, slip the animal bondage of the perpetual present to hear Lincoln's mystic chords of memory."[86]

Deep mapping provides mixed chords of memory that tap into the multitonal chorus of human history, underscored by natural history. As such, it is dialogical in nature, somatic by choice, and undergirded by an insistent regard for the land below and yet above human constructs. Deep mapping is an aesthetic and an ethos. Its stories, to echo Elliott West, are "built from the roots up." "We who would inhabit the grassland need a new story," Richard Manning declares, "a sort of illiterature that rises from the land."[87] Deep mapping the Great Plains, the signature effort of nonfiction writers of place, marks a significant new direction in this region's literary culture. Charting patterned textures of science, history, and human desire, Plains writers deep map a layered illiterature steeped in place. This study of an evolving genre unfolds a number of Great Plains deep maps and guides readers across many landscapes and diverse cultural and historical matrices. The chapters that follow attempt to give a closer reading of the most significant writers of this narrative form. As a rhizomatic genre, extending in infinite ways, the deep map resists any master paradigm. Deep maps are quirky, indefinite, and contrarian narratives, as individualistic as the varieties of grasses and forbs on the Plains. What they share is a desire to delve below the surface and the present, to challenge mythic renderings of place, and to destabilize established or dominant viewpoints. This study focuses primarily on writers from the central and northern Plains, ecoregions that have inspired the largest number of deeply mapped narratives.[88]

I start with Stegner and Heat-Moon because Stegner is the first western North American writer to initiate a book-length cartographic representation of a Plains location, southwestern Saskatchewan. His innovative methodology weaves memoir, history, geology, and fiction, an ambitious and wholly new narrative in the literary history of the Plains. Stegner's narrative is haunted by a double consciousness: that of the boy and that of the man. The childhood self, immersed in the landscape, allows Stegner to focus his mind, as Momaday advises, "upon the remembered earth." In his youth, Stegner was a participant in late settlement history: few white people wanted to farm or ranch in this arid corner of Canada before the twentieth century. The sensuous encounters with river, flora, and soil rise as vivid memory when the adult Stegner returns to this formative landscape. As a man, he can understand how much he did not know of himself or of the newly settled country, nor of the family problems that would drive his parents away and subject them to a peripatetic existence. Stegner's deep map presents the dynamic of roots—homesteading—and routes—migration—dramatically, but he layers this brief history within sediments that reach back into the history of First People on the continent and of earth's geologic eons. This grandly expansive time demonstrates earth's own mutability and mobility over billions of years. Against the backdrop of rapid modernity and deep time, Stegner understands that he, like all living things, exists in a transient, negligible, and changeable state.

Heat-Moon's *PrairyErth*, in which the metaphor of the deep map is invented, begins from a similar personal quest: he wants to know more of one county in Kansas, a place he remembers as a child.[89] In the opening section "Crossings," Heat-Moon recalls "when I first crossed Chase County, I was twelve years old and riding in the front seat as navigator while my father drove our Pontiac Chieftain with its splendid hood ornament, an Indian's head whose chromium nose we followed for half a decade over much of America."[90] Thirteen years later, the blur of grasslands "looked different to me," Heat-Moon explains, "so alive and varied" (27). By 1965 the twenty-eight-year-old author "began to see the prairies as native ground, the land my hometown sat just out of sight of" (27). Part of their fascination was that "they [did not] demand your attention like mountains and coasts but because they almost defy absorbed attention" (27). One has to intentionally "search out its variation, its colors, its subtleties" (27). One really has to concentrate the mind to make Chase County remembered earth.

Later, in middle age, Heat-Moon gives his full attention to Chase County, Kansas, on the central Plains, and the 624 pages of his narrative examine every possible scale of the landscape from the visible and invisible, the grand and the small, the native and the invasive, the human and the nonhuman, the finite and the infinite. He comes to Chase County to discover his roots in the grasses and his many routes over the grasslands. At the same time, he uncovers the many concealed realities and histories of this tallgrass prairie and reimagines the larger biome and the human dramas, now nearly traceless, that spun their short trajectories on the Flint Hills of Kansas.

Stegner and Heat-Moon play with an intricate methodology to disclose vastly different parts of the Plains. Each foregrounds unique materials, varied and variegated contexts, to give us as complete a picture of experience in a place as is possible. Other writers in this study follow suit but with their own distinctive foci. Another early experimenter in deep map writing, Loren Eiseley, turned to a construct that he called the "concealed" essay to present human consciousness within a temporal and spatial reality that folds and telescopes deeper histories.[91] The essence of time and space is among his obsessions. Eiseley's brilliant series of essays, collected in *The Immense Journey* (1957), examine a plethora of storied, remembered landscapes through the focused lens of scientific discovery. Among them are the Nebraska badlands, the Platte River valley, and the Wildcat Hills around Scottsbluff.

As a young physical anthropologist in the 1930s, Eiseley participated in summer field seasons that introduced him to the High Plains. A polymathic talent, Eiseley experimented in his field notes and later essay drafts with ways to frame multiple temporal realities, geologically reshaped landforms, imminent and transcendent experiences, and an energetic, imaginative, singular consciousness. This rich condensation of histories and perspectives gave rise to a new form of science writing that has proved highly influential within deep map writing. Through his career, in published and unpublished work, Eiseley would return to formative Plains landscapes, including childhood haunts in Aurora and Lincoln,

Nebraska, and field areas in north-central and northeastern Kansas. The concealed essay form allowed him to work his artistic alchemy on complex multilayered materials.

For the other science writers that I examine—John McPhee, John Janovy Jr., Don Gayton, and Wes Jackson—Eiseley's "concealed" form provides a jumping-off point for novel representations of the Plains. Chapter 3 examines writers of the Plains biome. Gayton, Janovy, and Jackson use field research as a contemplative spring-board into their unique deep maps. From the Canadian prairies (Gayton) to the Cedar Point Biological Research Station on the High Plains in Keith County, Nebraska (Janovy) to the Land Insti-tute in Salina, Kansas (Jackson), these biologists anchor much of their analysis into the evolutionary adaptations of flora and fauna. Deep time in their presentations is not just a facet of bedrock and tectonics; it is archived in the DNA of living things. Each scientist is drawn to his particular remembered landscape for different pur-suits, but each also shares an affinity for the grasslands and life on the grasslands. Contemplating his attraction to western Canadian spaces, Gayton realizes that "it is the patterns: they are what gives me this overwhelming sense of fulfillment. Architecture of grass and forb and rock and sky. Random patterns."[92] A few patterns he understands; many more are unrecognizable, "but there is a pleas-ant sense of potential" (13). The instinct and ability to retrieve the information of place "would have been a great survival asset in our nomadic antiquity," Gayton ponders, "and is no doubt coded into our genes" (14). All three writers share this "fine legacy"—to study the patterns, to discern the meanings, of a place (14).

At the same time, they also acutely perceive the dangers facing the Plains, accelerated by settlement, commodification, modernity, and indifference. Jackson argues, "It has never been our national goal to become native to this place. It has never seemed necessary even to begin such a journey. And now, almost too late, we perceive its necessity."[93] Janovy, who has brought scores of students to Cedar

Point, laments that many of his brightest students—those who could help decipher more of the biome's patterns—instead go on to medical schools, following what Jackson calls the "one serious major" in the modern university, "upward mobility."[94] The "small pothole microcosms of North American freshwater biology that dot the High Plains landscape," Janovy remarks, are rich sites of exploration and wonder.[95] But too few people express a desire to follow this kind of field-based research or even to value it or the landscape of Keith County.

Jackson argues that Plains communities need to embrace a "resettlement" project through knowledge of place and the varied Plains ecosystems.[96] All three writers celebrate the people who embrace resettlement, even if this perspective remains overshadowed by extractive industrial farming and ranching. Their science supports the development of sustainable Plains practices, built from the roots up. "The mindscape of the future," Jackson states, "must have some memory of the ecological arrangements that shaped us and of the social structures that served us well."[97] Janovy perceives that a species like a sandpiper "is also representative of that vast wilderness of everyday biology one finds anywhere—Kansas to Amazonia—that has no immediate political or economic importance."[98] But to ignore the fate of native ground may destroy that which is most valuable "about what it means to be human."[99] Deep mapping, then, supports bioregional resettlement, or what Gayton calls "rebalancing" work: "If we are ever to renew our earth bond, a rebalancing must occur. New bonds with the earth can now only be forged by personal explorations that go far beyond simple analysis and concern, into realms of imagination and myth."[100] In a large sense, these writers engage in the "ecotones" of culture, to borrow from Florence Krall, a position that "carries the connotation of a complex interplay of life."[101] The metaphor of the ecotone, what Gayton calls the "dynamic edge," presents "rich and dynamic transitional zones and may provide great learning as well as suffering."[102] Gayton, Janovy, and Jackson survey the Plains from the edges, sharing the bounty of their research, yet understanding that science, by itself, is not enough to guide communities into resettled futures.

Chapter 4 gives a comparative reading of Eiseley and John McPhee, focusing on time and space in the Plains deep map. As Eiseley was entering his mature years as a writer, McPhee was starting out, first at *Time* and then at the *New Yorker*. While Eiseley is a native Plains man, Princeton-born McPhee is not. What connects these two writers is their appreciation of time's linear and cyclical qualities and its embodiment in space. McPhee's *Annals of the Former World* (1998) presents an epic reading of North American geology in all of its glorious complexity. Each book of this collection follows a particular geologist or group of geologists, as McPhee discusses the theory of plate tectonics and its effect on revising the story of the North American continent. In *Rising from the Plains* and *Crossing the Craton*, McPhee considers the multiple stories of place as human cultures and geologic realities interface. His guide, David Love, preeminent Rocky Mountain geologist, is native to Wyoming and the High Plains and foothill grasslands of the West. Complementing McPhee's narrative of his physical journey across Wyoming and of geologic mapping of this state is the journal of Ethel Waxham Love, David's mother. Her migration to Wyoming in the early twentieth century (on a lark to take a position as schoolmarm in rural Wyoming, much like Molly Wood in *The Virginian*) brings the reader to the same historical moment as Stegner's *Wolf Willow*. Wyoming, too, was a last frontier in settlement history.

The creative interplay among voices is one of the pleasures of *Rising from the Plains*, a complex deep map that balances science writing with stories of human habitation and enterprise, whether boom or bust, and personal regret. Wyoming is one of the most industrialized landscapes in the United States, despite its tourist glow from Yellowstone and the Grand Tetons. It is a place where the imperatives of an extractive economy collide with homesteading dreams. While McPhee mutes his own presence in the text, *Rising from the Plains* is as plaintive and urgent, in its way, as the deep maps from the biome. In less than a century, the Love ranch devolved, the pioneering work of patriarch and mother diminished. Settlement's complicity with the rise of industrialism casts a shadow on McPhee's final pages. The author takes his readers through narratives of the deepest times, pressing these layers against human stories in a way that links stratigraphy to literary cartography. David Love's cautionary language about human ignorance and arrogance echoes Gayton's from western Canada, Janovy's from western Nebraska, and Jackson's from the Flint Hills of Kansas. Across the sciences, the jury is in and the message is loud in these deep maps: humans must reverse course now and learn from the land, give into the landscape, live within its contours.

If these writers foreground science in their cartographic narratives, the final authors, Julene Bair, Sharon Butala, Linda Hasselstrom, and Kathleen Norris foreground the familial and personal within the larger matrix of human habitation and natural history on the Plains. Their deep maps explore the self in place, whether attached or detached from a home place, and the repercussions of rootedness in a world of transit and translation. Their methods reflect what Claire Omhovère has called the "biotext": "works that exceed generic barriers and include heterogeneous documents . . . in order to explore a central question: how does a life translate into narration?"[103] Experiential, subjective, and meditative textures are amplified in these writers, emphasizing the sense of becoming in a place. Consciousness as a spatial mediator organizes the layers of their narratives.

For two writers, Bair and Hasselstrom, childhood memory disturbs much of the present in their texts, a *sub-rosa* force that pushes against the displacement and fluidity of adult existences.

Bair calls herself a "Plainsdaughter." Hasselstrom, across volumes, emphasizes that she is a rancher's daughter and a rancher herself. Both women present this childhood acculturation within a Plains matrix as central to who they have become. "My father's utilitarian blood runs through my veins just as surely as distance trained my eyes and this lofting, arid air taught me the pleasure of mornings," Bair writes.[104] In a similar vein, Hasselstrom declares, "I grew up absorbed in the arid landscape and its people. . . . All the elements that became part of my life when I first moved there—neighbors, cows, relatives, deer, weather, water, clods of dirt, and the connections between them—grew naturally into my writing."[105] As girls Bair and Hasselstrom rode their horses over the Plains, extending their understanding of the landscape and of their identities as Plainsdaughters. Indeed, both authors feature photographs of themselves with horses to underscore this empowered connection to the land.

Yet life has worked to distance them from home place. First, strong, patriarchal fathers could never see their daughters as true heirs of place. Continued connection to ranch or farm depended upon husbands or male children. Bair and Hasselstrom might have breathed the same arid air as their fathers, but that air did not create an egalitarian culture in which girls could easily follow their fathers into ownership. Familial relationships serve, ironically, to displace and alienate daughters. A deep connection to home country marks their writing, but this umbilicus proves a fragile tether to settled habitation on the Plains. The dissonance between the homonyms routes and roots instead unsettles and shakes their texts. Longing and disaffection coexist within their lived spaces.

Sharon Butala, in contrast, calls herself an "apprentice." While Alison Calder strongly rebukes Butala's construction of experience—"romantic explorations of the self and landscape . . . presented as the accidental experiences of a naïve narrator, untutored, and unschooled"—Butala insists that she is a newcomer, through marriage, to the High Plains, and thus an uncertain cartographer.[106] In several books, Butala explores her evolving perceptions of southwestern Saskatchewan on ranch country that has been in her husband's family since 1913. The Butalas, unlike the Stegners, gained a toehold in this sparse land and "had slowly built up their ranch on the wide grasslands of the northern Great Plains."[107] By her marriage in 1976, the Butalas owned "more than thirteen thousand acres" (1). Her childhood and young adulthood had been spent in very different places, "the bush country of northern Saskatchewan" and the city of Saskatoon (18). "I had come from the parkland area in Saskatchewan," she explains, "and I was used to a much different terrain, as well as to rich black soil in which crops and vegetable and flower gardens flourished with little effort" (19). The new regime of little rain, constant wind, and swelling horizon, a landscape of precision and limitation, is alien to her. Whereas Bair and Hasselstrom often long for return to their Plains homelands from their Wyoming locations, Butala longs for the deeper connection of the dweller. She wants to shed her greenhorns.

Butala deep maps, then, to become native to place, and building a new home serves as a metaphor in *Wild Stone Heart* of her longed-for emplacement. Yet the new home is haunted, its spirits loud in protest at these usurpers. It is as though the place itself were keeping Butala out. An unplowed field, outside of the new home, becomes her guide to habitation instead. The stones on the land suggest another story of habitation, that of the Siksika people who lost these thirteen thousand acres and more to white settlers like the Butalas. The more Butala seeks direction from the landscape, the more it seems to resist her, too. Deeper human and natural history—for the First Nations legitimately claim primacy as storytellers of the Plains—slip out of her reach.

Mystery and a sense of illegibility, of indecipherable layers of history, propel Butala's quest to map this smaller field within the larger ranch landscape. She wants to know the land intimately, to penetrate "this bedrock of mystery" with its strange stone patterns, First Nations' artifacts, and "enigmatic" structures (29). Penetration is itself a troubling metaphor. In wanting "to know more," Butala finds herself "losing energy" (31). Her very quest dis-eases her. As *Wild Stone Heart* unfolds, the story of settlement, conquest, and extraction connects to the writer's affliction, as she delves deeper into the ethnographic history of the Plains and the longer recesses of geologic time. Hers is a vexed, imperfect map that reveals the challenges of going off grid, Heat-Moon's metaphor for rejecting accepted, simplified versions of place. Constructing a deep map means accepting the complexities, paradoxes, and hard truths of messy history. By returning to Eastend, Saskatchewan, with *Wild Stone Heart*, the same territory as Stegner's *Wolf Willow*, I hope to show that the same place can be mapped in multiple ways.

Kathleen Norris's concept of spiritual geography provides this study's coda. During a decade in which many books about the Great Plains rose on the bestseller charts, Norris's book, *Dakota: A Spiritual Geography*, stands out. Published amid a burst of bioregional literary cartography, *Dakota* begins at the home place, anchoring narrative into individual experience and radiating horizontally and vertically into aligned, complicated material. "Map making can be an empowering tool of reinhabiting and reimagining place," declare Lynch, Glotfelty, and Armbruster in *The Bioregional Imagination*, "allowing us to visualize in a nearly infinite array of contexts and scales the multiple dimensions of our home places."[108] Part of this bioregional practice cultivates hope.

Norris's frank and often critical deep map, radiating out of Lemmon, South Dakota, never buries hope. Among her most memorable chapters is "Getting to Hope," a portrait of an inspiriting church congregation in South Dakota. Paradoxically, the church is facing erasure: "Hope Church, which fifteen years ago had a membership of 46, is down to 25 today," Norris laments.[109] Despite challenges and impending finality, the members of Hope Church remain intellectually alert, globally conscious, committed to social justice, and open to new ideas. Unlike Norris's town of Lemmon, where people often retreat into defensive hostility, Hope "does not suffer from tribalism, the deadening and often deadly insularity that can cause groups of people to fear or despise anyone who is not like them" (170). If Plains communities from the Southwest to Canada are to survive the pressing contingencies of twenty-first-century globalization, they need to consider embracing the "wide generosity" of a spiritual outlook like Hope's.

In the literary development of the deep map, spirituality is among the most salient features of the genre. By no means a religious person, Loren Eiseley still acknowledges the powerful spirits, the mysteries and graces, of the Plains landscape. In the final essay of *The Immense Journey*, "The Secret of Life," Eiseley professes "that if 'dead' matter has reared up this curious landscape of fiddling crickets, song sparrows, and wondering men, it must be plain even to the most devoted materialist that the matter of which he speaks contains amazing, if not dreadful powers, and may not impossibly be, as Hardy has suggested, 'but one mask of many worn by the Great Face behind.'"[110]

A generation later, Don Gayton speaks of the necessity of rebalancing priorities in the final chapter of *The Wheatgrass Mechanism* ("Hubris"). The hubris of human exploitation troubles him, and he admits that he has participated in the wounding of earth. In rebalancing and restoration work, Gayton seeks a path to earth bonding. "The grand sweep of western Canadian landscape is now before me," he concludes, "prairie, mountain, coulee, badland, floodplain, and outlier. The mechanisms of these places, those that are known to me pulse reassuringly. The whole landscape is now my dream bed, where I will seek a new relationship with earth, to be influenced by the flows of its nature and, if I am lucky, to spawn a few of its visions."[111] The ground itself, he acknowledges, resonates spiritually; to ignore its pulse means further ravaging of the landscape, further self damage.

Looking around her, perceiving "the losses we've sustained in western Dakota since 1980," Norris seeks a way out of "the human cost in terms of anger, distrust, and grief" (8). Her way embraces spiritual pathways within a landscape that has been a place of worship for millennia. "Standing on a hillside near the Grand River in central Perkins County," she tells us, "you realize suddenly that you are on the highest ground for many miles around, and the stones nearby are not random but were placed there by human hands long ago" (108). Native people have long understood that the "spirit of the land is not an abstraction in western Dakota, but a real presence" (128). Norris, an avowed Protestant attending her grandmother's Presbyterian church in Lemmon, must find her way into a spiritual geography through her own traditions and belief systems, not those of Indigenous communities. But she remains open to many traditions, most formatively the practices and communal rituals of Benedictine monks. Ending my own study on a grace note of hope, I underscore one of the compelling realities of twenty-first-century Plains life: increasingly, people and communities want to rethink and re-inspirit home. The deep map narrative, with its ability to limn storied places, supports this bioregional impetus.

This environmental genre demonstrates remarkable, generative qualities and adapts in idiosyncratic ways to the mapped landscape at hand. The Great Plains, for two generations of nonfiction writers, has proven anything but arid, hardscrabble, and marginal. In truth, it is rich soil for American and Canadian writers seeking to tell those stories that discern new ways into the heart of the continent.

CHAPTER TWO

DEEP MAPPING HISTORY

Wallace Stegner's *Wolf Willow* and William Least
Heat-Moon's *PrairyErth: (a deep map)*

A place . . . is much more than a point in space. To be sure, a place
is necessarily anchored to a specific location which can be identi-
fied by a particular set of cartographic coordinates, but it takes
in as well the landscape found at that location and the meanings
which people assign to that landscape through the process of
living in it. A sense of place results gradually and unconsciously
from inhabiting a landscape over time, becoming familiar with
its physical properties, accruing a history within its confines.
Kent C. Ryden, *Mapping the Invisible Landscape*

*Wolf Willow: A History, a Story, and a Memory of the Last Plains
Frontier,* the headwaters of extended deep map writing, takes us
into the multiple layers of remote Whitemud, Saskatchewan, Stegner's fictional name for the town of Eastend. This book is deeply
personal for Stegner. In 1914, Stegner's mother took her two sons
to the Canadian prairies, where her husband was attempting to
establish a wheat farm. The Stegners were part of a less-studied
northern migration of over a million Americans, who joined Europeans and eastern Canadians seeking "new opportunity in the
Canadian West."[1] Stegner's text encompasses memoir, Canadian

political history, natural history, fiction, and polemic. His narrative sweeps across geological and cultural eons, encompassing millions of years; yet the heart of his story telescopes the last two hundred years of contact, conflict, and colonization in North America. "As a literary cartographer," Rick Van Noy writes, "Stegner is concerned with writing the interior landscape, the 'deep maps,' stories, and myths humans develop about places, but he sees some versions as qualitatively better than others, adjusted for how they conform to the exterior landscape."[2] The Stegners' attempted relocation does not conform to the exterior landscape, and the family experiment proves futile. As an adult, Stegner returns to Canada to investigate the family's exodus from this desert and to confront a failure that has haunted him. Unearthed in the process is a young boy's longing for open spaces, riparian movement, and psychological integration with a primal space.

Stegner's interwoven narrative establishes many of the features of the deep map genre that persist into the twenty-first century. First, the strata of cultural and natural history meld with personal perspectives of one individual's life. In his attempt to understand place and his place in settlement history, Stegner resorts to somatic interchange, to intimate, physical contact with soil, grass, human structures—all of the material realities of Whitemud. His body, charged with sensuous stimuli and reawakened memory, becomes a vehicle for negotiating the many layers of space and time. Additionally, as Van Noy notes, in Stegner's text one finds fluidity between interior and exterior boundaries, between political and mythological borders, between memory, official history, and the imagination that later writers of Plains deep maps have adapted, as we shall see. Moreover, the cross-sections of story are grounded in a particular biome—grasslands—and its systematic transformation and exploitation when the era of government-sponsored settlement began. At the heart of *Wolf Willow* and of subsequent Plains deep maps is an accounting of loss brought about by the legal, political, and economic institutions of empire, which do not fit the aspects of place they are imposed upon.

Indeed, the dissonance between deep history and modern myth-making, between the grasslands biome and one frontier town, strikes a central irony in Stegner's vision of Whitemud. Frontier stories mythologize the imposition of white settlement on the Plains on both sides of the forty-ninth parallel, elevating the encroachers to epic stature and inventing a pantheon of settlement heroes and villains whose stories continue in permutated form to this day. But in Stegner's deep map, the perspective of geological history casts a cold eye on the mythmaking of Whitemud. Vulnerable, "as bare as a picked bone," Whitemud stands in contrast to the mythology that initially lured people to its streets and homesteads.[3] Nature eventually proves too stern a master to the Stegners and scores of settlers, failures as farmers and losers in the disruptive boom and bust of economic life west of the hundredth meridian. Cast out as a child, Stegner has never forgotten this place and his family's part in the homesteading experiment. Their story, however, is small compared to the larger displacement of Indigenous people and the disruption of a biome millions of years in the making.[4] Stegner's refusal to celebrate white settlement, his growing consciousness of his family's complicity in a historically brief land grab, his recognition of the racism that underlies the settlement project, and his concern for the environmental consequences of commodifying the Plains, establish a markedly critical tone that is reiterated in Plains deep maps ever since.

Stegner begins at the end, an adult returning to the formative, primal place of his childhood, seeking some sense of rootedness amidst a life of movement and flux. During his boyhood, Stegner often felt an absence of history in a town engulfed by space with few fixed points. Indeed, the first glimpse of Stegner's childhood landscape reveals hardscrabble, difficult, expansive country. Western Saskatchewan "is notable primarily for its weather," he discerns, "which is violent and prolonged . . . its wind, which blows all the time in a way to stiffen your hair and rattle the eyes in your head" (3). To a child recently transplanted, such buffeting enormity must have been daunting. Inventing a map of place, then, becomes necessary for psychic and physical survival. Returning in the late 1950s, Stegner notes the larger boundaries and visual markers first: "that block of country between the Milk River and the main line of the Canadian Pacific, and between approximately the Saskatchewan-Alberta line and Wood Mountain" (3). But almost immediately for Stegner the sensuous cues of boyhood take over. Memories bound up in somatic encounter overwhelm him in a process that Van Noy calls "experiential geography."[5] The child's map contracts into living, breathing, intimate space: "What I remember are low bars overgrown with wild roses, cutbank bends, secret paths through the willows, fords across the shallows, swallows in the clay banks, days of indolence and adventure where space was as flexible as the mind's cunning and where time did not exist"(6). It is a vividly remembered world, borne into the present on the scent of wolf willow. River, prairie, and "overpowering" sky provide the abstract perimeters of his boyish experiences, stable coordinates on which to build his narrative (7). "Once you have submitted to it with all the senses," Stegner writes of this landscape, its essence works on body and soul: "You don't get out of the wind, but learn to lean and squint against it. You don't escape sky and sun, but wear them in your eyeballs and on your back. You become acutely aware of yourself" (8). In "a land to mark the sparrow's fall," Stegner, unknowingly at the time, came of age (8). The first section of *Wolf Willow* develops a complex set of overlapping maps, a double consciousness that travels back and forth between childhood and middle age. Against these measurements and the land itself, Stegner attempts to divine his maturation and the growth of Whitemud. His evolving map of place reveals itself in fits and starts, in resolution and dissolution.

If the self came into clearer relief in a prairie world, the family foundations, decades later, are harder to find. In mapping White-mud (Eastend), Stegner discovers how ephemeral human habitation can be. The Stegner homestead, abandoned so many years ago, has left few, if any, traces. The writer, anxious about such nega-tion, resists a journey to this home place. "I can imagine myself bumping across burnouts and cactus clumps," he admits, "scanning the dehumanized waste for some mark—shack or wind-leaned chicken coop, wagon ruts or abandoned harrow with its teeth full of Russian thistle—to reassure me that people did once live there" (9). The contrast between forged selfhood—"the strongest feeling of personal singularity I shall ever have"—and negated family history—"every trace of our passage wiped away"—confounds Stegner, and he turns away from the old pathways (9). Town seems a surer direction.

Ambiguity, erasure, haunting emptiness: these evocative, ambiva-lent qualities prompt Stegner to restake and reclaim his history in western Saskatchewan. From such a tenuous toehold into the past, Stegner builds his deep map. The homesteading boom of the early twentieth century, which brought the Stegners and many others into western Canada, has left a shallow layer of record on the land. Returning to Saskatchewan as an adult, he also learns how limited and inaccurate his childhood memories, even vivid ones, can be: "He sees only what he can see," Stegner comments of the boy self. "Only later does he learn to link what he sees with what he already knows, or has imagined or heard or read, and so come to make perception serve inference" (12). The childhood map is imperfect and fragmented, pieced together through misperceptions and distortions. At the same time, what the man encounters in Whitemud—an established town with "hospital, Masonic Lodge, at least one new elevator, a big quonset-like skating rink"—has nothing to do with his memories: "I cannot find myself or my family or my companions in it" (13). Even the mythic river of childhood disappoints, "a quiet creek twenty yards wide" (13). The present landscape bumps uncomfortably against the remembered map of a distant place: "How could adventure ever have inhabited those willows, or wonder, or fear, or the other remembered emotions?" (13). With memory suspect, seemingly "fictitious," Stegner must reconfigure his personal map of place, layer it within other histories, other realities.

In town, Stegner drives to the house his father built, an artifact that documents their onetime existence in Whitemud. "Facing the four-gabled white frame house," he expects a stronger reaction than he feels. This house should be ground zero of his past: "It ought to be explosive with nostalgias and bright with recollections, for this is where we lived for five or six of my most impressionable years" (15). Memories of the 1918 flu pandemic, his grandmother's nervous breakdown, the plethora of holidays, celebrations, and parties now take effort to recall, to "pump up recollection" (16). The house "still has power to disturb," but in a way that is "dream-like, less real than memory, less convincing than the recollected odors" (16). The scent of wolf willow, then, in this opening foray into a deep map, remains one of Stegner's most effective guiding posts into place, into the many layers archived in soil and rock. But the recollected odor also reveals the gaps and erasures in his own sense of the past.

Exacerbating Stegner's initial cartographical bid is the incomplete education he received in his formative years, the absence of any serious study of Canada or the prairie. He and his family had participated in "a human movement" that would redefine the Plains. Whitemud, he now understands, represents "a belated concentration of Plains history" (20). As Stegner sees it, "the successive stages of the Plains frontier flowed like a pageant through these Hills, and there are men still alive who remember almost the whole of it. My own recollections cover only a fragment; and yet it strikes me that this is *my* history. . . . If I am native to anything, I am native to this" (20). Contradicting emplacement on the prairie, his early schooling focused on European history and culture: "In such a town as Whitemud, school superimposes five thousand years of Mediterranean culture and two thousand years of Europe upon the adapted or rediscovered simplicities of a new continent" (24). Looking back, Stegner sees clearly how inadequate this training was for his life and career. "I was educated for the wrong place," he concludes, and must turn to "something else in place" that animates his maturation in the last Plains frontier (24).

How might the contours of Whitemud provide an alternative view of history? How might Stegner overcome the dismissal of western Canadian history? A "palpable" sense of history eluded him and others: "We knew no such history, no such past, no such tradition, no such ghosts" (29). To his childish mind, the town dump provided the best evidence of history lived. "If the history of Whitemud was not exactly written," he remembers in one of *Wolf Willow's* most famous scenes, "it was at least hinted, in the dump" (34). In the dump, Stegner found "our poetry and our history" (36). What Robert Kroetsch has called "a kind of archaeological act," an "archival method . . . trusting to fragments of story, letting them speak their incompleteness," structures Stegner's presentation of Whitemud's rich layers.[6]

Indeed, Stegner himself turns to the trope of archaeology, to a rich Whitemud dig that unearths the multiple layers of story embedded in place. In completing section 1 of his narrative, "The Question Mark in the Circle," Stegner elevates the town's dumping ground to historical record, reassigns the detritus of settlement to archival status. The dump southeast of town was comparable to "archaeological sites potent with the secrets of ancient civilizations" (31). The dump gives the boy Stegner his first vertical examination of Whitemud and its surrounds, his first inkling that stories lie buried in the ground, ready for capture by uncovering imagination.

The dump site organizes a number of cartographical features in his imagination: the river running from the Cypress Hills; an old trail and still-useful campgrounds; and the irrigation flume where Stegner "could sit . . . and grab a cross-brace above him, and pull, shooting himself sledlike ahead" (32). Founded in 1888, the dump "was the very first community enterprise, the town's first institution" (33). A necessity for the town's adults, the dump serves Whitemud's children with a wondrous dive into the past. The relics that he and his friends uncover provide a lively catalogue in Stegner's imagination. Among their finds are "[s]mashed wheels of wagons and buggies, tangles of rusty barbed wire, the collapsed perambulator that the French wife of one of the town's doctors had once pushed proudly up the plank sidewalks" (34). The boys find melted glass, lead casings, telephone wires, as well as "plenty of old metal, furniture, papers, mattresses . . . and jugs and demijohns" that lured in the field mice and drowned them (34). Stegner was once shocked to find family books in the dump, volumes of Shakespeare that "had been carried from Dakota to Seattle, and Seattle to Bellingham, and Bellingham to Redmond, and Redmond back to Iowa, and Iowa to Saskatchewan" (35). Borrowed and accidentally burned, these volumes, family heirlooms, end up refuse. For the boy Stegner, seeing these throwaways is like seeing death; as an adult he understands that in new country "much is lost . . . much thrown aside . . . much carelessly or of necessity given up" (35). Among the most poignant relics in Stegner's listing is the skinned carcass of his colt, the victim of a dog attack. The dump's archive provides a historical overview of a young Whitemud that is both large scale and intimate. To Stegner and his friends, "this was the kitchen midden of all the civilization we knew" (35). It defined their world and their destiny. The intensely personal childhood survey of Whitemud that opens Stegner's deep map, recollected in later adulthood, ends on this elegiac note.

As a mature writer, Stegner returns to seek history beyond the confines of a junkyard, a record of the discarded. Memoir is an important feature of the history Stegner presents—it is the foundation of his narrative. Yet as John Daniel reminds us, "for Stegner the personal is not sufficient . . . he progresses to the larger weave in which his family's life is only one thread."[7] Stegner must move beyond the charged sensuousness of his own childhood to find the deeper history of a place so "marginal or submarginal in its community and cultural life" (306). The text transitions into a different sort of "contact," as Van Noy explains, "the [intellectual] contact made through understanding and interpreting the region's history."[8] As the "Herodotus of the Cypress Hills," Stegner must incorporate the longer history of the First Peoples of Saskatchewan and their contact with European adventurers, traders, and surveyors, and the even longer geological history of place.[9] He investigates the legal, political, and economic institutions of empire, "the problems of an expanding continental hegemony" (103). Oral history and personal artifacts like letters and journals contribute to Stegner's textured narrative.

Part 2 of *Wolf Willow*, "Preparation for a Civilization," starts with European contact and conquest, with the brutal subjugation of First Nations people and the dismissal of Indigenous knowledge and cartography. The Cypress Hills' anomalous geology provided its Indigenous population with a unique ecosystem. "Biologically they preserve Rocky Mountain plants and animals," Stegner explains, "far out into the Plains, and southern species far into the north" (45). This welcoming topography for the First Nations became "last home of buffalo and grizzlies, last sanctuary for the Plains hostiles, last survival of the open-range cattle industry, booby prize in a belated homestead rush" (45). One thousand feet of extra elevation made the hills desirable to flora and fauna and to competing human cultures. Seventeenth-century excursions stopped "several hundred miles of the Cypress Hills" (42). Lewis and Clark came close in May 1805 and noted the plethora of beasts and birds alike. They would name the Milk River but not explore the lands northward. Stegner celebrates this once "densely peopled" country of "small creatures": "prairie dogs, picket-pin gophers, field mice, weasels, ferrets, badgers, coyotes, jackrabbits, burrowing owls" (41). Across the sweep of grasslands, "even more homeless and fluid than the clouds," moved herds of bison and bands of antelope (41). The sloughs, grasses, and soil provided generous nesting grounds for varieties of birds. This land that only brought "unmitigated discomfort and deprivation" to Stegner's family once shimmered with fecundity (282). The "first look" of Lewis and Clark, an incomplete, from afar survey of the distant Canadian prairies, gave a teasing glance of a vast, dynamic landscape. In 1805 Lewis and Clark turned away from the Milk River portal, postponing white encroachment for two generations.

Surveying, one of the most powerful tools of hegemony, began in earnest with the arrival of Captain John Palliser in 1859. His surveying expeditions forever altered an ancient landscape and set the stage for the disruption of First Nations and métis communities in what would become the Province of Saskatchewan. In section 2, Stegner analyzes the complexities of this ecological and cultural change, attendant with the unexpected consequences and challenges to the Plains tribes. Fur trading gave way to new economies. Between 1872 and 1874, surveyors in this region mapped out the Medicine Line, the international divide, the forty-ninth parallel, and clarified the rule of law on both sides of the border. In 1879 Whitemud was established, and from that point on migration by cattlemen and then farmers transformed the biome irrevocably. Yet of this history, Stegner writes, "All of it was legitimately mine, I walked that earth, but none of it was known to me" (112). The phrase "I wish" acts as a refrain in the chapter "Capital of an Unremembered Past," underscoring the adult author's need to counter absence. Stegner admits that his boyhood knowledge of the First Nations came from popular culture and books. This "unnaturalized history" ranged from "Noble Savage sentimentalities" to local prejudices (49). In Whitemud, this attitude was bluntly racist: "An Indian was a thieving, treacherous, lousy, unreliable, gut-eating vagabond, and that if anything a halfbreed was worse" (50). In childhood, Stegner had little knowledge of deeper Native history—a far more significant stretch of history than white settlement represented—nor of the debasing effects of colonization and modernization.

The Stegners arrived in Saskatchewan a mere four decades after the mapping of the forty-ninth parallel and the Battle of the Little Bighorn. "We lived in the very middle of what had been for generations a bloody Indian battleground," he explains (53). Yet Stegner's understanding of the complex political and cultural realities of Plains tribes only developed in later adulthood. Similarly, his education concerning the mixed-blood settlements of Saskatchewan, communities that were twice suppressed, had been scant. "Once in 1870, on the Red River, and again in 1885, on the North Saskatchewan," these communities lost "their chance of independence" and "their chance of identity" (58). The onslaught of white settlement pushed aside this history and buried its uncomfortable truths.

Both First Nations and métis communities faced damaging cultural diminishment and displacement when the forces of dominion asserted themselves over Rupert's Land, the Northwest Territories, and British Columbia. "The métis themselves," Stegner asserts, "would help destroy the world that nourished them. Their bequest to this future would be death and emptiness; they would clear the grasslands and coulees for another sowing" (66). The Hudson's Bay trade monopoly that had organized much of Indigenous and métis life would shift after the great surveys to establish national boundaries at the forty-ninth parallel were completed and never regain its tight control.

A new kind of order, represented by the Royal North-West Mounted Police, appeared on the northern Plains: "a stream of scarlet tunics, white helmets, white dragoon gauntlets, gleaming metal, polished leather, 275 picked officers and men on picked horses, the most brilliant procession that ever crossed those yellowing plains" (105). Stegner gazes back at this history leading up to a new political, national order, and laments that "I wish I could have known it early, that it could have come to me with the smell of life about it instead of the smell of books" (112). Growing up on the vestiges of an ancient biome, First Nations and métis communities, and Fort Walsh, Stegner keens, "The very richness of that past as I discover it now makes me irritable to have been cheated of it then" (112). Despite Stegner's admission that the European settlers dismissed, devalued, and hated the Indigenous peoples, his version of this history is questionable, as Elizabeth Cook-Lynn has cogently argued. "A broader look at history," she counters, "might suggest that the idea that Indian hating was nonexistent and empire building less violent in Canada than in the United States is simply a delusion of the imagination. Racism and its relationship to colonization and nationbuilding on the North American continent," she concludes, "seem fairly pervasive and consistent."[10] Stegner's attempt to redress his inadequate education falls short, and Cook-Lynn chastises him for "a combination of compelling fantasy and bad history."[11]

Even in 1962, Stegner's outline of North American settlement, of the history he was denied, remains inadequate. Stegner's deep map writing from Saskatchewan, reflected in later non-Native writers of the Plains, is strikingly ironic for this reason: the colonization of settlement, continuing to the present day, has left a profound sense of loss and disorientation in the non-Native descendants of those who first homesteaded the Plains. These sons and daughters of settlement now seem willing to retrace the knowledge and values of the Indigenous Nations whom their ancestors helped displace. So far, as Laura Smyth Groening has documented, bridging the historical divide of colonization has proved complicated and fractious.[12] As Stegner dramatizes, settlement presence on the Plains is too brief to give any heft to the communities' experience or knowledge. Yet, from Stegner forward, the urge to connect deeply to place has been gripping the heirs of colonization. Stegner has diagnosed this dis-ease as "the dissatisfaction and hunger that result from placelessness," the disaffection of being "displaced" and "mythless."[13]

To become a place, Stegner asserts in his essay "The Sense of Place," memory must kick in: "No place is a place until things that have happened in it are remembered in history, ballads, yarns, legends, or monuments."[14] Rick Van Noy adds, "A place involves not only the fact that it is a name on a map, or the accumulation of events that happened on that spot of the map, but the meanings, perception, and emotion of individuals responding to their surroundings and events."[15] When the facts as lived, recorded, told, remembered, and published no longer suffice, Stegner turns to fiction halfway into this history, story, and memory. As Van Noy explains, fiction helps to "make geography meaningful."[16]

Section 3, "The Whitemud River Range," provides an initial reminiscence of Whitemud's folk culture and evolving narrative of community. The Lazy S Ranch housed a number of mythic personalities —"Big Horn, Little Horn, Slivers, Rusty, and Slippers"—whose exploits fascinated the town (128). These heroes found their counterparts in the town's despised; "[t]he cruelest and ugliest prejudices" followed Whitemud's minority population, Chinese, Jewish, Indigenous, and mixed-blood citizens. Even the overly Anglicized, "anyone with a pronounced English accent," were taunted (129). The town developed its own tense structure of insiders and outsiders, and among the most privileged insiders were "good shots, good riders, tough fighters, dirty talkers, stoical endurers of pain" (129). Usually white, these individuals confirmed the frontier mythology that celebrated muscular, masculine power and stand-alone integrity. Whitemud was at a crossroads in the early twentieth century between "horse and gun cultures" and homesteading, between "cowboy tradition" and domestication (133–34). The town's folklore celebrated cowboy ways, even though the reality often expressed "prejudice . . . callousness . . . destructive practical joking . . . the tendency to judge everyone by the same raw standard" (136). What tilted the balance toward the homesteaders and town folk, toward feminized culture, was "catastrophe," the killing winter of 1906–7.

Stegner's cowboy tale, "Genesis," and family drama, "Carrion Spring," relate human struggle against a fierce landscape during this infamous winter. In Robert Harlow's words, by entering a fictional landscape "we leave off remembrance and history and watch while the spirit and edge of the frontier are blunted by the hard facts of the climate of the region."[17] Through fiction, Stegner's deep map engages the reader in the immediacy and inchoateness of harsh living during the transition from nomadic communities to settlement.

In "Genesis," Stegner releases in the sound of a prairie blizzard "the voices of all the lost, all the Indians, métis, hunters, Mounted Police, wolfers, cowboys, all the bundled bodies . . . all the ghosts . . . all the skeleton women and children of the starving winters"(202). Wind, cold, and landscape overwhelm Stegner's protagonists. At one point, young Rusty Cullen, working his chores and chopping through the river ice to provide for the living, "watched the water well up and overflow . . . like some dark force from the ancient heart of the earth that could at any time rise around them silently and obliterate their little human noises" (150–51). "Without a better internal 'map' of the country," Rick Van Noy states in his reading of this story, "hopes about places are doomed to get lost."[18] Rusty, a greenhorn Englishman, faces a test of his internalized, shallow map of place. He has barely been in this country. The possibility of erasure, of disappearance, depresses him: "It was easy to doubt their very existence; it was easy to doubt his own" (151). Living and enduring, in sync with the cattle he watches, Rusty sees both human and beast "in league against the forces of cold and death"(163).

Taut and graphic, "Genesis" relives a killing winter in all its fury and "cosmic injustice" (196).

At story's opening, a cowboy crew headed by foreman Ray Henry departs for a roundup of cattle to winter pastures. No one suspects the dangerous weather that awaits them as they leave the T-Down Ranch. Young Rusty imagines what their cowboy parade must look like. "They carried no lances or pennons," he vainly thinks, "the sun found no armor from which to strike light, but in the incandescence of being nineteen, and full of health, and assaulted in all his senses by the realization of everything splendid he had ever imagined, the English boy knew that no more romantic procession had ever set forth" (140). In a matter of days, the T-Down procession would return, desperate and near frozen, their cattle scattered to face the killing snows and brutal temperatures.

November 1906 marks the beginning of a tragic winter. The men set out to complete a tough task—finding cattle on the vast open range and securing their return to the T-Down. Ray Henry, coolheaded and experienced, a quiet leader of men, keeps them focused and on track, wearing them out with persistent work. Rusty soon discovers that camping after a day's hard labor is no bargain. "He was tired, stiff, cold; there was no immediate comfort in camp, but only more cold hard work, and the snow that was only a thin scum on the prairie was three inches deep down here," Stegner tells us (150). Exacerbating the young man's adjustment, Rusty has no map of this place. He responds to the land's reality through the warped lens of European literature. Medieval literature cannot prepare him for the motley crew he works with, the challenging life of cowboying, or the implacable resistance of the cattle. The men tease him or ignore him, and when Rusty injures an arm, they offer no help or sympathy. These first days out on the range turn into an excruciating rite of passage for Rusty.

What the Englishman does not grasp is that this toughening will help him survive the ordeal of the impending storm. Ray Henry knows how to work men and cattle, but even the foreman's confidence in the efficacy of hard labor fails when nature turns up all forces. More than a week into the drive, watching his men huddled and dimming in the tent, Ray has to confront ground truth. They will die if they persist. A Montanan, Ray, unlike Rusty, is not alien to the Plains. His senses and mind respond to the land's cues, and Ray does not trust what he sees. "I don't quite like the looks of the sky," he concludes (186).

"Genesis" presents the men's harrowing return in gripping detail. Young Rusty inwardly rebels against Ray Henry's decisions and commands, but Ray's internalized map is superior and his instincts correct, even if his stubborn will wants to complete a job. What Rusty cannot grasp is that Ray's steadiness and environmental astuteness will save them all—all, that is, except the cattle. Their loss goads Ray, and "[for] the first time expression . . . flickered across Ray's chapped, bearded mouth" (218).

Out in the wind, cattle are dying. "Well," Ray considers with disgust and defeat, "the ones that ain't dead by the time this blows out may find some willows to gnaw in a coulee. . . . If we don't get a Chinook the wolves are going to be very fat by spring" (218). Ray cannot afford romantic illusions. He must steer his men back to safety, and in the end he does. Throughout the story, Rusty inwardly gnashes, pouts, whimpers, and sulks, an immature, inexperienced dude hand in terra incognita. Ray serves as the standard of manhood on the last Plains frontier. In silently mentoring the younger man, Ray teaches Rusty "that what would pass for heroics in a softer world was only chores around here" (219).

Ray's comments about cattle dying are prescient. In the paired story, "Carrion Spring," Molly and Ray Henry's dreams of participating in the epic construction of Whitemud are nearly defeated by the carrion stench "breathing out in the first warmth across hundreds of square miles," as the tally of dead cattle rises (223). The killing winter of 1906–7 did not end until May. Newlyweds at story's beginning, the Henrys leave for Saskatchewan in late October, taking a "buckboard honeymoon" (222). Along their journey, they discuss "the future settlement of that country and the opportunities open to the young and industrious" (222). Instead, they arrive in time to participate in the killing winter, to face six months "of desperate work and hardship and shortages and unmitigated failure" (222). What hope Molly has after these months focuses on one thing: "to take her man and her marriage back where there was a chance for both" (222). When she looks around at her homestead, Molly assesses things this way:

> The yard lay discolored and ugly, gray ashpile, rusted cans, spilled lignite, bones. The clinkers that had given them winter footing to privy and stable lay in raised gray wavers across the mud; the strung lariats they had used for lifelines in blizzardy weather had dried out and sagged to the ground. Muck was knee deep down in the corrals by the sod-roofed stable, the whitewashed logs were yellowed at the corners from dogs lifting their legs against them.... Across the wan and disheveled yard the willows were bare, and beyond them the flood-plain hill was brown. The sky was roiled with gray cloud. (223)

Molly cannot wait a moment more to leave this wasteland behind: "There was nothing left to do but go" (223). Life here has born nothing.

"Carrion Spring" reeks of death and irony and presents to us "a hopeless country" (227). As Ray leads their horses across the prairie to take Molly away from their failure, he sits "humped" and "impenetrable," protesting their retreat. He has worked hard to gain a toehold in this country. Hundreds of dead cattle line their route producing a stench that exacerbates the separation of husband and wife. The story may be framed through Molly's thoughts and feelings, but all the while Ray's laconic voice and silent stubbornness tug against her internal reality. In a stand-off reminiscent of

Robert Frost's poem "Home Burial," the Henrys hold oppositional dreams. She wants Malta, Montana, and the friends and family members they left behind; he wants to conquer this death and build his ranch. Molly perceives that "they had this antagonism between them like a snarl of barbed wire" (228).

Ray, infuriated by the land's resistance, argues that they stay: "We're never goin' to have another chance like this as long as we live. This country's goin' to change; there'll be homesteaders in here soon as the railroad comes. Towns, stores, what you've been missin'. Women folks. And we can sit out here on the Whitemud with good hay land and good range and just make this God darned country holler uncle" (237). He wants to buy the T-Down Ranch that he has been working for. To do so, Ray will need to go into debt to the tune of "six or eight thousand dollars" (238). To convince his wife to stay, Ray asks, "Haven't you got any ambition to be the first white woman in five hundred miles?" (238).

The hypermasculine world of "Genesis" is unsustainable if Whitemud is to prosper in the long-term. "Carrion Spring" brings us the transition to settled country, borne on the shoulders of women who acquiesce to their husband's dreams. A coyote pup that Molly has rescued from its den enacts her ultimate acceptance of Ray's determination to stay and fight, to stare down death and bring on life. A ranch hand kills the mother and other pups. The sole survivor, wild citizen of the landscape, becomes Molly's to "tame" (232). While feeding him tidbits from their packed lunch and touching its fur, Molly considers Ray's proposition. "All right," she says in the last lines of the story, "if it's what you want" (238). She gives in with the knowledge that they will be in debt "enough to pin them down for life," that they will face years of sufferance in exchange for a chance on this landscape (238).

If the story "Genesis" "shatters the romantic myth of frontier individualism," then "Carrion Spring" presents "a couple that decides to 'stick'—to make a living in that place even though they lost their cattle to the winter—while others are moving on."[19] The Henrys have seen the worst this place has to offer; they go into this new venture with a deeper respect for place. Perhaps, against all odds, the Henrys have learned the landscape lessons well enough to "provide better 'maps' in a journey home."[20] The Henrys' response to failure, guarded optimism, returns the text to memoir and the failure of the Stegners to make ends meet on the Plains, to make any durable mark on the landscape.

In his final chapters, Stegner comes full circle to the settlement town of his childhood and to the difficulty of presenting the history of a "discontinuous" place. Dreams brought homesteaders and merchants to remote Whitemud, but nightmarish reality drove many out. In the twentieth century, Whitemud became a town that doubted it would have a future, an evolving history. Like Ray and Molly Henry, Stegner's parents arrived full of hope; but the drought years following their arrival in 1914 would defeat them. Settling in a country "that hated a foreign and vertical thing," the Stegners attempted to establish themselves in resistance to "searing wind, scorching sky, tormented and heat-warped light," and the treeless terrain (278). The nature of the place—what Brett J. Olsen calls "that merciless expanse of earth and sky"—would win out.[21] In the 1930s, the Dirty Thirties, drought would again shrink Whitemud's population. "Dead, dead, dead, says the mind contemplating the town's life," Stegner keens (296). In light of such futility, the graveyard and the dump seem to Stegner the town's most permanent features. The town, at its 1955 jubilee, was but a shadow of its nineteenth-century expectations. This diminishment, after the town's early boosterism, provides material evidence of one of Stegner's major points in this multilayered text: frontier myths that belie facts on the ground cannot sustain community life. In Brett Olsen's assessment, "[as] his early life fell at odds with romantic notions of the West, a skepticism regarding western myth lay at the core of his environmentalism. Indeed, perhaps more than any,

Stegner understood, from both experience and observation, the environmental and human damage caused by blind adherence to frontier mythology."[22]

John Daniel sees in Stegner's historical narrative a purposeful pattern: "Memory gives form to the flux of subjective experience, history gives form to collective experience held in memory, and fictional narrative further forms memory and history into the wholer truth of art."[23] In an article devoted to Stegner's storytelling, Elliott West has underscored the essential deep mapping narrative elements that make place-based historical writing so vital: place "is the accumulation of all the things that people have done on that spot . . . a 'place' involves the meanings that humans have taken from an area and from what has happened there, the perceptions and emotions of individuals responding to their surroundings, and to events."[24] It is Stegner's genius that he presented "western history as a perceptual and emotional encounter."[25] Such narrative deep mapping works, in William Kittredge's words, to achieve exphrasis, to expose time's deeper connection in "moment[s] which [contain] the past and [imply] the future."[26]

In one of Stegner's most memorable metaphors, history is a pontoon bridge: "Every man walks and works at its building end, and has come as far as he has over the pontoons laid by others he may never have heard of" (29). Unknowingly, each step Stegner takes as a child covers space already inhabited, already built up around stories. Yet as a boy, Stegner, and the other children who "grow up in a newly settled country," suffered from "discontinuity" (111). The past was an "unremembered" thing, and Whitemud the capital of this absence. Unlike the descendants of "Gabriel Dumont or Big Bear or Wandering Spirit," he was unable to understand the longer history of this place, to feel "the passion of personal loss and defeat" (112). Only in middle age, Stegner confesses, did he miss history: "I realized that I didn't have a single place to which I could refer myself. I had no crowd, I had no gang, I had no sociological matrix or context except as I could find it or form it by going back along my life."[27] It was as a "middle-aged pilgrim," then, that he returns to the "monotonous surface" of Saskatchewan to look beyond the failure of the last Plains frontier, beyond the drought years that destroyed homesteaders' dreams.

What to do with this sense of loss and mea culpa, how to acknowledge it, mourn it, rectify it, remains incomplete business in Stegner's deep map and continues to press upon Plains deep map writing of this era. The current interest in bioregional narratives or environmentalist essays of place finds a resonantly firm foothold in Stegner's examination of the last Plains frontier land rush in Saskatchewan and its illusory mythology. He castigates the settlers' tragic detachment from the environmental realities of the northern Plains, their heedless, ruthless damage to arid land, and then clear-sightedly dramatizes the blowback from the Plains environment itself.

At the core of Stegner's critique, however contradictory, is a firm love of the landscape, a desire for restitution, and a need to redress loss. With the hindsight of later years, Stegner assesses the outcome and begins to articulate a grasslands land ethic, a Plains bioregionalism that marks deep map writing from the center of the continent. In reestablishing his roots in Saskatchewan, Stegner invents an innovative aesthetic to plumb a story that requires a complex matrix of connections, histories, feelings, temporal and spatial dimensions, and science.

In an interview with Richard W. Etulain, Stegner discusses the shallow vision of history among his neighbors in Whitemud: "All of those people were orphans of a sort. All of them had a very limited and almost completely unliterate kind of memory. More than that, the Indians before them had left no marks on that country, except a few tepee rings. There weren't many relics of the past, books or otherwise, and so I couldn't have learned anything about the history of that town, although I could now."[28] A similar sense of the elusiveness of history marks another deep map, William Least Heat-Moon's *PrairyErth*. Stegner begins *Wolf Willow* cartographically: he situates Whitemud on a map, giving us the highways and topographical features that lead us to his boyhood home. Indeed, as Rick Van Noy points out, "Stegner inserted such a map on the end papers of the book showing the geography of Eastern Montana and of Saskatchewan."[29] Moreover, Van Noy details, Stegner's very "first lines of the text acknowledge the importance of maps as the starting point for information about a place."[30] From this textual and visual map, Stegner advances his sense of history. Envisioned "personally and historically," he waxes, "that almost featureless prairie glows with more color than it reveals to the appalled and misdirected tourist. As memory, as experience, those Plains are unforgettable; as history, they have the lurid explosiveness of a prairie fire, quickly dangerous, swiftly over" (4). Stegner's map of memory and history clearly lies below the surface of Heat-Moon's text.

Deep mapping one county in Kansas, Chase County, Heat-Moon also turns to cartography to provide direction and stability to a place marked by transience, economic instability, and cultural erasure. The irony of mapmaking or map-reading, in both Stegner and Heat-Moon, lies in our complicit knowledge that a map, any map—like history itself—is an inexact representation. As much as a grid—on a map or in a text—structures perception, offers itself as guide and meaning, it also requires critical reading and revision. In O. Alan Weltzien's words, "as *moments* of representing any landscape, [maps] immediately and inevitably lag behind the living thing they purport to represent."[31]

In *PrairyErth*, the map becomes a visual signifier of history, of narrative that is itself lagging behind in representation. History and maps are never finished, never completed, always approximate. Yet if both are to work, we must trust in their efficacy, trust in their fragments, to repeat Robert Kroetsch. Thomas Fox Averill has noted the important ways maps connect with memory and imagined history. A map begs us to elaborate, refurnish, flush out the landscape it represents. Speaking of his deep connection to Kansas and his love of maps, Averill continues, "maps become more real as they are traveled and imagined (imaged), thus made both concrete and intuitive."[32] In such a process, history and cartography become necessarily "participatory."[33]

In creating the narrative structure of *PrairyErth*, in representing his deep map of Chase County, Kansas, Heat-Moon absorbs the culturally mixed cartographic traditions of the Plains. This history is fascinating in and of itself. Rock art, elk-skin celestial charts, birch bark scrolls, and other forms of Indigenous mapmaking preserve the spatial knowledge of diverse Plains tribes. Received visually or orally, Native cartography aided European exploration of the North American continent, and, in particular, provided Lewis and Clark with "an unparalleled grasp of terrain."[34] G. Malcolm Lewis ascribes "three broad categories of American cartography" in this summation:

> The first stage, precontact, predates even in direct European influence and is rooted in antiquity. Evidence of maps that were made largely independent of European influence, however slender, consists of rock art and man-made structures such as mounds, representing mainly celestial and cosmographical subjects. The second stage, comprising maps made at the time of first contact with explorers, traders, soldiers, missionaries, and early settlers for a variety of exploratory, economic, and political negotiations, dates from the mid-sixteenth century to the late nineteenth, depending on region. The main sources of evidence for such maps are accounts of ephemeral maps in early literature on discovery and exploration and very few surviving artifacts on birchbark, skin, bone, and wampum. The third stage dates from the establishment of the first permanent Euro-American settlements, the development of regular trade and communication

networks, and the beginnings of resource exploitation. In this category we find Indian maps made to aid communication with Euro-Americans and to satisfy their requests for information about routes, strategic relationships, and resource locations.[35]

This contact between cartographic traditions signals the political and cultural transformation of a landscape. From Indigenous mapmaking to the efforts of professional and amateur surveyors to contemporary GIS image-makers, Heat-Moon finds inspiration in tracing the thick description of a long history.

Heat-Moon's mapping metaphor is meticulously worked out in *PrairyErth*. His arrangement is purposeful and inventive. Though I am not persuaded by Pamela Walker's argument that *Prairy-Erth* is "randomly arranged," I do agree with her assessment that Heat-Moon starts with a visual icon of place, the map, features an interdependent, Bakhtinian representation of "time-space," and plays with a self-conscious, "writerly" narrative.[36] This purposeful structure, in Rick Van Noy's assessment, gives readers "a more profound and complex sense of place than maps, stereotypes about the prairie, or the flyover view from an airplane acknowledge."[37] Heat-Moon's critical consciousness is essential in questioning the assumptions that structure his map, and he asks his readers to test the grid right along with him.

A pivotal quality of maps is how they organize time. The casual map-reader does not usually mull over "the accumulated thought and labor of the past" distilled into a map's features.[38] But maps "make present . . . the past" as well as bring into being future understanding.[39] Maps infuse the present, "our living . . . *now . . . here*," with the past.[40] Cartographer Denis Wood eloquently explains, "We are always mapping the invisible or the unattainable or the erasable, the future or the past, the whatever-is-not-here-present-to-our-senses-now and, through the gift that the map gives us, transmuting it into everything it is not . . . *into the real*."[41]

Spreading twenty-five U.S. Geological Survey maps of Chase County over his floor, Heat-Moon walks the six-foot-by-seven-foot "paper land," trying to get a finger on the grid. Alan Weltzien's brilliant analysis of *PrairyErth's* grid structure asserts, "The book constitutes a gargantuan metaphoric extension of the USGS quad map," that "he writes his initial parables of cartography inside the primary American cartographic narrative."[42] Each chapter "contains six sections and of these, the first two and final sections—'From the Commonplace Book,' 'In the Quadrangle,' and 'On the Town' respectively—repeat themselves."[43] Gregory-Guider adds, "each of [the book's] chapters is devoted to the narration of the author's travels within one of the twelve quadrants that comprises his cartographic grid. These twelve sections are named according to the distinguishing topographic feature of the quadrant (e.g., Fox Creek, Elmdale, Gladstone), and each opens with a map that indicates the location of train tracks, road- and waterways, and selected sites of interest."[44]

Significantly, each chapter begins with a cartographic icon, an abstraction of the grid, which emphasizes the narrative's dynamic relationship to mapmaking. Yet this system born of the Land Ordinance of 1785 proves unworthy of Heat-Moon's task. The grid represents "arbitrary quadrangles that have nothing inherently to do with the land, little to do with history, and not much to do with my details."[45] On Roniger Hill, in Chase County, Heat-Moon tests the grid, "standing here, thinking of grids, and what's under them, their depths and their light and darkness," seeing if the "digging, sifting, sorting, assembling shards" of this county's past will come to life, will breath as living history (15–16). The grid is a starting point only. Chase County itself "is thirty miles long north to south, twenty-six miles east to west on the south border and a mile shorter on the north."[46] These literal dimensions embrace a complex mapping. Reading, thinking, imagining, walking, talking, and dreaming build the accretionary levels of his history. In both

Stegner and Heat-Moon personal, sensory engagement guides the initial mapping that leads to complex narration.

Like Stegner's deep map, Heat-Moon's "time-space" narrative radiates out from personal history to connect to deeper geological time and to a longer sense of human habitation. He interviews contemporaries to gather oral histories, anecdotes, and information. He reads history, geography, newspaper accounts, journals, and old letters to add to his store of knowledge. His feet take him many long miles over each quadrangle in the USGS maps, where vestiges of past worlds and lives haunt him. Hard to find are artifacts from settlement days; harder still are traces of the Native peoples of Kansas. Buried below the surface lie the telling layers of former worlds, "the crystalline basement" (156). As each section of the map is traced, researched, and walked, one gains a sense of gathering loss, of history losing its depths, of humanity's ephemerality. *PrairyErth* leaves a strong impression of impermanence and loss. Despite all the Geertzian thick description of place in Heat-Moon's text, Chase County remains elusive, so much so that by page six hundred of his story, he presents his readers with a blackened blank page. The Jeffersonian grid itself becomes implicated in boom-or-bust cycles, struggling, nascent ventures like the Emma Chase Café in the present or the Orient line in the past; the grid has damned Chase County.[47]

The grid, as imposed and imposing structure, provides an important portal into Chase County's considerable history that "sweeps from the distant past to the present."[48] Ronald Grim, examining the mapping of Kansas and Nebraska between 1854 and 1895, claims that such rectangular precision is "the dominant factor" of surveying and consequently settling the Plains.[49] The abstract, two-dimensional grid stands out even at cruising altitudes of thirty-five thousand feet. Its presence is ubiquitous. The elegance of the grid seemingly complements the emptiness of the place. Yet the grid is never ahistorical; as a human construction, it reflects the worldview of colonizers (the grid goes back to imperial Rome) who wished to turn *terra nullius* into production and to push "unproductive" Natives off the land.[50]

A U.S. governmental survey system implemented two centuries ago has sectioned off Chase County and "seventy percent of America."[51] The grid determines private and public ownership of our lands; it defines control and power. Contemplating the economic struggles countians face in Elk, Heat-Moon reflects on the grid and sees "a crimping of expectations and possibilities," a bitter irony "in this grandly open land" (427). No longer a mere abstraction that measured wildness and domesticated the heart of America—the positive spin on the survey system—the grid is a "curse . . . that has helped bring about the effective vassalage" of settlers' descendants (427–28). Heat-Moon's thick description, complex rambles, and amassed stories critically appraise the grid, a system that initially seemed "arbitrary," ahistorical, irrelevant to the author's "details" (15). As Heat-Moon's stories accrue, so, too, do the grid's effects over history: homesteads too small to sustain families; human vision fenced in and diminished; towns increasingly stripped of people and purpose. In Homestead, Kansas, the grid, "Jeffersonian perfection," transforms into a prison, into a net, into a blankness and a darkness: "In my time in the quad, I could never find a way to escape through the gaps into where the real place might lie, and I seemed equally incapable of turning the grid into a screen that might sift out artifacts" (364). What at first presented itself as an enabling metaphor seems to lead not to truth and to connection—to a sense of coherent history—but to absurdity and incompletion.

The grid cannot serve as the sole method of mapping because so much escapes its boundaries. As a parable of cartography, as O. Alan Weltzien interprets it, *PrairyErth* provides lessons in incompletion, limitation, and failure.[52] Other kinds of maps, other visuals to history, supplement the grid in this text: personal maps of peregrination, topographic dream maps, Native American circlings that "alter and often subvert the grid."[53] Heat-Moon scrupulously marks the state and county roads he follows—roads that tend to reproduce the grid in asphalt or dirt washboard—but just as often, he leaves them behind, discarding the map and allowing the body instead to guide his exploration. If one stays in the grid, much truth is lost; the grid conceals more than it reveals.

Acutely aware of any one map's circumscription, Heat-Moon, like Stegner, constructs his deep map to stretch boundaries, to enlarge vision and scale, to multiply perspectives, and to make the finite and infinite touch. His cartographic narrative expresses exactly the kind of new cartography geographer Alan MacEachren and others have called for: "cartographic research that attempts to merge the perceptual, cognitive, and semiotic issues of maps as functional devices for portraying space."[54] Cartographers, MacEachren continues, must understand "representation at many levels."[55] James Duncan and David Ley echo MacEachren's argument. Rejecting mimetic and positivist models of mapmaking, they champion a new hermeneutical method that is "interpersonal" and "intercultural."[56] In place of traditional representations of landscapes, contemporary cultural geographers and cartographers seek new metaphors: "text, theatre . . . and painting."[57] With the map now allied with narrative art forms, it can delve into complexities of space and of cultural conflict enacted in space. For the cultural geographer and cartographer to understand landscape from multiple angles, interdisciplinarity is de rigueur. Such theorizing over representation itself crosses disciplines. The ongoing dialogue in geography parallels those in both history and literary studies. Heat-Moon, with his ambivalent connections to academia and the University of Missouri, has created a multifaceted narrative in tune with poststructural debates yet independent of abstract, ivory tower obtuseness.

In her memorable study *Ghost West: Reflections Past and Present*, Ann Ronald locates those "places where something once happened, locales where people and events from the past still define and determine the aura of the present."[58] Such haunted spaces expose "something about the way ghosts from the past overlay a twentieth-or-twenty-first century sense of place."[59] Once Heat-Moon steps off the grid, he starts negotiating much of the "ghost West" in Chase County. Off-grid cartography requires attention to folklore, vestigial artifacts, the oral and written historical record, and sixth sense, dream sense. In mapping traces and hints, Heat-Moon attempts to understand the present-day landscape, where small businesses struggle, industrial agriculture pushes production beyond sustainability to the edge, and the population ages and shrinks. Heat-Moon tries to divine as much as he can from this invisible landscape.

In a book as long as *PrairyErth*, it is challenging to pull from the many details and episodes the most telling and pregnant stories. For Heat-Moon, Chase County is alive with stories, even if the casual traveler sees little in the rolling landscape to stop the eye and draw attention. So many other voices speak in *PrairyErth*, from the commonplace book refrains, to interviews, captured conversations, and unsolicited comments from strangers. In his dream moments, Heat-Moon seems to hear from the landscape itself. The density of vestiges in this narrative is daunting to the scholar attempting to distill a reading. That a number of scholars have chosen to focus primarily on the grid and the USGS map is understandable because the ghost map of Chase County resists mapping in any traditional sense.

Early in the text, Heat-Moon comes upon old U.S. 50, two miles east of Saffordville, Kansas. Even the "countians don't know it still exists" (46). A newer highway has taken its place and, Heat-Moon adds, "its toll" (47). The new highway is one of the most dangerous stretches in the state. Heat-Moon prefers "this ghost of a road, the one under my boots, this one quiet for thirty years and starting to disappear under sediment and scrub" (47). Old U.S. 50 goes nowhere, but in his imagination it goes back to "the birth of the tallgrass prairie, that epoch when turfy perennials—bluestem and gramas, panicums and ryes—began covering the American interior as the old sea, now turned to a limestone anchor, once did" (47). Ironically, the ghost road is allowing the ancient prairie to return, blade by blade, through its disintegration. In Heat-Moon's ghost map, "prairie birth" is day one for the future Chase County. "Here," he explains, "inches of evaporation and precipitation are nearly equal, and here, above my head, the rain-shadow of the Rockies meets in commensurate strength the humid Gulf fronts," a balance that supports tall grasses and tall trees (48). Without this foundation, the flora and fauna and human habitation of the tallgrass prairie would suffer. The old highway is now off-grid or off-map, but its crumbling surface bespeaks eons of change.

The grid, then, is the visible, surface landscape. The deep map exists to support the many off-grid or ambiguously gridded realities. The grid, too, faces modification as people experiment, dream, and adapt in place. As Buell puts it, Heat-Moon

> clearly relishes pointing out cases where symbiosis of land and settlement has occurred, as in the planting of Osage orange trees as natural hedgerows or the adaptation of the hardy cottonwood, now the totem tree of the state of Kansas. When settlers modify regional ecology in such a way that nature flourishes and the people intertwine with it, that is not imperial imposition; for the grid itself is modified, biologized. The author is not at all disposed to deny bona fide deeply rooted place-sense to 'countians' because of their culture's gridlike inception, least of all when the grid begins to soften and dissolve.[60]

Thus the grid is not monolithic, but bends to off-grid sensibilities. Towns that existed because of the grid and the building of the railroads also speak to softening and dissolution, to the nonlinear cycles of off-grid time and space. Thurman, early in the book, stands as a ghost town. Almost all of Thurman has disappeared. His guide Joe Hickey, a local academic anthropologist, tells Heat-Moon that Thurman is now "go-back-land" (102). Founded as part of a speculation, Thurman has suffered the fate of many boom towns; it went bust. Joe says, "One thing has been consistent through all the years of white settlement: just about everybody has treated the land as only a commodity to make a buck off of" (103). Elmdale, another "place of erasure," is further evidence of decline (309). Heat-Moon describes "the vaporish citizens," the shuttered Main Street, and the low pulse of habitation here (309). Is Elmdale where one crosses into eternity or a limbo place where the dying live before actual death? "Maybe I've already, so to speak, gone west in Elmdale, Kansas," Heat-Moon playfully contends. "Maybe *I'm* the wraith here, a temporary ghost" (310). Yet another place, Wonsevu, speaks to the many Kansa and Osage who came to the agency building, now a ruin. "A few cabins remain in this valley," Heat-Moon observes, "where the people who gave their name to the state watched a ten-thousand-year-old way of life disappear, and with it their hopes for continuance" (550). At this temporal distance, however, the replacement culture seems as vulnerable as the Indigenous people who were so forcefully and violently removed from their traditional lands to reservations.

In Kansas, a number of famous routes and trails associated with white settlement and nation building traverse its terrain: the Santa Fe, the Overland, the Oregon or California Road, the Underground Railroad, the Chisholm and Great Western Cattle Trails, the Pony Express, and later mythic auto routes like U.S. 50 and 66. John C. Frémont's published expeditions and Francis Parkman's *The Oregon Trail* immortalized Kansas. The Flint Hills preserve traces of a number of these storied routes. Each has accrued its own narratives of creation and passage. When relevant, Heat-Moon marks the imprint of a famous route across Chase County. However, it is a different sort of ghost route that claims the author's fascination: the Orient Line.

Leaving Cottonwood one morning, Heat-Moon happens upon "a tall and marvelously laid stone abutment with a matching one on the bank opposite, the cut rocks as big as any you can find here" (245). This railroad fragment takes on signification as his deep map expands. The Orient grade was an investor's dead dream, a proposed rail route to connect Kansas City to China's markets. Climbing onto the grade, Heat-Moon "[hikes] down another man's dream" (246). Arthur Edward Stilwell "designed a railroad sixteen hundred miles long which will bring the Pacific Ocean four hundred miles nearer to Kansas City" (247). Topolobampo, Mexico, would be its western terminus. As Heat-Moon recounts this story of dream defunct, he notes this irony: all of the proposed route was eventually built but other railways gained the trackage. Stilwell's vision never came to fruition, and his "dream route was complete except for a hundred and some miles across the Flint Hills" (251).

The uncompleted traces of dreams, the finished, dying towns along the way, the erased signs of human presence, Indigenous and settler, speak loudest of the past to Heat-Moon. The fabric of time and space folds in his pliable mapping, the haunted and living layers touching in uneasy relationship. Imperial gestures like the Orient grade lie like the ruins of Shelley's "Ozymandias," vain efforts of grandeur and railroad baronetcy. Haunted coordinates in the county presage similar fates to modern human enterprises if Kansans steer into the future on the roads of the past.

In the "topographical dreamtime" of Chase County, one spot expresses a different sort of grandeur: Diamond Spring. Along the trade route, this location was "the most famous oasis on the Santa Fe Trail" (448). As "last home port" on the road to La Villa Real de Santa Fe, this spring loomed large in travelers' accounts. It became a place of gathering caravans set for disembarking westward across the expansive grasslands. As jumping-off point,

Diamond Spring marked the divide between plenty and scarcity. Beyond lay "uncertain supplies of water, grass, and safety: from the spring westward, the trail passed through the fierce land of the Comanches, Apaches, and Kiowa" (449).

Visiting Diamond Spring in the late twentieth century, Heat-Moon experiences what "would have been the grandest disappointment in my million miles of American travel" (448). Ranching has negatively impacted this historic site "so that few springs flow as they once did" (448). Today a "concrete stock tank . . . only a little larger and deeper than a coffin" replaces the spring (449). Cattle hooves cut into the soil. This place of national importance, barely viable, is nearly impossible to find, map or no map. Maps of old, vital to travelers' survival, are now off grid in the modern world.

The ghost world of discard, bust, and neglect speaks directly to national mandates, ideas of progress, development, and property, which once seemed so promising but now leave residues of doubt and concern. Countians seek new solutions amid the detritus of dead ideas and dreams. Late in his text, Heat-Moon finds his way to Wes Jackson, who is attempting a new map of place that bends to place. Attempting to create a "domestic prairie," Jackson and his fellow scientists seek answers in the oldest map of life, DNA (494). In the chapter "To Consult the Genius of the Place in All," Heat-Moon takes backstage and allows Jackson's voice to prevail. Jackson examines the legacy of the grid and proclaims, "*[We] destroyed most of the original relationship we had with nature as we expanded our gardens and plots into fields*" (497–98). The patterns we have embraced, like the grid, are entrenched "old inclinations" that need to be rooted out and replaced with restorative measures (499). Jackson's dream map, the future landscape of place-based agriculture, looks like this: "*I imagine keeping the grasslands intact, planting bottomland to a greater diversity of species, and farming it in somewhat different ways to try to be much less extractive*" (500). This new map does not exile the heirs of settlement or argue a return to buffalo commons. Instead, Jackson seeks efficiency in sustainability. His *"new world view"* maps *"the second coming of the homesteader"* (504).

This map-to-be precedes Heat-Moon's final map, his map of circlings and return. Exploring the ancient Kaw Track with his friend Clive, or "the Venerable Tashmoo," Heat-Moon explains, "The track we intended to follow was not a narrow, trodden depression but a direction. . . . We were hunting the idea of the trail" (609). Perambulation throughout *PrairyErth* has given Heat-Moon the most direct access to the tangible ecology of Chase County that inspires his off-grid imagination. As Eamonn Wall explains, "walking goes hand-in-hand with writing."[61] Heat-Moon's feet trace the ghost steps of Indigenous travelers and bring him sensuous guideposts to place. In walking, he is also connecting to the first North Americans, who embraced a vertical life in grasslands. In circling back to the oldest Plains inhabitants, Heat-Moon ponders the incomplete nature of his journey and his deep map.

His intensely stratigraphic rendering of Chase County, Kansas, concludes enigmatically. Sitting around a campfire, the two men lift glasses and honor aspects of the genius loci. Heat-Moon declares, "I'd say I've found a place willing to reveal itself" (621). The landscape apparently responds:

> Then came something I'd never seen before: a bird flew into the small cottonwood, and from its silhouette against the moon I could see it was a jay. We stared at it in disbelief, and finally the Venerable whispered, *Since when do birds fly into campfire circles?*
> —Isn't just a bird.
> The Venerable slowly stood, pulled me up, raised his arms, I did too, palms outward, and he said, *Old Ones.*
> A circled presence, like a miasma, pressed in, and how long it remained I don't know, but a meteor, the slowest falling one I ever saw, dropped right across the Great Bear like a thrown

spear, and then the circle seemed to loosen, and things regained their accustomed positions, dispositions. The jaybird was gone. (621–22)

For this dreamlike moment, they stand in the fold of the deep map, contemplating the power of memory and imagination, of a shared cosmic consciousness.

Essays of place, Kent Ryden reminds us, attempt "to replace a static, two-dimensional, cartographic view of cartography with a living world of narrative."[62] Ultimately, Heat-Moon must abandon the grid in order "to both feel the life and meaning of a place and to inscribe its patterns on paper," even if that paper must turn infamously pitch black on page 600.[63] "My explorations quite early began forming into a gestalt," Heat-Moon explains, "that seems to control what I am capable of writing about" (598). In a land "where openness can sometimes begin to seem like blankness," the grid provides a toehold for understanding; but Heat-Moon's forays off the map, into a complex gestalt both physical and imaginative, finally allow him to enter fully into place (547).

Michael Kowalewski has noted that "[literary] 'mappings' of American places have increasingly involved an interest in metaphors of depth, resonance, root systems, habitats, and interconnectedness."[64] Stegner's *Wolf Willow* reminds us that Canadian places also inspire deep maps. Indeed, Stegner and Heat-Moon embed all these various transferences and more. In order to organize their vast, overarching histories, they have turned to parables of archaeology and cartography to make sense of complexity, to account for absence, and to reclaim the significance of human efforts. *Wolf Willow* and *PrairyErth* are monumental, significant efforts themselves. In a different context, scholar Krista Comer has argued that "[landscape] is not just mystified text; rather, it *makes* history."[65] Through studied and innovative storytelling, steeped in the nuances of place, of landscape, Stegner and Heat-Moon make history. In the preface to *Under Western Skies*, Donald Worster remarks, "the history that most excites me is . . . physical, ecological, earthy, complex as only nature can be complex."[66] Indeed, a major argument running through this series of essays is a call for "a new past."[67] Additionally, Jamie Robertson reminds us, "Such a mixture of fact and fiction . . . is a poetic creation, both real and imaginary, that explains our relationship to a place and its past."[68] Deep maps, then, follow a new aesthetic and connect to this urgent call for renovated stories and revamped histories. *Wolf Willow* and *PrairyErth* stand as signature efforts of creative artists to join this chorus for a resonant past.

CHAPTER THREE

DEEP MAPPING THE BIOME

The Biology of Place in Don Gayton's *The Wheatgrass Mechanism*, John Janovy Jr.'s *Dunwoody Pond*, and Wes Jackson's *Becoming Native to This Place*

While according postmodernism its due for showing us very well the roles that culture, imagination, and words have played in creating the world, I am convinced that there are tangible ecologies of place out there, and that one of environmental history's tasks is to fold the stories of those ecologies into human history. The word "plains" may carry cultural freight, but it still denotes a different ecology, and a tangible and real one, from "mountains." And we remain biological even with all our bewildering array of cultural dressings.

Dan Flores, *The Natural West*

As the first two chapters reveal, the deep map has undergone a long gestation and its origins lie in the Great Plains straddling both sides of the forty-ninth parallel. Following *Wolf Willow*, nonfiction writers published significant experiments in place-based writing, and the decade of the 1990s was particularly fruitful. The deep map genre has claimed practitioners from many disciplines—journalism, poetry, science, and ranching, for instance—for a reason: the flexibility of a cross-genre, cross-sectional narrative provides a format that revels in the nuance and power of idiosyncratic experience, training, and appreciation of landscape. This form of literary stratigraphy shapes a distinctive kind of "articulated geography."[1] That texts as diverse as Sheila Nickerson's *Disappearance: A Map* (1996), Ian Marshall's *Story Line* (1998), and Matt White's *Prairie Time* (2006), for instance, stand alongside Stegner and Heat-Moon's deep maps signals the growing appeal of this genre across regions.[2] Lawrence Buell has argued that environmental literature in general "increases our feel for both places previously unknown and places known but never deeply felt."[3] The deep map makes the "deeply felt" its forte.

Increasingly important to scholars of the deep map are the innovative, extended essays by professional scientists whose fieldwork gives them a unique understanding of a significant layer of the deep map, the biology of place. Laurie Ricou has argued that "students of literature interested in writing about place . . . need now to be students of ecology on some level," an argument echoed in historian Dan Flores's search for "tangible ecologies of place."[4] In modern environmental nonfiction, the participation of men and women trained in biology and blessed with writing talent has added considerably to our understanding of place and of life's interconnectedness. Aldo Leopold's lyrical celebration of Sand County, Wisconsin, and cogent argument for the land's inherent value in *A Sand County Almanac* is a watershed moment in American letters. Additionally, Rachel Carson's *Silent Spring* galvanized environmental writing, added urgency to the environmental movement, and changed the political landscape. In more recent years, Wes Jackson has attempted to redefine stewardship of the land in influential essays, arguing that the art and science of agriculture must bend to the "realities in nature."[5] *The Rites of Autumn* and *Buffalo for the Broken Heart* have made Dan O'Brien a significant voice in restoration efforts, as communities across the American and Canadian Plains attempt to heal broken land. Biologist Terry

Tempest Williams's poetic essays from the American Southwest spiritualize the science of ecology, blending the intangible with the tangible. Ethnobiologist Gary Paul Nabhan, studying the borderlands between Arizona and Mexico, presents what he calls a "marriage of science and poetry" in books like *Cross-Pollinations*.[6] This brief catalogue of scientist or scientifically trained writers is but a sketchy outline of the invaluable contribution science writing has made to environmental writing.

Only recently have people who make their living as scientists experimented with the deep map genre. Drawn to the genre's hybridity, these scientists delve into the biological mechanisms of place, presenting the interaction of natural forces (climate, geological history, and other evolutionary stresses) upon flora and fauna; re-creating lost worlds and memorializing extinct creatures; musing about the present and its effects on the future; and positing the imposition of human activity on a living place. Science is at the heart of this literary enterprise, but the art of translation, the memorable strokes of metaphor and analogy, and the panache of a well-turned phrase and lyrical moment are not lost on these narrators of place. Intellect, imagination, and passion fuse in their deep maps.

Once again, Great Plains writers have led the way. A contemporary of Heat-Moon's, plant ecologist and Canadian writer Don Gayton has experimented with deep map form in his groundbreaking analysis of grasslands ecology and homage to *Wolf Willow*, *The Wheatgrass Mechanism: Science and Imagination in the Western Canadian Landscape* (1990). In the same years, parasitologist and celebrated essayist John Janovy Jr. was drafting his own deep map, a sustained examination of Sand Hills country to be entitled *Dunwoody Pond: Reflections on the High Plains Wetlands and the Cultivation of Naturalists* (1994). Wes Jackson, from the Land Institute in the Flint Hills of Kansas, was also studying the biome and attempting to redefine agriculture on the Plains. His extended bioregional argument published in 1994, *Becoming Native to This Place*, promotes a new "mindscape" on the Plains informed by memory, social justice, imagination, and science. As a subject in *PrairyErth*, Jackson serves as a cartographic guide for Heat-Moon. While Jackson's own writings are not technically deep map narratives, they work in tandem with those of Heat-Moon, Gayton, and Janovy and serve to underscore the urgency of deep map writing of the 1990s.

Focusing on the science of plant ecology, parasitology, and genetics, these three writers open up to a larger biological canvas that forces us "to think about ourselves as inhabitants of places, of watersheds and topographies, of an evolving piece of space (with an evolving set of fellow inhabitants) different from every other one."[7] Navigating the Great Plains biome, these trained biologists illuminate the ways in which we are native to place at a basic cellular level and at a larger mythic one. They bring us into a microscopic world that escapes the unaided human eye; yet this microworld is fundamental to life and to place. Their biological explorations demonstrate ways in which "the inner landscape is symbiotic with the outer."[8] In so doing, Gayton, Janovy, and Jackson force us to decenter the human, to reconsider the primacy of a larger biological reality, and to reexamine the political and cultural precepts that attempt to control natural systems. They add vital pieces in the ongoing effort to reimagine and revalue a biome that, in writer John T. Price's words, "has suffered such an enormous loss of life with so little protest."[9] Topophilia as necessary affiliation anchors the narratives of these three writers.

Gayton's exploration of the Western Canadian Interior, Janovy's decades' long examination of Sand Hills country in Nebraska, and Jackson's understanding of prairie ecology in Kansas serve to engage readers in central issues of evolutionary biology, habitat destruction and transformation, human choices and their effects on the biome, and the need for a sustainable economy and ecology of the Plains. These "landscape lessons," to use Gayton's phrasing, combine science, history, polemic, and myth in an effort to map the flora and fauna of a region.[10] Such scientific mappings "inaugurate new grounds upon the hidden traces of living context," bending to the physical place but also seeking the invisible, "the various hidden forces that underlie the workings of a given place."[11] The materiality of place incorporates a textual "fusion of flesh, ecology, and culture," an immersion into life forms that fine tunes each writer's moral response to a changed and changing land.[12] Each writer guides us through a specific landscape or site of engagement, often providing maps or highway directions, directly or indirectly inviting the reader to make a physical journey to the grasslands. Somatic, sensuous connection to land, sky, and climate of each locale receives considerable attention. Eastend, Saskatchewan, Keith County, Nebraska, or Salina, Kansas, are sites of fieldwork, and nature is the laboratory, or in Jackson's words "the standard."[13] The work of a plant ecologist, a parasitologist, and a plant geneticist depends on supplementary lab work, but first and foremost, one must become intimate with the laws of integration that operate in real ecosystems.

Gayton walks and bikes through prairie sites in Saskatchewan and Manitoba; Janovy and his students muck about in ponds, wade into rivers, enter into miasmal canyons; Jackson and his colleagues at the Land Institute live and work within the native prairie. Bodily and intellectual immersion guides their experiences in these places. In his essay "The Lady Whitetail," Janovy explains, "The biologist approaches nature in the form of a plant or animal and immediately begins asking questions about the innermost soul, the innermost characteristics, the true spectrum as well as the immediate traits, of the living thing."[14] Perhaps then, too, places "have innermost characters, innermost souls, and whether by simply peeling off the layers one might find that innermost nature that dictates not only our impressions of the place, but indeed our way of approaching and regarding and treating that place."[15] Gayton admits to an "urgency"—what Kristie S. Fleckenstein would call a "permeable materiality"—in a "heart-rending landscape . . . wanting to embrace the land, to couple upon it, to quickly learn the meaning of its antelope and its burrowing owls, and to understand how living things were made from the brittle bunchgrasses."[16] Jackson seeks knowledge that honors "where we come from, counting that as baseline information, essential to our journey toward nativeness."[17] The desire to know intimately, to step into the thing or the system, comes first, before a study is constructed, before lab work is planned and equipment organized. From the singular and specific—a species, a field, or a pond—biologists trace the larger system. Dragonflies of the genus *Anax*, for instance, can help map evolutionary and geologic history. Western wheatgrass connects one to "genetic identity" and to "a very fundamental prairie timeline."[18]

To borrow from cartographer James Corner, Gayton, Janovy, and Jackson present "grounded sites" that help map "a multiplicitous and complex affair, comprising a potentially boundless field of phenomena, some palpable and some imaginary."[19] Their literary cartography—deep mapping genetics and geology, charting ecologies of place, and situating human history and mythology—presents "a fertile heterogeneity."[20] Terrain, then, from this perspective expresses "a complex and dynamic imbroglio of social and natural processes."[21] In the vein of bioregional storytellers, their essays depict particular landscapes as rich sites of "interpenetration," in Dan Flores's terms, which expose layers "of topography, climate, and evolving ecology."[22] The inclusion of science has become a de rigueur stratum of literary deep maps, but in the hands of scientists, this layer gains the foreground. Through the deep down realities of Plains life—root systems, cellular structures, DNA—readers gain a profound understanding of time's passage and life's pageantry, and of human interference with a biome's integrity. This knowledge embodies, as Yi-Fu Tuan gracefully phrases it, "place as time made visible, or place as memorial to times past."[23]

In 1990 Don Gayton published *The Wheatgrass Mechanism: Science and Imagination in the Western Canadian Landscape*, a milestone in Great Plains nonfiction and a significant contribution to the then evolving deep map genre. Western wheatgrass provides his central metaphor in this examination of grasslands ecology. As a native species of grass, western wheatgrass helps define the larger natural system of the Great Plains, a region that extends through much of North America, crossing political boundaries in its expanse. Its plant mechanisms have evolved in a hostile climate, bitterly cold in winter months, subject to cyclical drought in scorching summers and freeze-drying snowless winters. Western wheatgrass has evolved "multiple systems of endurance and individual survival."[24] When stressed by drought and heat, western wheatgrass will curl its leaf edges, "allowing the leaf to function but reducing drought exposure" (22). Miniscule wax plates on its leaves "help seal off water loss" (22). Even in extreme conditions, western wheatgrass functions and reproduces itself. Rhizomes extend under the soil, eliminating the need to reproduce by seed, a riskier proposition "in the ever present summer sun" (22). Western wheatgrass is a survivor in a "ravaged" Plains landscape: "Between plowing and overgrazing, it is perhaps the most extensively altered biome on the planet, and we know very little of its original ecology and function," Gayton laments (25). Yet lowly grass extends our understanding of the larger "architecture of grass and forb and rock and sky" (13), of a landscape "ancient and silvery" (9). If grasslands were the original habitat of hominids, then the western wheatgrass also links us to our earliest, most primal cultural memories. In linking a native species to a larger nexus of natural history and human occupation, Gayton creates a thickened, layered narrative as dynamic as the landscape he analyzes.

The Wheatgrass Mechanism, empirical and lyrical, presents a wealth of information on grasslands ecology to counter indifference, to provoke concern, and to encourage "earth-bonding" (143). The deep map of place, from Gayton's viewpoint, contains a database both genetic and mythic necessary for a continued human presence on the prairie. At Lethbridge, Alberta, stiff winds buffeting him, Gayton surveys deeper history that underscores contemporary loss. The tallgrasses "are history" (41). The introduced earthworm has made native soils less stable. European colonization "nearly extinguished" Indigenous peoples (42). Farmland has obliterated traces of their cultures as quickly as it has changed the soil structure and original biome:

> Teepee rings, dream beds, buffalo jumps, turtle effigies. Marks on the land: myth. These things are not found on farmland, only on the dwindled remnants of native prairie, along with the burrowing owl, the crocus, and the horned toad. The symbols and essences of our natural bioregion are slowly being traded off in our dubious quest to be the world's breadbasket. Somehow we must find room for both the natural essences and the wheat. They need each other. (44)

Yet the severity of weather, the cycles of drought, the rising cost of machinery and repairs, the stagnation of market prices, and a complex of other factors economic, social, and natural, keep many Plains people living, in Donald Worster's phrasing, "on a thin edge."[25] Without substantial adaptation, without attending to the lessons of the Plains past, chronicled in its soil, its remaining native remnants, and its cultural artifacts, modern Plains culture could face its own diminishment and reach the tipping point of failure.

Grasslands provide a challenge to historical ecologists, those who attempt to reconstruct the evolution of a landscape (25). Transformed so irrevocably in 150 years, the Plains elude scientists who have had little time to understand "its original ecology and function" (25). But research to encourage sustainable economies and restored cultures on the Plains depends on scientific rooting in many fields. Gayton's narrative weaves together the knowledge of diverse scientists, but like Stegner in his definitive deep map, he also follows the imperative of his own instincts and desires, and listens to the experience of long-time inhabitants. He, too, imbibes the touch, color, and smell of place, kneeling down into the grass to gain perspective that "opens up and fills in the prairie" (10). From the microscopic view of prairie to panoramic sweeps of grassland history, Gayton seeks the patterns of place, "scans for lines of landscape, patterns of rock, assemblages of vegetation," and decodes the smallest cellular functions (14). His quest is restorative as he re-creates and maps the biome.

Richard Manning tells us that the term *biomass* "describe[s] the weight of life of a place."[26] In a grasslands ecology, the roots represent the major part of biomass, engendering "the center of the life of the place" from which "all else flows."[27] Indeed, Elliott West tells us, "a square yard of grass might have twenty miles of roots in a foot of its topsoil."[28] In the prairies that Gayton has studied, the harsh climate has encouraged "tough, minimalist above-ground structures" balanced by "massive root systems" (21). A fundamental mathematics drives life in the grasslands: the moisture that the sun evaporates must be replaced by the moisture that the deep roots suck out of the soil. Without this exchange of water, the plant cannot survive. Wheatgrass becomes an index species on sustaining life in dry land. To deep map plant phylogeny, one must unravel one essential "mechanism of landscape," phloem. "It is," Gayton asserts, "the heart, vessel and living sap of all regional floras. A journey toward understanding forest, desert, grassland or wetland," he concludes, "must ultimately pass through phloem" (30). Inside any plant is "an extensive trade of liquids and nutrients across membranes, down gradients of concentration, and through changes of physical state," he explains (31). In the earth, roots search for water that will then circulate like a cooling system through the plant's surfaces. Without such plumbing running through the xylem of a plant, it could not proceed successfully with photosynthesis. Phloem, on the other hand, "transports the sap plants produce for their further growth" (32). In the main stem of wheatgrass, phloem "nourishes new shoots, or tillers" (32). How this happens exactly remains a mystery, one of the hidden things of the landscape that even the electron microscope has yet to solve.

A plant's full functions are complex. "A grass leaf," Gayton proposes, "is essentially a four-story, double-sided, solar-driven manufacturing plant, suspended in space" (89). Extending this metaphor, Gayton limns the plant factory: cuticle cells make the roof; just below, in "a palisade layer," photosynthesis proceeds; spongy mesophyll, the third floor, oversees transpiration; the next two levels are the leaf undersides; stomata, up and down the roof, "vent gases and vapors to and from the mesophyll layer to the outside" (89). In the "utility space" between the second and third levels, xylem and phloem run "liquid supply lines" (89). Water evaporates, carbon dioxide is fixed. Rarely is this manufacturing plant idle: "Except in periods of prolonged drought, cold, and darkness . . . there is nearly always something to do" (91).

In a review of Gayton's work, Heather Pringle writes, "[In] the study of tiny details, ecologists, biologists, geologists perceive the underlying order of nature."[29] The minutiae of grass, its dynamic particulars, allow Gayton to sample the pulse of the larger biome. Yet he must do so understanding that "a definition of plant growth is elusive" (92). Repeatedly Gayton reminds us that at the heart of any deep map is mystery. Imagination, one of the key words in Gayton's subtitle, "in this deep-time travel . . . is almost all we have."[30] Imagination guides us through the multiple functions of grass, through the complex of symbiotic grasses, forbs, and legumes on the prairie, and through the fractal reality of landscape. Patterns both minute and grand, the micro and macro mechanisms of place, capture Gayton's imagination and structure his text.

Among the formative patterns Gayton traces is that of erasure; loss, too, leaves a mark. An ancient landscape underlies Gayton's modern, "ravaged" prairie. The late Pleistocene in particular attracts him, a period spanning thirty thousand to nine thousand years ago: "The late Pleistocene was a curious and changeable time, just on the cusp of recorded history, simultaneously ancient and modern" (126). Ice sheets scraped over the Western Canadian Interior "at least three times" in these years, producing vastly different landscapes of tundra, spruce forest, and "a new phenomenon," prairie (126). Advancing ice sheets drew down ocean levels, creating land bridges over which "shadowy human figures" crossed (126). With the entrance of humans to the North American continent, species extinction accelerated. The dynamic nature of this period animates paleontologists, anthropologists, glacial geologists, and historical ecologists: "The Late Pleistocene is essentially a lost memory to us, one that begs re-creation" (126). Adding to the challenge of piecing together this interdisciplinary narrative is the reality of glaciers, enormous grinding machines that build and destroy "on a continental scale" (127). Little evidence survives of early human settlements in North America. "With one or two notable exceptions," Gayton informs us, "the North American new and old have been relentlessly ground together" (127). If the glaciers erased evidence left on the ground, pulses of human migration added to the destruction. Like "Hells Angels on a church picnic," human newcomers descended "fast, destructive, and unexpected" (132). Megafauna—"mastodon, woolly mammoth, short-faced bear, ground sloth, superbison, saber-tooth tiger"—disappeared "almost overnight" (130).

Fast forward to the eighteenth and nineteenth centuries, when exploration into the interior regions of North America accelerated, and a new era of species diminishment and disappearance began. This time waves of European settlers followed their own mandates of survival. Fauna continued to diminish—the bison being the most famous species brought to its knees—but the introduced technology of the plow, far more destructive than the technology of fire, overturned ancient roots, the heart's blood of the prairie, and in a heartbeat—150 years—99 percent of the grasslands ecosystem disappeared. One million square kilometers of tallgrass prairie were rubbed out in a nanosecond, existing now only in the imagination, a haunting presence in the centers of Canada and the United States. Along with this change came the erasure of First Nations cultural artifacts, "thousands of [teepee] rings, wheels, pictographs, and boulder effigies," now "victims of our continuing need to consume land" (42). Such losses are profound.

Lording over this once vital landscape was the bison, the "ur-creature of Western North America," Gayton suggests. "His time was from the last of the glaciers until the first of the white men. That era is like a distant symphony for us; we hear a phrase here, a chord there. When that music is finally reconstructed, buffalo is sure to be the coda," Gayton laments (99). The vestiges of buffalo trails, though "disappearing through cultivation," slash through "ridges and river valleys" (100). Aerial photography arrests their fading. The sizes of the original herds can only be guessed. Twenty-five million? Fifty million? Buffalo once held up "a westward train trip . . . for *three* days" (100). The remnant herds still have their genetic history, Gayton writes, because "10,000 years loose on the prairies have left their stamp. Corrals and holding pens must be made from telephone poles and two-by-tens. Calves that are tied up frequently kill themselves trying to get free. The genes for this wildness run deep: it takes two and three crosses with domestic cattle before the offspring—beefalo—are tractable" (101). Photographs from the nineteenth century provide us as intimate a look as we will ever get into the process of near extinction. Among the most haunting of these scenes are the "fuzzy photographs" of a bone depot near Regina, Saskatchewan, "a place that became known as Pile o' Bones" (101). Bone piles, stacked "neatly," contrast with dark freight cars. "The scene," Gayton tells us, "is strongly reminiscent of Dachau" (101). The year 1891 marks the fatal culling of the final free-ranging herd in the United States. Of the tens of millions of bison that once roamed the Great Plains, scholars suggest that somewhere between 100,000 to 350,000 remain, and most of these are managed animals.[31]

The grasslands evolved together with the bison, their relationship symbiotic, mutually enhancing. As Elliott West has written, "[The] story of the buffalo, like that of its homeland, is one of seemingly unconnected parts that turn out to be inextricably bound together."[32] Part of western wheatgrass's original mechanism—and that of other forage species—would have been periodic grazing by bison. Western wheatgrass undergoes a period of rapid growth during spring months (103). Bison would have arrived to graze in the summer months, making little impact as the grasses "coast toward maturity and senescence" (103). The cool-season grasses would sustain the herds, allowing warm-season grasses to grow undisturbed until needed later in the year. Migration patterns of regional herds, scientists speculate, would have taken advantage of shelter, insulating snow, seasonal forage, and running water.

The replacement herds of cattle and sheep developed in a different landscape, where grasses evolved to withstand the stresses of year-round grazing. The "indigenous consumers" of North American grasslands were once "buffalo, grasshoppers, and fire," a triad that helped develop "a subtle biogeographical transaction" (106). The genes of both "grazed and grazer" evolved together and faced diminishment together (106). Some grasslands fell to the plow, others to the cutting hooves and persistent grazing of cattle or sheep. Introduced grasses, invasive grasses, and opportunistic weeds now prevail on North America's rangelands. Speaking of the fate of one native grass species, Gayton informs us that "[the] bluebunch has given way, gradually but profoundly, to the invading cheatgrass, another Eurasian alien. Now bluebunch is a pathetic remnant, and cheatgrass dominates some 40,000,000 acres of its original range. Knapweed, a thistle-like European broadleaf, commands another 2,000,000" (108). Deep time natural processes and historic waves of migration and colonization that have transformed the Canadian interior must be understood, Gayton argues, if restoration efforts on this landscape are ever going to succeed.

Patches of prairie are all that remain, comparable to the "fossil landscapes," the "small prairie 'islands,'" that survived in Ontario after boreal forests reasserted themselves following the Altithermal period circa five thousand years ago.[33] Such remnants, Gayton argues in his essay "Tallgrass Dream," exist under "the imminent threat of losing entire ecotypes."[34] These fossil landscapes hold on tenaciously amidst fields and rangeland, prospering particularly near railroad rights-of-way and cemeteries. They exude "a buffalo-energy" not felt on "the grid roads and wheat fields" (108). No longer wild or free-ranging, buffalo wander no more "the old trails" nor roll on the "rubbing stones" that "mark one of the world's greatest migration cycles" (108).

The diminishment of the North American bison has discernible if complex effects and provides one kind of moral tale in Gayton's bioregional analysis. But nature can throw some wild, nasty punches that defy clear understanding. Old Wives' Lake, the fourth largest saline water body in North America, dried up in 1988 (45). No one could remember if it had disappeared in the Dirty Thirties. As Gayton explains, scientists debated possible causes: diverted water from its only water source, Wood River; "[a] shift in weather patterns, excessive summerfallow in the region, a cycle of dry years, slough drainage, the greenhouse effect" (46). All were candidates, but none were clear picks. This seemingly random event brewed huge "greasy clouds," sickened cattle, and damaged already "drought-stunted grain crops . . . by the salty deposits" (45). To communities, it "was a politician's nightmare" (46); but to a plant ecologist, it was a unique opportunity to study "a brand new and absolutely empty niche" (46). From a singular event in a particular grounded site, biologists could learn lessons as old as "the beginning of life" itself on "a cooling, juvenile earth" (46). Old Wives' lakebed became a field laboratory "for natural plant succession, from the earliest pioneer species up to stable climax" (47). With a salinity of ninety units, Old Wives' lakebed was an inhospitable foundation for life. Excess and extremity marked its boundaries. In a landscape already minimal, Old Wives' projected a "profound emptiness" (50). Its detritus evoked a complex history:

> It has swallowed buffalo herds and World War II military aircraft. Some say the cackle of the old wives can be heard in the wind. A derelict sodium sulfate extracting plant molders on its southeast shore, the corrugated tin of its decrepit buildings flapping loosely in the ever present wind. The few farmsteads along the shoreline are mostly abandoned, recalling Palliser's dictum that the area was uninhabitable. (50)

Yet a grass species had found a toehold, a niche. *Niche*, Gayton explains, is fundamental to understanding ecology: "It is the multidimensional space that a plant (or any other living organism) fills" (46). Niche, in a flourish of metaphor, "can be thought of as the abstract address at the intersection of a hundred biophysical streets" (46). In this tangible, saline ecology, Gayton connects the landscape lessons of Old Wives' to wheatgrass, bison, human adaptation and maladaptation, and invisible evolutionary directives.

A pioneer annual species, kochia, took root at Old Wives'. Then suada, "a salt-tolerant perennial forb," found its place (51). Desert salt grass began to form a mat of vegetation. Bit by bit, over a few years, the less stable annual grass, kochia, gives way to perennials; but its presence has reduced wind speed, cycled soil-to-plant nutrients, slowed down salt accumulation, moderated soil temperature, and held snowfall (51). The pioneer, kochia, has sacrificed its reproductive energies to form the surface of a new landscape. Such adaptations display "a certain elegance and forward harmony" and reveal "the technologies of a niche-based ecological engineering . . . that we would do well to study" (52). From the micromap of Old Wives' lakebed, Gayton extends his vision to the mechanisms of a larger grasslands ecology, the deepness of evolutionary history, and the troubling short-sightedness of modern human solutions and economic contingencies.

Niche thus operates as metaphor for the deep map process itself, a form that represents a multistoried place. *The Wheatgrass Mechanism* highlights a number of unique, niched places in the Western Canadian Interior that illuminate multiple measures and layered histories: Bragg Creek, Alberta, an ecological "zone of tension" (53); the Cypress Plateau and its hidden near-monoculture of lodgepole pines; Don and Dorothy Swenson's farm in sandy land near Moose Jaw; Roy La Motte's rangeland near the Okapan. The Great Plains biome is a composite of rich, interesting microenvironments worthy of study and storytelling. In the heart of his text, Gayton pays tribute to Wallace Stegner's formative deep map, *Wolf Willow*, by traveling to the Cypress Hills and Eastend, Saskatchewan. In a chapter that distills much of Stegner's own cartography, Gayton muses over geologic history from the Cenozoic to the Pleistocene; ranges over John Palliser's *Report to Her Majesty of 1860* and his considerable surveying accomplishments; and studies a modern hydrological map in an effort to trace the divide. His chapter "Analogues and Desires" layers map upon map in an effort to reexplore a landscape both "physically and symbolically" (82).

The Cypress Plateau seams together as a "geographical clasp . . . the Gulf of Mexico to the Arctic Ocean, and the Rockies to the prairies" (82). Canada's last wild bison once grazed here together with "the last of the non-reservation Indian bands" (82). The Cypress Plateau escaped glaciation, adding to its uniqueness within the larger grasslands biome. Choosing a bicycle to convey himself over the landscape, Gayton straps a topographical map to his handlebar, "following its sinuous isolines" into an immersive exchange between place, imagination, and body. "There was much to experience," Gayton relates, "not the least of which was the simple passage of rough grid road underneath my front wheel. I was totally alone on the landscape" (85). The plateau represents a classic zone of tension, the interface between forest and grassland, what Gayton calls "the dynamic edge" (139). Up in the Cypress Hills, one finds the "deep green of lodgepole on north faces" and white spruce (84). Descending the plateau, he enters "plains rough fescue country, with admixtures of silver lupine, cinquefoil, and prairie sage" (85). He joins the Frenchman River at Ravenscrag, entering yet another landscape, "a glacial meltwater channel that had cut deeply into the prairie" (86). Erosion has exposed "Cretaceous shales and Jurassic coal seams" (88). Echoing Loren Eiseley's famous somatic immersion in his essay "The Slit," Gayton offers his own metaphor for the deep time etched on the slopes: "These valleys are the intimate labia of the earth itself" (86). In a symbolic gesture, he detours off of Eastend's main street to see Wallace Stegner's old home, connecting his chapter to the work "rooted in land" that Stegner produced. As he rubs against the physical remains of other eras and eons, Gayton's language enters into an intertextual intimacy of its own.

The dynamic edge takes on extra meaning from such encounters in *The Wheatgrass Mechanism*. In the meeting of forest and grass, humans were cradled (139). Something about the juxtaposition of open and closed spaces "feels right" to Gayton (139). The creative juxtaposition of histories embracing the natural and cultural realms becomes yet another edge, a textual one from which his deep map evolves. Within a narrative's embrace, other, older texts and oral tales edge in, furthering the dynamic tension and interface. In his introduction, Gayton speaks of creativity as a "catharsis for scientists" (12). "These aged realms of 'science' and 'the humanities' hide a very fertile ground at their mutual border, a narrow seam that may someday blossom into a domain itself"

(12). Into such fertile ground has blossomed a narrative domain, the deep map, and Gayton's book demonstrates that even humble grass rooted in a prairie soilscape lives within a historical matrix as deep and complex as the original grasslands biomass itself. In the emergence of contemporary deep map writing, Gayton's text complements Heat-Moon's *PrairyErth*. If Heat-Moon foregrounds human acculturation over natural history, Gayton inverts this positioning. In his narrative, the imperatives of natural processes ultimately determine the viability of human communities.

Toward the end of *The Wheatgrass Mechanism*, Don Gayton considers the forty-ninth parallel and the range of reptiles and amphibians. Though the political border remains an artificial construct in examining the Great Plains biome, it does provide "a real boundary in the West" when considering geography and fauna: "It tracks the southern extent of continental glaciation, and it is close to the northern limit of range for nearly all reptiles and amphibians" (109). The very existence of tiger salamanders, western painted turtles, horned toads, and other "saurian personalities" seems a bonus to Gayton. "They are not pests," he asserts, "they have no real economic value, they are just *there* as quirky and vastly distant life-forms" (115). If we can somehow not harm them, perhaps, Gayton suggests, "we will have achieved a sort of wisdom" and gained what Buell has called "environmental consciousness and commitment to place" (115).[35]

John Janovy Jr.'s central works on Great Plains fauna, *Keith County Journal* (1978), *Back in Keith County* (1981), and *Dunwoody Pond* (1994), concur with Gayton. "If we are ever going to place the kind of value on our world that is required to preclude its total destruction as a planet, then we must be able to find the love and joy in a dickcissel," Janovy argues.[36] As a parasitologist, he could have also added the multitude of microscopic animals that live inside even the smallest of animals. The "earth-bonding" these writers seek leads them to both widen and narrow their focus.

Janovy boasts, "[We] have seen the world through a quarter-inch seine and have been impressed with what we've seen" (136). Following a spore through a single amoeba as it waits "to receive the environmental cue that will unleash its genes," proves as elegant in its way as following a lonely highway to a rare vista of wide Sand Hills country (132). Scales small and large stretch the imagination and help unravel the primal bond between organism and environment, between body and place.

From his earliest work, Janovy has been fascinated with deep mapping place, in particular how fauna reveal the essence of a place. "A site," he explains in *Keith County Journal*, "can preempt our thoughts and direct them to the animal, just as the animal can preempt our thoughts and direct them back to some place in space or time" (130). Keith County itself "has a way of inundating the human with nature," of provoking immersion and curiosity (114). But as Gayton has insisted, even the deepest inquiry leads to mystery. In Janovy's words, "There may be some unwritten rule that says a biologist is forbidden to know everything about a creature, and that rule may be what follows from the ever-enlarging interface between known and unknown that is generated by the study of even a single one of these inhabitants of the Sand Hills" (114). Yet experiencing ineffable, unknowable things does not negate what one does discover. The intestine of an animal is a record of encounters, a series of environmental "memories" (89). A one-celled gregarine in a grasshopper's intestine illuminates "not only the animal but the obvious significance of that animal's position in nature," Janovy relates (89). The body of a grasshopper is a micro-landscape, "a veritable community, with other insects' larvae in their bodies and external parasites of all kinds" (90). The context of this community extends out to the grasslands that grasshoppers eat and to the birds that eat grasshoppers. An ecosystem, and all of its interconnections, is mindboggling the farther one tracks the spores of a one-celled animal.

Lawrence Buell has pithily argued that "[there] never was an is without a there."[37] To understand creatures' destinies, one must discern that "their bodies are physically located somewhere, in particular locations."[38] *Stagnicola elodes*, a snail species, require calm, warm waters. Killifish in the Platte thrive in "a perfect combination of shallowness, warmth, current" (80). Herbivore dung provides the moisture and darkness termites need, who might otherwise perish on the dry Sand Hills. Survival has "everything to do with being in your own place, the place that is for you at the time that is for you," to do with "a built-in mechanism, for finding one's place in the world" (30). Over the years, in trying to discern an animal's place and point of view, Janovy has also learned to feel like the animal. Walking the waters of the Platte, for instance, he "stopped looking for the killifish compartment and began feeling for it" (80). His legs pick up the right warmth, the exact speed and shallowness of water that killifish inhabit. Fine-tuning his own somatic responses, Janovy lets his body select the place most likely to yield specimens.

In his famous encounter with swallows in *Keith County Journal*, he inches down into the colony to "intrude deep within an organism" (65). Immersed in the motion, smell, and sensuous feel of the colony, Janovy realizes he is touching "one part of a naked flowing animal," much like "the feeling of having depolarized a three-hundred-foot-long nerve cell with one's finger" (66). Face-to-face with the swarming, complaining colony membrane, Janovy senses "having been here before" (66). The encounter, though strange, even "surreal," provokes a distant, perhaps cellular connection to the imagination. A cliff swallow colony underneath a twentieth-century highway bridge leads back in evolutionary time to "something vaguely familiar" (66). In rivers, under bridges, or exposed in higher country, Janovy relies on experience, imagination, and instinct to understand the multiple dimensions of a being's emplacement. The writer is on-the-spot, himself a part of this logic. Janovy's writing confirms Kristie S. Fleckenstein's assertion in "Writing Bodies" that "[as] writers and as knowers, we come to be *only* by our engagement with(in) a multilayered corporeal scene."³⁹

Janovy's early Keith County essays establish his interest in deep mapping a particular ecology of place. *Dunwoody Pond: Reflections on the High Plains Wetlands and the Cultivation of Naturalists* is his most sustained effort at deep mapping. In its range through time, its concern with evolutionary and cultural change, its illumination of one microenvironment's mechanisms, and its presentation of what Dan Flores calls "an occupied landscape," *Dunwoody Pond* stands as Janovy's highest literary achievement thus far.⁴⁰

Published after such works as John McPhee's four volumes of *Annals of the Former World* and William Least Heat-Moon's *Prairy-Erth: (a deep map)*, *Dunwoody Pond* shares with these texts the experimental, cross-sectional narrative of the deep map as well as its attention to science, social history, and environmental ethics. What Janovy brings to the deep map genre, however, is a remarkable clarity about the enduring yet fragile genetic, evolutionary undergirding of a biome's identity. Moreover, the acute sense of life's impermanence and of time's irreversible nature that marks Janovy's early writings becomes amplified in *Dunwoody Pond*. One senses as well Janovy's profound connection to place after years of fieldwork, his increasing moral concern about human practices and politics, not unknown in his earlier works but certainly intensified in this later text. Science teaches us that nature is not static, nor is an ecosystem closed; still, shortsighted human policies are promoting changes that are not all benign. Janovy laments,

> There was a time when I would see a sandpiper and feel excited, pleased. Then there came a time when I would see a sandpiper and feel privileged. Nowadays, as often as not, when I see a sandpiper I feel sad. Where have they gone, I wonder, those

Dunwoody Ponds, Martin Bay Ponds, Nevens well tanks, Roscoe river beds, Monkey Rocks, and Ackley Valley Souths?[41]

Reflecting the bereft tone of much deep mapping, Janovy is at times elegiac, mourning the loss of biodiversity, the narrowing of vision, and the imperatives of land "use" in an extractive economy. The "vast wilderness of everyday biology one finds anywhere," Janovy argues, "has no immediate political or economic importance" (277). Yet in devaluing the intricacies of biological mechanisms, we stand to lose our own humanity. The Platte River, a legal and environmental battleground, no longer resembles the river of centuries past. Imagining its killing, Janovy projects a Platte that "is finally dry, when Denver's sewage is washed away with water that once flowed past Roscoe, when the cranes no longer darken Nebraska's March skies"(265). A plaster cast he made of killdeer tracks along the river suggests just one species facing possible extinction if the Platte dies because "we let the wrong people tell us what we were wasting" (265).

Thus *Dunwoody Pond* weaves in many stories, some of science, some of scientists, some of the land that inspires their quest for understanding. Its reflections reveal the formative nature of deep time history, much of it still alive in the genes of organisms, and ponder the changes brought to the land by climate and human migration. A celebration of topophilia, its deepest current is a love of this place, a unique biological site in beautiful country. Dunwoody Pond provides a peephole into life itself. On its shores, one finds that "[the] mystery of the universe, written small and near, surrounds you, crawls up your leg, flies into your ear, bites you on the neck, and leaves black muck under your toenails" (12). In entering its space, in interpenetrating its intricacies, Janovy and his students come into contact with "an extraordinary array of life in constant motion" (10), part of "the deep prairie and the microscopic worlds that occupy its seeps" (62).

In the spirit of deep mapping, Janovy represents the truths of place cartographically. Movement, migration, and road systems convey the compass points of scientific exploration. Building upon patterns of roads, towns, and fieldwork in the Keith County books, *Dunwoody Pond*'s narrative literally moves over the physical landscape. To find the pond, one travels "[two] miles down a sand and gravel road, north of a town with no grocery store, in the middle of the sixty-eighth most populous county of the thirty-fourth most populous state" (4). Another field site near Nevens Ranch requires particular attention to roads. In Keystone, Nebraska, blacktop changes to gravel road and deteriorates from there until "the washboards become brutal and dangerous" (46). At the Buckthorn Springs ranch gate, the road narrows, a devolving structure that leads to a well tank teeming with microscopic life. Similarly, to study the Platte River and its branches, specific state highways and Interstate 80 provide access. Janovy's text marks bridges, access roads, county highways, and roadside ditches; he even revisits Highway 61 in his closing chapter, "The Blue Mustang," to interpret an earlier symbolic journey in *Keith County Journal*. With a detailed Nebraska map, the reader can literally follow the author, his colleagues, and his students as they stake out study sites in the vicinity of Cedar Point Biological Station.

This contemporary map, however, tells only part of the story, for blacktop and gravel lead back in time, shadow migratory routes, and cover the tracks and footprints of other eras. The hydrologic map takes us into an ancient world of "[volcanoes], meandering streams and rivers, wandering underground seeps and springs and eastern glaciers" (195). Ditches and access points give way to genetic maps that allow a glimpse into "the intertwined mass of causes, effects, and evolutionary histories" (184). Duane Dunwoody's pond exists on land that came to be through ancient winds, far-off volcanic activity, and lifted, airborne sands. Megafauna once lived here. Modern landscapes overlap the ancient. Fossil water "lies in a porous sandstone, filled with cold and crystal water . . . left behind when the glaciers melted and the mastodonts died" underneath Janovy's feet, an "underground freshwater ocean" extending all the way to Texas (54). The Platte River, north and south, carries ancient orogenies and cultures in its waters. The North Platte, with its "granite, basalt, quartzite and slate slivers," tells the story of the Laramide Revolution, "one of America's most persistent geological anomalies" (60). The South Platte sands are interspersed with cultural detritus, "stone points and ceremonial knives, deer bones, patent medicine bottles, bison teeth and rusted out early seventies car bodies" (61).

Each site of study plumbs deeper, connects to other maps, and links to "ultimate questions . . . of phylogeny, of evolutionary relationships, in which deep causality is sought in the unique geological history of the planet" (160). Such ancestral connections may be disturbing to those who want "safe and servile science," but they lie at the heart of Janovy's and his students' quest (160). The heterogeneous environments studied in *Dunwoody Pond* parallel the heterogeneous histories of place. Janovy's complex narrative reiterates Gayton's insight that the deep map, as generic niche, can connect "a hundred biophysical streets."

Dunwoody Pond, then, is a matrix containing all of the possible meanings of *pondness*. The pond is an archetype, a mold so to speak of primordial dimensions; it is embedded with natural forms; it is the material enclosing objects of study. It originates, embeds, embraces life-forms. As a matrix of study, Dunwoody Pond becomes the central metaphor in a far-ranging narrative. Though other places receive attention, all these storied paths lead back to Dunwoody Pond. Janovy lyrically celebrates the pond's profuse energies:

> There is a movement; the sunfish strikes. Death comes to another larval dragonfly, as swiftly and unemotionally as it comes to

the hundreds of smaller scuds and wigglers consumed by the dragonfly over the past months. Sunlight pierces a small gap in the vegetation, a ray slices down into the weeds. Fine particles and diatoms drift in clouds throughout the light shaft; along a *Ceratophyllum* leaf, a busy microscopic, telescoping rotifer swirls a tiny current around its head, sucking in the diatoms; worms, smaller than bits of thread, pack the dense leaf tufts at the end of a stem, secreting mucous tubes, and pulsating, always pulsating, pushing, swallowing, pushing, swallowing, eating the drifting dirt from Dunwoody Pond. (9)

It is a world of constant "grabbing, gnawing, sucking, stabbing, swirling, licking, biting, chewing, rasping, and scraping" (9). The biologist's imagination takes such seemingly chaotic life force and abstracts measurements, ponders theories, and seeks partial answers for "complex mysteries" (10). Science and art converge at Dunwoody Pond. Scientific problems "originate inside a human mind; they are made of experience and curiosity mixed in with a dash—sometimes a sizeable dash—of naiveté and aesthetics, the building blocks of wonder" (12). Thus Dunwoody Pond becomes the matrix of imagination and inquiry, of the "digging and netting for questions" that fires a scientist's career. "All we need is a source of exotic puzzles," Janovy confides. "A Dunwoody Pond" (15).

Such a matrix, however, serves at the behest of climate and human desire. Dunwoody Pond could dry up or become contaminated, reminding us that the landscape body is not timeless. "Nothing's permanent except the memories and the meanings," Janovy concedes (230). A rich field site, Ackley Valley South on Highway 61 was once "a perfect classroom" (281). But when it began to dry up, life receded. A sandpiper, looking for its kind, calling and circling "thirty or forty times," must give up its search and fly on (282). Change and movement, the rise and fall of species, the passing of eons and landscapes find their mark in Dunwoody Pond. It, too, is mortal. The Sand Hills landscape lessons capture this poignancy: the deep structure of place lies under surface ephemerality. The Platte River waters, bearing down on the wader's feet, announces, "deeply and powerfully, that the passage of time like the passage of sand and water, is completely, totally, and finally, irreversible" (250).

Scientists work to capture this matrix in experimental form, gaining partial knowledge of the deeper biological mechanisms. Janovy's student Rich Clopton attempts to reproduce in his city lab some of the High Plains conditions that influence the lives of darkling beetles and their corresponding parasites. His surrogate environment duplicates the dark, murky, moist realms of the beetles' homeland. If Rich combines the right properties, he will be rewarded with chains of parasite spores: "For a parasitologist seeking to control a wild animal, spore chains might be a gift from God" (226). An early photograph of Rich in the field "shows him alone, on his knees, in a vast sea of mixed grass prairie, nothing behind him but a flat line and empty sky. His face is low, almost down in the ground, and his hands are hidden" (215). In this posture, Rich is emblematic of the creative, somatic encounter that guides Janovy's and his students' science. Immersed in the beetles' ground, Rich learns to feel like the beetle and thus solves a puzzle that has "baffled science for a century and a half": controlling the production of spore chains (226). He has tapped into an evolutionary mechanism, sensitive to select environmental cues, that has allowed parasites to "blow with the wind and wash with the rain across vast reaches of the continent" (221). He has uncovered a little of the mystery of one kind of body, the darkling beetle, in its place, the High Plains, over time.

Incredibly powerful tools now aid the ecologist in exposing the features of the smallest structures: the scanning electron microscope (SEM) and the transmission electron microscope (TEM). SEM pictures produce a "shocking" enlargement of familiar features, reminding Janovy of Gulliver's travels to lands big and small

(204). TEM pictures reveal the "ultrastructure—the finest, most minute, cellular architecture observable by existing technology" (205). The ultrastructural views are abstract art: "In the TEMS we see the various granule types, deep invaginations of epithelial linings, mitochondria, folded cell membranes, cellular junctions, ultrathin slices of secretory granule-packed salivary cells looking like flagstone-paved floors" (205). TEMS expose a colorful, textured landscape that is "living tissue" (204). They extend our knowledge of the biome's deep map in important new directions.

Both kinds of microscopic images reveal the deepest internal structures of life itself. Miles from Dunwoody Pond, Janovy and his students explore these miniscule surfaces, yet "the memories of prairie wetlands remain" (205). The abstraction of living forms still has a potent connection to "the ever-fluctuating matrix of water, mud, worms, fish, and algae" (186). To represent this matrix, Janovy shares the narrative strategies of other contemporary nonfiction writers. In Kent Ryden's words,

> Instead of adopting and adapting a ready-made history, they continually construct the past anew from the materials at hand, thinking not of the entire region and its abstract history but of the places most immediate to their lives, looking and listening and remembering and then filling the emptiness by applying their own imaginative overlays to the landscape, locating regional identity not in a spot in the past but in the spot on which they stand.[42]

Dunwoody Pond ranges over many landscapes, some corporeal, some earthbound, to construct the past from cellular memory, geological remains, cultural traces, and the lingering of potent moments in a scientist's imagination. But Janovy, located in a spot in process, emphasizes the present and the future as well.

His backward glances are balanced by projection: What is the future for curious young scientists? Will basic research lose out to economically motivated science? What human-use pressures will exacerbate environmental crises on the Plains? What next will be discovered about this "Camelot" of landscapes (xvi)? Janovy defends science as "a state of mind, 'a way of knowing'" (xv). To seek understanding of life, Janovy gives this advice: "Follow a piece of the natural world in order to find out where it goes. Period. For no other reason" (281). *Dunwoody Pond* gives testament to this scientific journey, charting the "looking and listening and remembering" that lead to informed and inspired deep mapping.

Nebraska biologist Paul A. Johnsgard points out that at seventy-five miles per hour, a person traversing Interstate 80, a main artery across the Great Plains, need not "[pause] to think of the state's geological history" nor consider "the many ecological zones and habitats" one passes through.[43] In Nebraska, as in other Plains states and provinces, a complex story

> hides among the head-high prairie grasses and wildflowers that bison once tramped through and slept in as they rested from their long migrations to and from the Platte and Republican River valleys. It can be clearly heard in the song of a meadowlark perched on a roadside fencepost, should one only take time to stop and listen. It is present in the gently waving grasses of the green-capped loess hills and the yucca-peppered Sand Hills that are easily visible from the noisy interstate, beckoning one like quiet oases in a cacophonous bedlam. It silently calls out in the smell of ponderosa pines among the Wildcat Hills, along the Pine Ridge, and on the crest of Scotts Bluff. The story is there and always has been. How long the story may last and what lessons we may learn from it are up to us.[44]

Yet the larger biome of Nebraska, its system of diverse ecosystems, now faces "fragmentation" and "degradation."[45] Its story, along with that of the entire Great Plains, has been complicated by urban growth, industrial agriculture, and other economic pressures. Biome, as Johnsgard defines it, is "[a] major regional ecosystem, including both the plants and animals," the flora and fauna emphasized in Gayton's and Janovy's literary biology. Assessing such large-scale changes in the biome, Johnsgard comments, can cause a "jaundiced" eye.[46]

But sanctuaries, wildlife refuges, wild river protections, prairie preserves, and other acts of conservation, protection, and restoration are increasing across the Great Plains. Hope lies in those places "where one can lie back on a fragrant bed of last year's bluestem in early April, with the half-intoxicating odor of freshly germinating grass invading one's nose, with the shrill but majestic music of cranes almost constantly overhead."[47] Such tangible ecologies—bluestem, bison, cranes—inspire "the passion for preservation" that is itself a quest for "a sense of identity" rooted in place.[48]

Learning how to live in and with the land is an imperative more Plains inhabitants are hearing. Gayton's and Janovy's deep maps, though critical of human decisions and desires, endorse Dan Flores's assertion that "we remain biological even with all our bewildering array of cultural dressings."[49] Humans are not outside the biome; they are part of it. Biological deep maps can help guide human inhabitants toward wiser adaptation, toward "earth-bonding," toward their niche in the landscape. In *The Wheatgrass Mechanism*, Don Gayton celebrates the farming practices of Don and Dorothy Swenson, "the farmers of one possible agricultural future, where management is focused on living and microbial systems, where recycling is not a frill but a serious undertaking, and where land is not continuously besieged by chemical inputs and the heavy metal of large-scale tillage implements"(94). Janovy acknowledges the local ranchers in Keith County, residents like Duane Dunwoody, who know and love their land and "remain incredibly generous people" to the biologists who want to study upon it (292). Such men and women, "survivors in the strongest sense of the word," have become part of their place, "not easily dislodged" (14–15).

As an integral part of the modern Plains landscape, they are, in Wes Jackson's memorable phrasing, "native" to the land, part of the biome.

Jackson's work focuses specifically on how human habitation must change its farming economy on the Plains to assure long-term survival of communities all across the semiarid reaches of the West. While *Becoming Native to This Place* is not a deep map narrative, Jackson's participation in Heat-Moon's journey across Chase County and his bioregional focus complement *PrairyErth* and other Plains deep maps. His writing works in parallel with Gayton's and Janovy's oeuvre and gives a lucid presentation of the land ethic.

A series of connected essays that delve into the social, economic, biological, and ecological layers of Plains life, *Becoming Native to This Place* argues for a new sense of home, a revisionary resettlement of the landscape. "This book is dedicated to the idea that the majority of solutions to both global and local problems," he presents in his prologue, "must take place at the level of the expanded tribe, what civilization calls community."[50] He proposes that universities in the United States tackle ideas of home and homecoming and calls for a national movement to make all of us native to our regions and our continent. Jackson is an unsentimental rhetor, rejecting "mere nostalgia" (4). Resettlement, as a modern project, "is a practical necessity for everyone, including people who continue to live in cities" (4). Identifying the generation now in power as "prodigal," Jackson gives his deep map a Jeremiad tenor, but he is no prophet wailing from the wilds of Kansas (5). He is a brilliant, accomplished, and thoughtful scientist working from his corner of the Plains to give communities new tools for and scientific insight into adaptation and survival.

Like Heat-Moon, Jackson highlights Kansas history because it exemplifies "The Problem," the title of his first full chapter. When the Spanish conquistadors began their "*entrada* into the New World half a millennium ago," they spread across the North American continent, reaching Kansas during the Coronado expedition of 1540–42 (6). Searching for untold gold, thirty-one men (including Coronado) eventually reached an Indian kingdom called Quivira. Jackson writes,

> All were irritated that they had not found the rumored wealth they sought when they finally arrived at Cíbola, now the Zuni Reservation in Arizona. They had been enticed off on this second wild goose chase into what is now Kansas by the lies of an Indian slave who wanted to go home to his people, the Harahey, a people who resided in either northeastern Kansas or southeastern Nebraska. . . . Quivira had plenty of people and good land. They were tall people; one stood six feet eight inches. But the houses of Quivira were built of grass and sticks. There was no gold. (7)

Jackson begins with this tale of conquest and lust to make a point about the effects of colonization. When Quivira existed, "well over 25,000 people" lived there (11). In 1927, ten thousand fewer people called this part of Kansas home. By 1990 only 10,400 people remained. The Indigenous people thrived here; the white settlers, as one neighbor, Nick Fent tells Jackson, "devoted their lives to losing this land" (10). Something in the social and economic fabric of modern life—the result of colonization—has diminished the potential of this region. Jackson wants to reverse this "ecological illiteracy."[51] Those who pushed the Native people aside ignored their considerable landscape lessons and misread the message whispered in grass and forb.

If Gayton retraces the steps of an earlier deep mapper, Wallace Stegner, Jackson can lay claim that he is an important subject in Heat-Moon's influential *PrairyErth*. In the section "To Consult the Genius of the Place in All," Heat-Moon meets Wes Jackson at the Wagon Wheel Café in Stone City, Kansas. From there the two men travel the short distance to Salina. In extended, italicized monologue, Jackson explains to Heat-Moon his land-based philosophy, his critique of modern industrial history, and his drive to find sustainable solutions for Plains communities. "If we are to get serious about an ecological agriculture," Jackson asserts, "where nature is the standard and native prairie serves as our analogy, then we have to think about the basic unit of our study: the community—a diversity of species living together."[52]

Writer John T. Price clarifies Jackson's idea of community in his study *Not Just Any Land*: "In this new community what are often represented as opposites—the past and the present, humans and nature, traditional and technological cultures—will be made to cooperate, to connect, in the name of diversity and sustainability."[53] The *entrada* of centuries ago signifies the divisive effects of colonization across North America. The result all these centuries later? "We have *sent* our topsoil, our fossil water, our oil, our gas, our coal, and our children," Jackson laments of modern Kansas, "into that black hole called the economy."[54]

Jackson's work returns us to aftermath, the effects of the Jeffersonian grid on the landscape. He recalls *Wolf Willow* and the 1869 order "to select 'the most suitable localities for the survey of townships for immediate settlement.'" Those métis communities in Saskatchewan that had adapted to life on the northern Plains found their settled spaces cut into, fragmented, and diminished to make room for maladaptive structures. Similarly in Kansas, an 1874 survey group, under Captain Short's authority, began to divide up section lines. The six men in the party were killed in what has come to be known as the Lone Tree Massacre. Jackson adds, "The surveyor's instrument was symbolic" of the cultural divide and devastating consequences of settlement on Indigenous Plains nations (16). Spaces that Indigenous and métis people made into commons gave way to a system of property rights and the "immutable givens" of federal cartography (17). As settlers filled up the quarter sections, cultural options to become sustainable and native closed, too. The result is predictable: "Though we are regaining some wild animals now through game ranching and wild species reintroduction, we have less and less topsoil, fewer species, less germ plasm in our major crops, and more shopping centers" (18–19). Ignoring the dictates of nature, the heirs of nineteenth- and twentieth-century settlement on the Plains are reaping a lesser crop.

Like Gayton and Janovy, Jackson provides plenty of science to limn his portrait of a landscape in crisis. Too often modern science has dismissed the complexities of "the profound reality of interpenetration of part and whole" (19). It has followed the pressures of markets and money. "There are ensembles of genes in our major crops that would not exist in their particular constellations were there not a Chicago Board of Trade . . . or fossil fuel to make and run farm equipment, or computers to assist agribusiness" (21). An ecological science that bends to context, that "honors woods and stream, tropical rain forests, and also Kansas prairie" will be essential to steer grasslands farmers and ranchers to wiser production (42). The Land Institute has made nature its "standard" (44). They are developing methodologies that are informed by roots-up ecology.

Working and living on the grasslands opens up Jackson's scientific inquiries and nourishes his imagination. Writing in an older home, he catalogues the layered stories of this house, of others he has lived in, and of adjacent buildings, many in disrepair, monuments of "a failure of imagination" as well as "the tyranny of disregard by something we call 'the economy'" (57) Abandoned oil fields, Depression and Dust Bowl relics, an old creamery, an abandoned gas station and barber shop speak to a larger cultural abandonment of places like Matfield Green, Kansas. A few short generations ago, still in the memories of old-timers, this town "had been part of the first long-distance pipelines that delivered natural gas from the large Hugoton field near Amarillo to Kansas City" (54). Extractive businesses like oil and gas leave ruins all over western landscapes. Jackson's Land Institute itself would abandon the buildings in Matfield Green, putting them up for sale in 2008.[55] The realities of reinhabiting a place are challenging even for Jackson and his colleagues.

Still, Jackson envisions another kind of prairie town. "Imagine this human community as an ecosystem," he suggests, "as a locus or primary object of study" (55). Lives organized around ideas like renewability and sustainability would produce a radically different community. Over a century's worth of grid-based homesteading has left fragile settlements. The structure of this failing settlement, Jackson concludes, must give way to resettlement along new cartographic lines. If human communities are to last on the Plains, they too must follow biological imperative and adapt.

The landscape lessons offered in two deep maps, *The Wheatgrass Mechanism* and *Dunwoody Pond*, and in their complement, *Becoming Native to This Place*, weld science and imagination, pulling us into the living tissue of place, into the storied past, into the dynamic edge, as Gayton puts it, of "myth and mechanism."[56] These scientist authors push us to see anew, "expanding the notion of community so that it becomes situated within the ecological community."[57] Their biological narratives chart multiple levels of knowledge and experience; they delineate vertical and horizontal axes that geographer Yi-Fu Tuan has argued define archetypal dimensions in space—the human desire for emplacement that is both sacred and profane, transcendent and imminent.[58] The many questions and mysteries these narratives raise serve to provoke, inform, and inspire the readers' own cartographic, participatory explorations of place. In the end, Gayton, Janovy, and Jackson leave us our humanity to ponder, and the possibility that we as a species are at a defining crossroads.

CHAPTER FOUR

DEEP MAPPING DIMENSIONS

Excavating Time and Space in Loren Eiseley's
The Immense Journey and John McPhee's *Rising
from the Plains*

Scientific research is an art form in this sense: It does not matter how you make a discovery, only that your claim is true and
convincingly validated. The ideal scientist thinks like a poet and
works like a bookkeeper, and I suppose that if gifted with a full
quiver, he also writes like a journalist. As a painter stands before
bare canvas or a novelist recycles past emotion with eyes closed,
he searches his imagination for subjects as much as for conclu-
sions, for questions as much as answers.

E. O. Wilson, *Consilience: The Unity of Knowledge*

At the start of "The Gravel Page," an essay on forensic geology,
writer John McPhee ponders a collection of petri dishes "full of
Platte River pebbles."[1] Sixteen years earlier, he had collected the
pebbles from "a gravel bar in Nebraska, near the river's right bank,
not far from the hundredth meridian" (82). McPhee is precise
about this location, near modern Cozad, Nebraska, where the
Platte River, "[c]hoked with rock . . . cannot transport its load in
any but an awkward way, so it subdivides and loops and braids,
and hunts for passage through its own bed" (82). The collection

site is an exact pinpoint on the map of the Great Plains. McPhee even remembers that he was lying "thirty-six centimeters from the river gravel" (82).

The pebbles themselves, however, defy such empirical mapping. Sitting now on a desk in New Jersey, these pebbles reveal the complexity of any place on a map; they represent "distinct terrane in widely separated distant worlds" (82). The riverbed that gathered them, itself an ephemeral feature, opens up vistas, earlier manifestations of mountains and plains, traces of lived worlds, storied landscapes. Imaginatively, McPhee travels from a spot in time and place into millions of years of deep time. The riverine landscape reveals multiple stories of uplift and erosion, of "ancient vanished rivers" and once active volcanoes (82).

Any map is a composite of maps, every place contains memories of other places. Cartographer Alan MacEachren argues that cartography itself "is more akin to literature than to astronomy or geophysics."[2] Moreover, he calls for a new sense of cartography that embraces an "integrated view" of space, considering "multiple levels" and "multiplicity."[3] Literary cartographers of the Plains, like McPhee, are in sync with this way of constructing maps and are experimenting with exactly this new sense of cartography. Among McPhee's most salient points is that no matter how deep we map, we never get to the end of a place. A gravel bed in western Nebraska becomes a portal into many dimensions.

Taking his pebbles to stratigrapher James Swinehart of the Nebraska Geological Survey, McPhee seeks to identify the fragments of places marked in each stone. Among his pebbles are banded and burgundy cherts, gneisses, schists, hard shales, quartzites, red-bed sandstone, and Sherman granite (83). The pebbles had traveled hundreds of miles from their sources in Wyoming and Colorado. Some are as old as "two thousand million years" (86). Swinehart can identify some pebbles' provenance with certainty: "acidic volcanics" from the Rabbit Ears Pass area, Sherman granite from the Laramie Range, anorthosite from the Laramies, and green chlorite from the Medicine Bow Mountains (84–85). From a single collection site "on a gravel bar in the main stem of the Platte River west of the line of glacial advance and east of the hundredth meridian," McPhee transports his readers across and deep into geological history, before North America and the Great Plains existed (87). Landscape, in his able hands, becomes a fascinating chronicle of time and space.

As the deep map genre has developed in the last fifty years, explorations of time and space—landscape as archive—have offered new understanding of the Great Plains. Springing from developments in anthropology, evolutionary biology, geology, and astrophysics, these narratives highlight deep time and decenter human history. A heightened awareness of mutability, tectonic instability, and extinction—that other worlds preceded this one, just as the human era will precede many more worlds to come—marks this scientifically informed deep map writing. As Loren Eiseley proclaims in "Little Men and Flying Saucers," one of his essays in *The Immense Journey*, "[t]he chill vapors of time and space are beginning to filter under the closed door of the human intellect."[4] The human ego "learns that the world supposedly made for its enjoyment has existed for untold eons entirely indifferent to its coming."[5] From this long-view perspective, a petri dish full of pebbles discloses both unsettling and illuminating news. The many worlds of the Great Plains' past are wondrous in their own right.

At the same time, Eiseley, McPhee, and other deep-time excavators open up their cartography to what Barbara Stevens has called "a restless reformulation of the interpretative terrain."[6] This cartographic reformulation privileges dynamism, spatial complexity, and open-ended dialogue. Evoking Edward Soja's metaphor of Thirdspace, Stevens argues that literary cartographers like Eiseley and McPhee (her particular subject) present "a multiplicity of detailed and chaotic histories and space" that resists coherence and totality.[7] Citing geographers Henri Lefebvre and Derek Gregory, she outlines a practice "that is inherently difficult to understand, traversing the story line laterally, and taking into account extended possibilities."[8]   As Eiseley explains in "Days of a Doubter," part of his memoir, *All the Strange Hours*, "I have come to believe that in the world there is nothing to explain the world. Nothing in nature that can separate the existent from the potential."[9] Put more bluntly in "The Badlands and the School," he declares, "I don't believe in simplicity."[10] Mapping spatial and temporal complexity becomes his signature move and thus positions Eiseley at the headwaters of Plains deep map writing. His influence across decades of nonfiction writers of the natural world is considerable.

From the 1940s on, this Nebraska-born writer worked on an innovative essay form that he called the "concealed" essay. Eiseley biographer Gale E. Christianson explains that the concealed essay's adaptable, assembled structure integrates "fictional and autobiographical material . . . with scientific fact, literary allusions, and poignant quotations."[11] Eiseley's editor, Jack Fischer, notes that the concealed essay "moves in the borderland between science, religion, philosophy, and poetry; this is terrain of the first importance, but it is difficult country and the reader needs to be led into it slowly and carefully."[12] A signature movement in Eiseley is to begin at a moment of intimate encounter and to journey from there into an expansive meditation of scientific or metaphysical, cosmological significance. The beauty of this form, in Dimitri Breschinsky's assessment, is that "the time frame can be considerably broader, extending back indefinitely into prehistoric times."[13] In doing so, Breschinsky concludes, Eiseley produces "an atavistic experience . . . opening up new vistas of space and long-forgotten dimensions of being."[14] Paying close attention to time's arrows and cycles, to the linear and nonlinear structures of time, Eiseley imaginatively and artfully carries his readers across spatial realities as small as an atom or as vast as a cosmos.

In a number of essays grounded in his experience living and working on the Great Plains, Eiseley explores the cartographic and cosmological entry points where past, present, and future landscapes conflate. Eiseley explains, "I was a child of the early century . . . [a] creature molded of plains' dust and the seed of those who came west with the wagons."[15] Dust and seed, deep time and human time, define his embodiment. As a child playing in the sewers of Aurora and Lincoln, Nebraska, he discovered the lure of dark passages where time collapses into space, "in some unwary instant," he explains, "to telescope fifty thousand years."[16] Later, as an adult, he became a surveyor of depths, a guide to undecipherable terrain. In his memoir, *All the Strange Hours*, Eiseley recalls the excitement of fieldwork with C. Bertrand Schultz as part of the South Party excavating sites in western Nebraska:

> Few people outside of the realm of paleontology realize that these runneled, sun-baked ridges which extend far into South Dakota are one of the great fossil beds of the North American Age of Mammals. Bones lay in the washes or projected from cliffs. Titanotheres, dirk-tooth cats, oreodonts, to mention but a few, had left their bones in these sterile days. The place was as haunted as the Valley of the Kings, but by great beasts who had ruled the planet when man was only a wispy experiment in the highlands of Kenya. These creatures had never had the misfortune to look upon a human face. Most of what we knew of mammalian evolution in North America had come from this region. All the great paleontologists had worked here.[17]

As Eiseley puts it, the place "enchanted" him and proved formative in exercising his imagination.[18] In these field sites, reworked in his essays, he ponders the web of connections between his body and fossilized bones, his life and ancient life forms, his consciousness and animal awareness, past and present. Time becomes fluid in his meditations, space plastic. The field notebooks that he kept to record these insights reveal poems and fragments of essays, early experiments in deep mapping across dimensions.

By the time Eiseley collected a decade's worth of essay writing into *The Immense Journey* (1957), he had perfected his multifaceted approach. In these brilliant essays, he guides his readers through space and time, what he calls in one essay "The Great Deeps."[19] But these deeps do not confer special status to humans. As he concludes in "The Snout," humans "are one of many appearances of the thing called Life; we are not its perfect image, for it has no image except Life, and life is multitudinous and emergent in the stream of time."[20] Humans, the "dream animal," however, do have consciousness and the gift of narrative, and through the mystery of the human mind, *Homo sapiens* "escaped out of the eternal present of the animal world into a knowledge of past and future."[21] Eiseley's essays are always cognizant of time's passage and begin with one life, one mind—Eiseley himself—in transit. Perhaps a memory jars a connection or a physical, somatic experience releases the synthesizing imagination; sensuous engagement, often at the borders of culture and the wild, provides an initial measure of familiarity and assurance before Eiseley plumbs the deeper recesses of his essay. In moving through multiple dimensions, Eiseley charts revelation and attempts a clearer map of meaning than "the maps we carry in our separate pockets," with their "contradictory . . . indecipherable" landscapes.[22]

Two of Eiseley's most famous essays in *The Immense Journey*, "The Slit" and "The Flow of the River," trace their origins to Eiseley's formative experience as a member of the South Party. His notebooks and sketchings from this period uncover his preferred contact zone in which to generate ideas and connections: the interface between the physical and the imagined, between sensuous stimuli and interior response. In "The Slit," Eiseley famously descends into a crack in the earth to discover "a perfect cross-section through perhaps ten million years of time."[23] In this tight, darkened space,

Eiseley reflects that even his own body archives the deeper history of earth's life forms, eyeing a hand "that has been fin and scaly reptile foot and furry paw."[24] At this moment of somatic joining, body and earth commingle, connecting material, corporeal essences to deep history and deeper mysteries. Bobbing in the Platte River, in the essay "The Flow of the River," Eiseley again experiences a collapse of time and space as he "slides down the vast tilted face of the continent."[25] His body closely touches "the immense body of the continent itself" in a physical choreography that stirs images of "the broken axles of prairie schooners and the mired bones of mammoth," of ancient orogenies and evolutionary adaptation (19). "I *was* water," he exclaims, "and the unspeakable alchemies that gestate and take shape in water" (19).

Had Henry David Thoreau understood the deeper mapping of place, Eiseley comments in this essay, "he would have seen, as the long trail of life was unfolded by the fossil hunters, that his animalized water had changed its shapes eon by eon to the beating of the earth's dark millennial heart" (21). Instead, it is Eiseley in a new century—what he calls in another collection *Darwin's Century*—who invents a new kind of narrative cartography, attuned to the intersections of geological and human time dimensions. He guides the literary cartography of the Great Plains into Soja's Thirdspace, the realm of the "real-and-imagined," a space where "*everything* comes together . . . subjectivity and objectivity, the abstract and the concrete . . . the knowable and the unknowable, the repetitive and the differential, structure and agency, mind and body, consciousness and the unconscious, the disciplined and the transdisciplinary, everyday life and unending history."[26] Here, where man is beast, is water, Eiseley successfully practices literary alchemy that not only augments but revises the essay of place.

Kent Ryden has argued that "an essay of place is a trial, an attempt—an attempt to lay bare the meaning of a place. It is a trying out of narratives, of possible interpretations; it is an earnest stab at the difficult work of making maps speak, of turning names into stories."[27] To ascertain the essence of place, its many layerings and unseen landscapes, Ryden argues that the modern essayist is "at once a cartographer, a landscape painter, a photographer, an archivist, and a folklorist, as well as a storyteller."[28] He recognizes the significant accomplishment of Eiseley's translation of place:

> Place grows out of life and sustains life, as Eiseley comes to understand; it provides a stable imaginative refuge from change and flux. It pins down and organizes images and history, preventing memory from becoming random, identity from becoming episodic and fragmented. Time alters and transforms the world and the self; geography shifts and scrambles; landscapes scrape off old familiar surfaces and accrete new ones in a sort of fantastically accelerated man-made process of erosion and sedimentation.... Place anchors the filament of continuity which runs through our lives, providing a rich evocative connection to the pasts which create us.[29]

In some of Eiseley's greatest essays, the High Plains of western Nebraska provide his narrative anchor and channel his evocations. At the same time, he is keenly aware of shifting and transformation, of the discontinuity that separates eons, that resists tidy configuration. The slit gives him a tight structure of earthen walls that may suggest a determinative frame, but the ambiguous play of dark recesses and open sky above the slit resists easy definition. The Platte River's waters also deny Eiseley any slender, elegant understanding of time and space. Fluidity tends toward the amorphous and indefinite. In becoming water, Eiseley merges into Soja's comprehensive *Everything*.

"The Slit" begins with an appraisal of landscape, of a "flat and grass-covered," seemingly eternal sun-touched prairie as it abuts an outcropping "of naked sandstone and clay."[30] Eiseley's senses are on heightened alert, seeking the dark recesses where time's artifacts reveal themselves. In this border landscape, he discovers the slit, a point of entrance into deep time. Eiseley describes the slit in Styx-like terms, a liminal passageway between the living and the dead, between the real and the dreamlike phantoms of lost worlds; the slit is the realm of the "real- and-imagined." Suddenly the sky itself morphs into a new timescape, and Eiseley becomes aware of "some future century I would never see" (4). Time becomes surreal for him; the borders between the past, present, and future dissolve in his descent. The slit of the present slips into a world tens of millions of years old. In this imagined, challenging Thirdspace, "all-inclusive simultaneity opens up endless worlds to explore."[31]

Here Eiseley discovers the skull of an early mammal, a "shabby little Paleocene rat," also a creature of the grasslands (8). The oreodont skull contradicts its deadness, becoming for Eiseley all of those adapting and surviving species that would lead to his humanity and his moment on the Plains. In the nexus of place, Eiseley comments, "I had come a long way down since morning; I had projected myself across a dimension I was not fitted to traverse in the flesh" (11). The same can be said of the "shabby pseudo-rat" (10). Yet both signify life on the Plains, the life of "sunlight and . . . grass" that stretches across epochs (10).

In this malleable space, Eiseley also discovers the mappable nature of flesh and the body. Part of the Plains landscape through time is embedded in the DNA of flora and fauna. The basic component of life, in contact with the physical challenges of emplacement, of living in place, charts a succession of evolutionary history. Early grasslands mammals and modern humans share a cellular deep map. As Eiseley elucidates,

> Though he was not a man, nor a direct human ancestor, there was yet about him, even in the bone, some trace of that low, snuffling world out of which our forebears had so recently emerged. The skull lay tilted in such a manner that it stared, sightless, up at

me as though I, too, were already caught a few feet above him in the strata and, in my turn, were staring upward at that strip of sky which the ages were carrying farther away from me beneath the tumbling debris of falling mountains. (5)

Stirred by this revelation, Eiseley acknowledges "that we are all potential fossils still carrying within our bodies the crudities of former existences, the marks of a world in which living creatures flow with little more consistency than clouds from age to age" (6). Despite their ephemerality, though, living bodies preserve a history of adaptation to place and even reflect the chemical components of place.

The prairie dog towns of the modern grasslands continue this mammalian journey. So, too, do the towns and highways of modern humans. Where these modern species will end up is a mystery, but both carry the map of the future in their bones. Rodents and primates took different evolutionary paths on the grasslands, but in the slit Eiseley holds them up together, signifiers of chance, selection, and connection.

The slit contains the passing show of grassland life, the deep map of many worlds, distant and near, bound together yet separate and distinct. The slit also embodies the starker truths of history. Thinking of the oreodont, Eiseley remarks, "Like the wistaria [sic] on the garden wall he is rooted in his particular century. Out of it—forward or backward—he cannot run" (11). Eiseley is similarly circumscribed. What releases them both is the synthesizing mind capable of producing a multifaceted, multilayered Thirdspace inspired by Eiseley's vertical descent. From a "remote age near the beginning of the reign of mammals," Eiseley charts an "immense, at times impossible" journey (5–6, 12). He tells the reader that this particular record is one of the many "prowlings of one mind which has sought to explore, to understand, and to enjoy the miracles of this world." (12). It is also a journey that demonstrates humanity's integral connection to the natural world, a connection that allows each person to "possess" a "wilderness" from which to observe "marvels" (13). Ultimately, though, the new map he conjures up must remain incomplete; our ability to see into the mystery of all things is limited. As Eiseley discerns this voyage, "[we] have joined the caravan, you might say, at a certain point; we will travel as far as we can, but we cannot in one lifetime see all that we would like to see or learn all that we hunger to know" (12).

The slit can only give a starting point for a map into unknown country, a commencement point into an ever-vanishing and changing landscape. Eiseley apologizes for this "inconsistent record," the musings that have "grown out of the seasonal jottings of a man preoccupied with time" (12–13). His perambulations keep him on an unceasing journey "forward and backward" across dimensions.

Peter Heidtmann, in his study *Loren Eiseley: A Modern Ishmael*, emphasizes Eiseley's intimate exploration of landscapes, real and imagined. As a "literary naturalist," Eiseley had a long apprenticeship. As a boy in Nebraska, he "[forayed] into geographical wilderness areas."[32] However, his "most significant wilderness" as an adult "was the realm where the individual soul encounters the world."[33] As "The Slit" and "The Flow of the River" demonstrate, Eiseley's sense of the world is complex, multidimensional, and abetted by physical immersion in the dynamic edge of place. While the *Mauvaise Terres*—the Badlands—receive much attention in *The Immense Journey*, "The Flow of the River" reminds us that Eiseley's landscapes range from the cavernous abysses of sewers and underground cavities to the riverine and grasslands ecosystems of past and present. His essays map the diverse landscapes of his Plains years in Nebraska and Kansas, connecting the Paleozoic depths to the quaternary years of modern humans. In the Platte River, Eiseley touches all of this deep history.

Ephemerality and mutability are writ large on the surface of moving water. Whether a rain puddle or the deepest ocean, water in Eiseley's appraisal is "magic," a medium on which life itself is in translation.[34] Eiseley presents a naturalist's baptism in "The Flow of the River," his recollection of a High Plains day in the Platte River. He frames his experience as extraordinary, "once in a lifetime," when "whole eons . . . might pass in a single afternoon without discomfort" (16). Water's atomic structure "reaches everywhere," Eiseley muses, "it touches the past and prepares the future" (16). Like the earth medium of "The Slit," the Platte River enfolds temporal and spatial dimensions and transports the author's imagination across an entire continent. In this particular cartographical essay, Eiseley first maps the contours of the Platte and "the extension of shape by osmosis" (16). Then, in a colder season on the Platte watershed, he collects a river dweller, an old catfish, and removes it to a tank in his city basement. The fish, embodying a cellular deep map, surprises Eiseley with unexpected knowledge of place.

Before Eiseley's appropriation of this catfish, however, he must become the fish in his imagination; indeed become all of the fauna and the very earth that supports life. Usually fearful of the water, Eiseley uncharacteristically trusts his body to the water's energy and experiences "the meandering roots of a whole watershed," his fingers "touching, by some kind of clairvoyant extension, the brooks of snow-line glaciers at the same time that you were flowing toward the Gulf over the eroded debris of worn-down mountains" (16). At this moment, Eiseley slips into "a philosophical category of daydream" that Gaston Bachelard calls "intimate immensity."[35] In a sense, he has entered in Bachelardian terms the vast "non-I" of the river and the life it supports in his somatic encounter.[36]

The Platte River, its north and south branches originating in the Rockies, cuts into the foundations of three major mountain-building orogenies spanning hundreds of millions of years. Its "rambling . . . streamlets flowing erratically over great sand and gravel fans," the river follows an older vestigial passage "of a mightier Ice Age stream bed" (17). The "vast tilted face of the continent" that

Eiseley rides carries the echoes of former worlds (19). The "grain by grain, mountain by mountain" texture of river and bank, urged eastward and then southward to the Gulf of Mexico, provides an expansive view of the watershed. Spatially, Eiseley imaginatively merges into North America; temporally he "was streaming over ancient sea beds thrust aloft where giant reptiles had sported" (19). He was "wearing down the face of time and trundling cloud-wreathed ranges into oblivion" (19). Amid detritus of modern and old, he becomes the element declaring, "I *was* water" (19). Eiseley shifts his perspective from a species-centric to a biocentric one. As in "The Slit," Eiseley's humanity becomes decentered, and he imagines the evolutionary and geological processes that produce and destroy life, the forces of adaptation that connect humankind to various life forms and that presage *Homo sapiens'* demise: "I was three fourths water, rising and subsiding according to the hollow knocking in my veins: a minute pulse like the eternal pulse that lifts Himalayas and which, in the following systole, will carry them away"(20). Eiseley acutely understands the passage of life on these Plains, which are themselves ephemeral. Had Thoreau lived long enough to grasp the nascent curve of Darwin's century—he died in 1862 just as *The Origin of Species* (1859) was generating controversy—he might have penetrated the deeper truths of American landscapes, "developed an acute ear" for Kansas wheat that echoes "the sound of surf on Cretaceous beaches," the grasslands that replaced "the swamps of the low continents" (21). As modern scientist, Eiseley is privy "to the beating of the earth's dark millennial heart" in a way that eluded Thoreau (21).

Thoreau's insight into "animalized water"—his perception of a Walden Pond emerald pickerel—sets up Eiseley's transition to his catfish story (20). Floating on the Platte River, he muses, "I, too, was a microcosm of pouring rivulets and floating driftwood gnawed by the mysterious animalcules of my own creation" (20). His capture of a fish tests this insight. In another season, Eiseley journeys to one of the Platte's tributaries. The landscape, frozen, "stark and ice-locked," is disorienting; "the willow thickets made such an array of vertical lines against the snow," he explains, "that tramping through them produces strange optical illusions and dizziness" (21). Strangeness frequently projects Eiseley into unexpected insight or connection. Caught in a block of "wind-ruffled" ice lies a huge catfish such as accompanied Eiseley the day he flowed with the river. Trapped or bedazzled into its predicament, the catfish suggests a sudden intimacy between the human and the piscine worlds, between "bleak, whiskered face" and clean-shaven scientist, both mortal and stuck in time (22). "Struck by a sudden impulse," Eiseley removes the fish to his car and brings him home "to test the survival qualities of high-plains fishes" (22). This impulse foretells a new immense journey, one that makes science the essence of Eiseley's artful imagination.

The fish surprises Eiseley. As the ice melts, the catfish awakens from hibernation, "the selective product of the high continent and the waters that pour across it" (23). Unlike introduced cattle that die "standing frozen upright in the drifts" of "prairie blizzards," the catfish is the progeny of species adaptation through deep time in a particular place (23). For the winter, housed in a tank and placed in a basement, the catfish accepts with docility its existence. Come spring, however, the fish surprises again. Pushed by "a migratory impulse or perhaps sheer boredom," the catfish leaps from its tank and dies on the floor (23). Animated with Eros and instinct, it "gambles" in a dramatic leap and loses all (23).

Its symbolic movement—a leap of faith—invokes Eiseley's penchant for telescoping temporal and spatial dimensions: "A million ancestral years had gone into that jump . . . a million years of climbing through prairie sunflowers and twining in and out through the pillared legs of drinking mammoth" (24). The leap, like his day of floating on the river, opens up landscapes for Eiseley, brings past, present, and future into "the momentary shape I inhabit," he muses (24). Once again, he sees "fin and reptile foot" etched in his hand (24). Fish body, scientist's body: they are overlays of a deeper, longer landscape and contain the imprint of a "mysterious principle known as 'organization'" (26). Eiseley concludes with a meditation on water that hints at deeper divinations: "No utilitarian philosophy explains a snow crystal, no doctrine of use or disuse. Water has merely leapt out of vapor and thin nothingness in the night sky to array itself in form" (27). Snowflakes, catfish, river-riding men: all are "apparition[s] from that mysterious shadow world beyond nature, that final world which contains . . . the explanation of [life]" (27).

Across his career, Eiseley returned obsessively to questions of life's origins, life's patterns and illegible plans, to explorations of deep time and space. As a writer preoccupied with time, he sought to perfect an essay form that accommodated immense, imagined journeys. To the end of his life in 1977, Eiseley mulled over time's artifacts and mysteries in his essays and poems. Inspired by the geographical particularities of a formative Plains landscape, he invented new narrative routes for his readers to follow. His distinctive approach in *The Immense Journey* set the stage for innovative literary cartography. Five years later, in 1962, Wallace Stegner published *Wolf Willow*, and the nascent narrative design of Heat-Moon's deep map was set. Eiseley's influence on a number of nonfiction genres—spiritual nonfiction, nature writing, environmental essays of place, science writing, to name a few—cannot be overstated. He is a monumental figure among modern essayists. My particular interest in this chapter, however, is deep map writing that foregrounds temporal and spatial dimensions, that places the science of geology front and center, juxtaposing contemporary human issues and queries in creative tension with deep time.

John McPhee, a child when Eiseley's first essays gained a national readership in the 1940s, turned his eye to "storied landscape" as the older essayist left the scene.[37] Like Eiseley, McPhee is fascinated with narrative that emerges from an intimate encounter with place; he, too, teases out the oldest layers of time, engaging in a narrative practice that is richly geological and stratigraphic. As Norma Tilden explains, in analyzing *Rising from the Plains,*

> As a nonfiction writer, McPhee . . . is crossing discursive boundaries onto suspect terrain, recreating geological processes in a narrative performance that the reader is challenged to experience as well as to understand. In so doing, McPhee creates a stratified discursive frame which contains a multitude of stories—of a Western woman, a contemporary nonfiction writer, a number of working geologists, and Wyoming itself—intersecting in an aggregate structure.[38]

In this and other volumes of his Pulitzer-awarded collection *Annals of the Former World* (1998), McPhee positions himself, itinerant journalist following professional geologists across the North American continent, as mediator of temporal scales and spatial histories, a liaison between deep time and human time.

For over a decade of his career, McPhee shadowed dozens of geologists in an attempt to understand their work, to unravel the "lingering remains" of geologic history, and to confront the changes wrought upon the continent by long-term, natural processes and by ephemeral human migrations.[39] His contemporary expedition, made possible by ongoing modern roadbuilding, allows him to touch upon competing concepts of history: history as deep time, history as local phenomenon, history as ongoing collaboration between the dead and the living, and history as necessarily incomplete, dependent upon vestigial traces and unknown future processes.

To make such a vast project decipherable, he "explores the overlapping of two different epistemologies: the more abstract measuring of space by scientists and the cognitive mapping of poets and writers."[40] As Barbara Stevens argues, McPhee adds another epistemology, that of Thirdspace, "a realm with affinities to the juxtaposed, conflicting, and mixed spheres of [his] landscape."[41] On a continent that is literally moving and changing, there is no steady ground. McPhee's cartographic excavations of North America reveal that maps must leave room for the unmappable. Echoing Eiseley's slippery terrain, McPhee's travels into the deep past leave his readers pondering an open-ended, inconclusive, "still moving . . . Big Picture."[42] McPhee's temporal and spatial journeys epitomize what geographer Derek Gregory has called "cartographic anxiety."[43]

The Great Plains, at first, seemingly defies such anxiety. As part of the Stable Interior Craton of North America, the Plains landscape rolls and dips, its surface covered in crops, grasslands, and wooded patches. "Crossing the craton," McPhee wryly declares, "you don't see a lot of rock."[44] Some of the land on the Plains was once glaciated; other parts owe their existence to wind-borne loess soils or to sand dunes once active like the Sahara. But the whole of this region, America's flyover zone, draws a big yawn; its farm- and ranchland and undramatic rises suggest predictability and stasis. Starting in Illinois and traveling to Wyoming, McPhee notes that "in the fifteen hundred miles of the mid-continent there is a great deal less rock to see on the surface than you would see in Wyoming if you opened one eye."[45] Rocks reveal the "lithic archives"; rocks spell out stories.[46]

The stable craton conceals much from the opened eye and thus preserves a deceptive stability. "As you cross Iowa and approach Des Moines," McPhee continues, "nothing on the surface—not a streamcourse, a fault line, an outcrop, a rise—so much as hints at what is now beneath you."[47] Sophisticated technology penetrates the surface and uncovers a spectacular story. Interstate 80 follows part of an ancient rift zone that "split North America right up the middle and down one side, threatening to scatter it to who knows what distant corners of the globe" (628). Once the center of the continent featured a rift zone comparable to modern-day plate junctions like the meeting of "[t]he Red Sea, the Gulf of Aden, and the East African Rift Valley" (629). Rifts, with their deep abysses or rift-depressed lakes, volcanic activity, and tectonic temblors, defy stability. Lincoln, Nebraska, sits atop the southwestern edge of this buried rift. "On modern gravity maps and magnetic maps of North America," McPhee tells us, "it is the single most prominent feature that you see" (628). In the assembling of North America, one needs to peer below the Plains to find evidence of ancient Archean landforms or cratons that once collided, "building mountains where they hit, and sometimes trapping between them volcanic-island-arcs" (636). When these cratons closed, removing "abyssal ocean," they compressed "the crunched remains of oceanic islands" (636). In his narrative *Crossing the Craton*, McPhee juxtaposes ancient orogenic revolutions with the modern "stable" continental core. The dissonance between time scales, the radically different spatial configurations, startles and unsettles the reader unfamiliar with this deep history. The midcontinent has been "quiet for half a billion years" (660). Will it remain so?

Crossing the Craton, the final book of *Annals of the Former World*, completes McPhee's epic cross-section of North American geology. As coda, this book provides reflection on the four preceding books: *Basin and Range* (1981), *In Suspect Terrain* (1983), *Rising from the Plains* (1986), and *Assembling California* (1993). McPhee explains in his "A Narrative Table of Contents," "*Crossing the Craton* describes Nebraska by visiting Colorado, because in Colorado you see the basement of Nebraska bent up into the air."[48] The modern western American landscape makes no sense without the long view that geology gives us. Moreover, in juxtaposing human and deep time, in analyzing the geological landscape that determines human activity, McPhee creates a dynamic interplay between regions that helps define both and proves central to our understanding of the American West. The mountains literally rise from the plains, but the plains, as McPhee's Platte River pebbles demonstrate, have built up from mountain erosion. Human history, enacted on this complex geological stage, dependent upon its resources, adds threads that alternate among mythic, political, social, and scientific perceptions.

Interstate 80 serves as McPhee's principal artery into North American deep history. This interstate follows other, older portals into the West, from the Union Pacific Railroad to the Platte River waterways of beaver trappers. Older still are Native pathways and bison trails. This stretch across the Plains and into the mountains channeled much human history. It provides a cross-section of these interrelated landscapes.[49] Geographer David J. Wishart, in *The Encyclopedia of the Great Plains*, explains Wyoming's unique position as a Plains state, where the clarity of the western boundary along the Rockies blurs: "In the Wyoming basin, for example, where the Great Plains rise to more than 7,000 feet and merge less perceptibly with the Rocky Mountains" one sees places where mountains "interpenetrate with the Plains" (xvi). Standing in Pine Bluffs, Wyoming, not far from Eiseley's field sites with the South Party, McPhee and USGS geologist David Love, with a clear perspective east and west, observe what would have been the nineteenth-century emigrants' "first view of the front ranges of the Rockies."[50]

Looking back, one could see the immense level horizon of the Plains, a familiar view from the emigrants' jump-off point in Missouri. In the late Cretaceous time, McPhee muses, he, Love, and those emigrants would have needed a boat to cross this eastern part of Wyoming; at present-day Rawlins, the landscape turned into "flat marshy terrain" all the way to Utah (46). The current synthesis of plains and mountains is a relatively—in geologic terms—new configuration. Wyoming's mountains trend in distinctive ways, the result of "one of the oddest occurrences in the tectonic history of the world" (48). Emerging from the "heartland of the continent, the Stable Interior Craton," the Wyoming Rockies "moved in highly miscellaneous and ultimately perplexing directions. The

Wind River Range crept southwest, about five inches every ten years for a million years. The Bighorns split. One part went south, the other east. Similarly, the Beartooths went east and southwest. The Medicine Bows moved east. The Washakies west. The Uintas north" (48). Much of this geological history is cryptic, illegible, imperfectly mapped. While all of this information might strike the reader as esoteric, McPhee demonstrates persuasively that the "odd syncopation" of the Wyoming Rockies, the contingencies of deep time, structure many of the realities of modern American history on the Plains and westward (49).

For a time, the Rockies were buried deep "in their own debris" (51). An "aggradational plain" covered much of Wyoming for thirty million years. Then something began to elevate this ancient great plain—most likely the Yellowstone hotspot—and lazy waterways turned into streams that "began to straighten, rush, and cut, moving their boulders and gravels in the way that chain saws move teeth" (52–53). One place east of the Laramie Range "somehow escaped exhumation" (54). This "one piece of the Great Plains—extremely narrow but still intact—extends like a finger, and, as ever, touches the mountain core" (54). Geologists named this feature "the gangplank," and its rise in Nebraska and Wyoming determined the route of the Union Pacific.

Today Interstate 80 shares "the narrowest point on the gangplank. . . . The tracks and lanes are so close that the gangplank resembles the neck of a guitar" (58–59). This extension of the Plains into the Laramies, a fortuitous discovery for Major General Grenville Dodge and his surveying company, accelerated the forces of modernity that altered the Plains and the intermountain West. The gangplank, an ancient bison trail that led Native people to hunting grounds in the Medicine Bows, changed American history. David Love explains, "This is the only place in the whole Rocky Mountain front where you can go from the Great Plains to the summit of the mountains without snaking your way up a mountain face or going through a tunnel. This one feature had more to do with the building of the West than any other factor" (59–60).

The gangplank establishes early in *Rising from the Plains* McPhee's method, his nonlinear narrative of deep time and human time and creative juxtaposition of stories. The gangplank provides an interesting geologic narrative, a chronicle of mountain building, mountain deroofing, and resumed uplift that leaves behind a vestige of a former world. It also frames a story transformed into myth: the building of a nation. Muted, but not lost, are the traces of Native people whose ancestors populated the Plains and Rocky Mountains for many thousands of years. Older, still, are the North American mammals and their antecedents going back tens of millions of years. Journeying all over late twentieth-century Wyoming, where the Great Plains and the Rocky Mountains merge, John McPhee and his guide, David Love, seek multiple stories, including the Love family's connection to pioneering myth.

Love is the son of homesteaders, of an itinerant cowboy-turned-rancher father—Johnny Love, born in Wisconsin on his uncle John Muir's farm and later kicked out of the University of Nebraska—and of a well-educated easterner, Ethel Waxham, who arrived in Wyoming sporting her Phi Beta Kappa key from Wellesley College. Johnny Love, rebel collegian, left his sisters in Broken Bow, Nebraska, to seek his fortune over the gangplank. Ethel Waxham journeyed by train over the gangplank into new country. Her desire to seek adventure as a schoolmarm in rural Wyoming resulted in a long-lasting marriage and a fascinating journal. Her journal's words keep company with McPhee's, giving firsthand accounts of settlement life in early twentieth-century Wyoming, only four decades after General Dodge's discovery of the gangplank. In retelling the Love family saga, McPhee conflates geologic and human history, demonstrating complex links between land and community. Brought up at Red Bluff Ranch, near the Gas and Rattlesnake Hills, David Love remembers that "everything depended on geology. Any damn fool could see that the vegetation was directly responsive to the bedrock. Hence birds and wildlife were responsive to it. We were responsive to it" (103–4). To survive the harsh conditions of central Wyoming, the Loves and others had to open up to the terrain, to learn from the flora and fauna. "If there was one thing we learned," Love concludes, "it was that you don't fight nature. You live with it. And you make accommodations—because nature does not accommodate" (104). Accommodations, however, do not necessarily convert to long-term viability in volatile, changeable human society. Like the passing show along Interstate 80, the recent past is quickly receding, taking Johnny and Ethel Love's history with it. Their son's words will come back to haunt him later in McPhee's deep map of Wyoming.

The ancient landscape that David Love guides McPhee through is everywhere inscribed by human time. Not only does he recall his own family's ranching history, Love also comments on the public stories that loom large in the nation's imagination: the Oregon Trail, the Mormon relocation, the transcontinental railroad, the Indian Wars, the discovery of oil, gas, and uranium, the outlaw exploits of Le Roy Parker and Harry Longabaugh, or Butch Cassidy and the Sundance Kid. Love's father knew both of them and was friends with Chief Washakie (of Crowheart Butte fame) and famed stagecoach driver Peggy Dougherty.[51] Vestiges of human making, from wagon ruts to deserted ranches and towns, and more recently deserted beer cans, signify ephemeral human passages. Gazing upon a strip mine, McPhee muses,

> This strip mine, no less than an erupting volcano, was a point in the world where geologic time and human time had intersected. Ordinarily, the close relationship between the two is masked: human time, full of beepers and board meetings, sirens and Senate caucuses, all happening in microtemporal units that physicists call picoseconds; geologic time, with its forty-six hundred million

years, delivering a message that living creatures prefer to return unopened to sender. In this place, though, geology had come out of its depths to join the human world, and as Love would put it, all hell had broken loose. (185)

Eventually this story, too, will recede as coal is depleted. Only historic snapshots will remain in the human memory, and those for only a few generations. McPhee defines the geologic record as "front-page science": because "every scene is temporary," only fragments remain, summations, moments (29). Human time similarly loses focus. McPhee's human stories, like Eiseley's, share in this compression and fragmentation, "a multiplicity of detailed and chaotic histories and space" woven together in deep map narrative.[52] The Love family saga is unfolded piecemeal and in nonlinear fashion. David Love, in his private and public roles, mediates all the disparate passages between Wyoming's geologic and human cross-sections. McPhee transcribes them. Love has spent his career traveling and studying this state, becoming "the grand old man of Rocky Mountain geology" (5). As a field geologist, he has pursued the story of plains and mountains from one end of Wyoming to the other. In his mind resides thirty years of work that has created the best narrative of Wyoming geology, a geology that is "[an] authentic enigma on a grand scale" (48). At the same time, Love encapsulates the recent microtemporal settlement of the West. His family, a representative "founding" family, delineates "a stratum of the region" (127). His memories, and his mother's daily jottings, provide a context for the complicated cross-currents of human habitation on the High Plains and the mountain West.

Among McPhee's essential stratum is the laminate of Ethel Waxham Love's journal (since published by the University of New Mexico Press) into his larger narrative plan.[53] Her detailed, personal record, in Norma Tilden's assessment, "is almost off-putting in its dailiness, its attention to the local and mundane."[54] Waxham Love's daily recordings and musings counter the geologic Big Picture with "comings and goings across a local landscape."[55] Locality, however, helps McPhee's readers cope with the overwhelming scale of deep time. His ability to present and articulate such differing spatial and temporal dimensions allows McPhee to "[cross-cut] the layers of Western landscape, from observable surface to geological depth; at the same time it cross-cuts stories of geologist Love and writer McPhee with the history of Love's mother."[56]

Quite purposefully, McPhee's multilayered deep map is multivocal, across generations. Love and McPhee's traversing of Wyoming traces Ethel's and Johnny's individual journeys across the Great Plains and into Wyoming's high country. On one scale, these private passages are short-lived and idiosyncratic. On another scale, their local realities connect to many stories, echo many journeys, giving their movements across time and space a larger, communal significance. Waxham Love's writings tune in on early settlement history; her son's and McPhee's observations bear witness to the aftermath of that pioneer era. Putting all in perspective is geologic time, with its etchings of former worlds and intimations of epochal mortality.

Rising from the Plains, in geologic fashion, ingests Waxham Love's trenchant, carefully wrought portraits of Wyoming settlers and settlement life into a complex textual landscape. Her firsthand account of history-in-the-making complements McPhee's other lithic archives. Like the author himself, she represents the stereotypical easterner who gives up comfort, security, and convention for the greater freedom of open spaces. As schoolmarm, she plays Molly Wood to Johnny Love's cowboy allure.[57] After a long wooing, he finally ties her down to the ranch and connects her to the West. She confronts illness, wild bulls, murderers, mad dogs, near bankruptcy, and death. When a cowboy mangles a hand in a roping accident, she "snipped the tendons, dropped the finger into the hot coals of the fire box, sewed a flap of skin over the stump, smiled sweetly, and said: 'Joe, in a month you'll never know the difference'" (89–90). Early in her journal, she comments, "It is a cruel country as well as beautiful. Men seem here only on sufferance" (36).

While providing a chronicle of her family's challenges, from educating two sons in isolation to aiding her husband's efforts to stay afloat financially, Waxham Love also comments on the social and economic history that would industrialize much of Wyoming. "Oil to us," she writes, "was once just a word recurring through the story of Wyoming" (106). Noting the tales of Native people, trappers, Captain Bonneville, Jim Bridger, and the many emigrants to California and Oregon, she lists the early uses of oil in the state—a remedy for cracked hooves, harness sores, human aches and pains, a recipe for axle grease when mixed with flour, and a starter fluid for buffalo chips (107). By 1917, oil derricks were going up everywhere. "Such excitement," she adds, "was contagious. . . . Almost every herder had his own oil dome. We took up oil claims" (107). With oil and gas come boom-and-bust times. The Mineral Lands Leasing Act of 1920 gave oil and gas corporations enormous power over the landscape. Uranium discoveries and massive coalfields became part of the corporate spoils, too.

Her son David, PhD Yale, working for both industry and government, would be a participant in the land's transformation into an extractive economy. His complicity in this change has made Love, a passionate lover of Wyoming's diverse lands, a man of contradictions; "he carries within himself the whole spectrum of tensions that have accompanied the rise of the environmental movement," McPhee discerns. "He carries within himself some of the central paradoxes of his time" (180). Reared in central Wyoming, where much "energy colonization" has occurred, Love now finds himself defending the landscape (180). Trained to delve deeply into earth's history, Love perceives the ephemeral nature of much human activity; but short-term activity can cause long-term problems.

The geologic scale overshadows Wyoming's current social, political, and economic landscape. The earth is ever changing. Near Rawlins, an outcropping displays twenty-six hundred million years. In one glance, McPhee relates, "we were looking at many moments in well over half the existence of the earth" (23). On the entire stretch of Interstate 80, between the Atlantic and the Pacific oceans, no other suite of rocks reveals so much time. Most people, speeding by on their picosecond journeys, are unaware of the narratives preserved in these granites, sandstones, and limestones. Wyoming itself has moved over time, riding the restless North American plate, sometimes south, sometimes north.

In the Tetons, where Precambrian rocks over one billion years old as well as young rocks only a few million years in age lie exposed, Love "can watch the landscape change, see it move, grow, collapse, and shuffle itself in an intricate, imbricate manner, not in spatial chaos but by cause and effect through time" (137). Wyoming has housed numerous mountain chains, ur-Rockies that weathered and were buried by sands. Shallow inland seas have washed over Wyoming's surface several times. The climate has been by turns like Malaya, the Sahara, and the Pacific Northwest. Enormous volcanic eruptions have disrupted the terrain, and massive intrusions have lifted up miles of buried sediment. Sculpting, by river and wind, exhumed the recent Rockies from an ancient high plain. The Laramide Revolution, the parent event of the mountains we now know, created "rootless sheets of whole terrain . . . sliding like floorboards, overlapping, stacking up, covering younger rock, colliding with the rooted mountains, while to the east more big ranges and huge downflexing basins appear in . . . random geometries" (139).

Wyoming's geologic chronicle is so complex, Love has spent his whole life attempting to understand it. Before him other geologists, storytellers of deep landscapes, men like F. V. Hayden, Clarence King, John Wesley Powell, Charles T. Lupton, and Charles J. Hares, attempted to piece together parts of the Big Picture, itself always changing. With the advent of plate tectonic theory, McPhee explains, the story "coalesced . . . and drew together in a single narrative aspects of geology that almost no one had guessed were related" (158). But that narrative can never be complete—too much is gone, too much will never be known. As William Howarth notes in an essay on McPhee, "Itinerant Passages," texts can be "chain[s] . . . road[s] . . . voyage[s]" along "a linear matrix."[58] But they can also be "web[s] . . . maze[s] . . . dark and tangled forest[s]."[59] In unraveling the complex story of plains and mountains, McPhee, like Eiseley, must embrace time's arrow and the cycle, using imaginative Thirdspace to discern the gaps, inexplicable realities, and unconformities in his map of natural history.

McPhee suggests that human stories share this slippage. David Love serves as a narrative anchor in the flux of Wyoming history. McPhee portrays him in mythic terms, a son of pioneers, solver of geologic puzzles, scientific guru of the Rockies. Referring to rocks that never move, McPhee labels him "autochthonous" (4). The Bronco he drives cannot contain Love's formidable energy, "a restlessness that derived from a lifetime of travel on foot and horseback" (5). Viewing Wyoming with Love is "analogous to walking up and down outside a theatre in the company of David Garrick" (10). Near the beginning of McPhee's narrative, Love stands on a rise in eastern Wyoming, a latter-day Natty Bumppo, surveying the territory. He looks west, toward the Rockies, for the settlers a symbol of "hope and courage" (43). Love is McPhee's touchstone, a wise man who lives not in caves but on the High Plains and the tops of mountains.

The Wyoming maps that Love has twice compiled garner more than respect—they inspire others to proclaim his irreplaceable essence: "'Dave has his hand on the pulse," exclaims Malcolm McKenna of the American Museum of Natural History in New York. "He knows geology from having found it out himself. He has set an example of the way geology is done—one hell of an example'" (144). Love, like his ranching father before him, is a dying breed, a field geologist in an age of "black-box" laboratory geology (147). David Love's kind "'is being diminished," laments a colleague, "which is a major intellectual crime'" (147). Mythic figures disappear fast in the modern West—in nanoseconds. For this reason, their stories must be collected. Underlying McPhee's deep map is a sense of urgency. Just as a geologic theory can "collect in one story numerous disparate phenomena," so, too, can the embodiment of one man (164). Gathering together the disparate, sorting out the multiple stories of place, stitching together fragments of space and time: for Eiseley and McPhee, the deep map narrative gives structure to retreating, echoing realities and voices concerns over humanity's long track record.

The geologic record, its lithic archives, reveals much that is "randomly assembled, subsequently arranged and filed," an incompleteness that should give arrogant humans pause (135). Love's favorite fable of the blind men and the elephant "allegorize[s] for him the history and practice of his science" (145). The final sections of *Rising from the Plains* reflect Love's concerned, at times bleak, assessment of the modern human history that has unfolded in Wyoming. Human endeavors to extract from the land, to uncover uses in the rock and to exploit them for profit—even a large segment of modern geologists follows the money and aids extractive industries—now disturbs Love's recollections and memories.

Much of Wyoming is now "acupunctured for energy" (179). Eocene lacustrine (oil) shale in southwestern Wyoming "contains more oil than all the rock of Saudi Arabia" (180). The Overthrust Belt produces new oil fields. Enormous coalfields near Rock Springs support the energy needs of many American cities outside of Wyoming. In Love's assessment, Wyoming is "at the mercy of the East Coast and West Coast establishments" (180). Near-constant train traffic to and from the coalfields rattles through Wyoming towns into Nebraska and eastward. Point of Rocks, east of Rock Springs, boasts "the tallest building in Wyoming," the ironically named Jim Bridger, "a coal-fired steam electric plant" that generates "four times what is needed to meet the demands of Wyoming" (182). At twenty-four stories, it towers over other commercial buildings in the state. Built near the coalfields, Jim Bridger exemplifies the extractive nature of much of Wyoming's economic foundation. But in Love's assessment, "This place is smoking the hell out of the country. . . . The wind blows a plume of corruption" (182).

The social effects of Jim Bridger and other big energy projects—part of boom times—is significant—"twenty-eight percent of the people of Wyoming were living in mobile homes" (185). Instability, crime, and overwhelmed social service agencies have disturbed Wyoming's communities. Moreover, these energy projects require steady water supplies. A constant stream now travels forty miles from Green River to Jim Bridger. Water for the human population is declining in quantity and quality. The end result of energy colonization, in Love's opinion, is this: "Wyoming's ox is being gored" (185).

Trona mining in southwestern Wyoming posits another kind of challenge. Industrial production depends upon it: "ceramics and textiles, pulp and paper, iron and steel, and, most especially, glass" (195). Its sodium enters the watershed, feeding into the Green River and thus into Lakes Powell and Mead. These bodies, Love attests, are "turning into chemical lakes" (195–96). A trona refinery west of Green River belches out a polluting cloud tainted with fluorine. Its haze travels the entire state and may "be damaging forests in the Wind River Range" (196–97). If a proposed geothermal project receives a green light, Love wonders, what further damage might Wyoming suffer? Might the geyser fields of Yellowstone cease activity, as has happened in New Zealand and Nevada when similar projects were built? Geothermal wells also expose the ecosystem to radioactive water and pollute watersheds "a thousand miles downstream" (199). Wyoming's geologic bounty, fueling a number of boom-and-bust cycles in the last century, is also a curse. The consequence of extracting deep time's products is pitting proindustry groups against others. "It isn't all or nothing," Love insists. "It doesn't have to be" (202). Humans, driven by complex motives, have yet to figure out how to avoid short-term thinking and solutions that negatively affect future generations' resources and environmental health.

McPhee's deep map ends by examining decay. Love takes McPhee to his father's Red Bluff Ranch, now abandoned. It is currently leased to cattle companies who overgraze the range. Muskrat Creek, which drains into the ranch from the nearby Gas Hills, has been polluted by uranium mining. "Fifty open-pit uranium mines were round about us," McPhee comments, "and in the low middle ground of the view to the north were [the creek] and Love Ranch. . . . The place was an unearthly mess. War damage could not look worse, and in a sense that is what it was" (210). Moreover, thieves have plundered the ranch house, stealing bookcases, furniture, and anything that could be moved. Looking around, McPhee observes, "Of the dozen or so ranch buildings, some were missing and some were breaking down. The corrals had collapsed. The bunkhouse was gone. The cottonwood-log granary was gone, but not Joe Lacey's Muskrat Saloon, which the Loves had used for storing hay. Its door was swinging in the wind" (213). Other vestiges of the Old West remain. McPhee finds fragments of newspapers once used for insulation; these scraps preserve stories now forgotten. Cedar and pine posts hewn by Johnny Love stand rot-free, testaments of a hard but satisfying life no longer extant. The old sod-covered storage cellar remains. But nature is rapidly tearing down Red Bluff Ranch: wind, short rain bursts, and wild animals now rule. McPhee tells us, "cattle chips and coyote scat were everywhere on the floors. The clothes cupboards and toy cupboards in the bedroom [Love] had shared with [his brother] were two feet deep in pack-rat debris" (214). Walking out of his old schoolroom, where

Ethel Waxham Love homeschooled her boys, Love insists, "I can't stand this. Let's get out of here" (214). The ranch, homesteaded in 1897, is dead. In the shadow of mountains signifying eons of time, how puny human productions appear. McPhee concludes his deep map on a troubled note. In the convergence of geologic and human time that is modern Wyoming, the original quest of settlers now seems problematic. Grandeur, beauty, and promise have been squandered in only a few generations. Homesteaders, who severed ties to create themselves anew in a "new" land, in reality brought the same sad human story: greed, waste, corruption. "At places like this," Love posits, "we thought we were doing a great service to the nation. In hindsight, we do not know if we were performing a service or a disservice. Sometimes I think I might regret it. Yes. It's close to home"' (214). On this mournful note, *Rising from the Plains* concludes.

When McPhee completed his assay of plains and mountains, he had yet to complete his larger goal of reading a cross-section of North American geology. The 1989 Loma Prieta earthquake, which famously rattled San Francisco's Candlestick Park on national television, helped determine the terminus of his project: *Assembling California* (1993). At this point, McPhee explains, he returned to a stretch of Interstate 80 from Chicago to Cheyenne that he had barely touched upon. With W. Randall Van Schmus of the University of Kansas, he returns to the Stable Interior Craton, in *Crossing the Craton* (1998), to gain new perspective on the grasslands, where few outcroppings disturb the interstate or reveal their histories. Even geologic textbooks have devoted few pages to this region. Van Schmus explains, "You need to wait for the development of techniques. We're still dealing with a frontier in continental evolution. The information's there; we just have to figure how to get it out."[60] Until recently, the deep time story of the Great Plains remained illegible and vastly simplified: "First there was the basement, and on that grew the world" (626).

At the end of the twentieth century, technical innovations have started to uncover the complexity of deep time below the Plains. McPhee presents a catalogue: "There have been inventions or advances in metamorphic petrology, in samarium/neodymium geochronology, in argon/argon thermochronology, in uranium/lead dating, in zircon dating, in aeromagnetic mapping, in filtered-gravity mapping, in trace-element geochemistry, and in the isotopic monitoring of the crustal history of rocks and their origins in the mantle" (628.) This revolution in ascertaining the deeper story of the Stable Interior Craton has brought "a new and rapid sketching-in of whole Precambrian scenes" (628). Since 90 percent of the earth's history is preserved in the Precambrian, these techniques are generating significant geologic stories for mapping.

As deep map writers from the Great Plains demonstrate repeatedly, the horizontal perspective must be countered and tested by vertical descent. These two planes together make possible the deeper stories of place. Van Schmus adds that sometimes to know a place, you have to travel horizontally and visit your neighbors: "If you want to see what's under Interstate 80 in Nebraska, you're seeing it right here [in Colorado]. There's basically no substitute for being able to see the rocks and walk over them. Nebraska is like *this*—a few thousand feet down" (641).

Vertical drilling for oil has also provided invaluable information on the Plains' deep time and space. Texaco drilled twelve thousand feet down in Kansas; Amoco drilled seventeen thousand feet into Iowa; Nebraska has been drilled, too (655). The Geology Department at the University of Kansas houses a "comprehensive rock archive" from these efforts (655). These lithic archives reveal stories of ancient island arcs, rift zones, plutons, and ocean spreading. As the island arcs docked some 1.8 billion years ago, the landform of future Nebraska and North America began to organize itself. When rifting threatened this continent building at 1.1 billion years ago—the result of a thermal plume or hot spot—the nascent landform began tearing apart. Had the rifting continued, McPhee explains, "a great bay would have developed, with a shoreline of a thousand miles" (658). Instead, the hot spot fizzled out, and Lincoln, Nebraska, and Des Moines, Iowa, are now three hours apart instead of an ocean apart. The modern travelers speeding back and forth across the Plains most likely know little of this earthly history. By spotlighting such newly emerging knowledge, McPhee's textual map helps readers to perceive the deeper realities of the places they traverse or inhabit.

In their deep time excavations, Loren Eiseley and John McPhee lead their readers through fascinating, immense journeys into the geologic depths of the Great Plains. These journeys underscore the complex connections between the past and the present, between temporal and spatial dimensions that are both alien and familiar. For much of earth's existence, human history has presented the most slender of laminates, the barest of layers. Of Eiseley's *The Immense Journey*, Michael Bryson has commented that it is "thus a series of many interlocking journeys—a walk in the woods, an anthropological expedition to the Plains, the course of one's lifetime, the evolutionary development of diverse species, and the process of scientific inquiry itself."[61] McPhee, too, integrates many journeys into his narratives of the North American West, of plains and mountains, basins and ranges, and the Stable Interior Craton. Following his geologist guides, he creates interwoven textual passageways, innovative literary cartography, which opens up, but leaves inconclusive, a deep map of the world we paradoxically rely upon, cherish, and destroy.

CHAPTER FIVE

DEEP MAPPING LIVED SPACE

"Layers of Presence" in Julene Bair's *One Degree West*, Sharon Butala's *Wild Stone Heart*, and Linda Hasselstrom's *Feels Like Far*

As the colonial culture of the West, we have no culture, which is just the same problem as having no story that tells us how we fit in the place. This is not an original idea, and in fact there is a self-conscious and active movement among western writers to invent a literature for the place. We need stories that will settle us to the land, not more stories reacting to those who would and do destroy it, but as long as the destruction goes on, these accounts of our struggles will be our only story.

Richard Manning, *Grassland*

Wallace Stegner has famously commented in *The American West as Living Space* (1987) that rootlessness and a desire for freedom have made mobility and motion principal elements of western American and Canadian life. Movement opposes community, memory, and "the gods who make place holy," causing a condition Stegner calls "spiritual pellagra."[1] In much western American and Canadian writing, as scholar Neil Campbell has noted, the "interplay of roots and routes" unsettles literary narrative.[2] This dynamic often leads to an insider-outsider animus within a work that reveals a sense of alienation from home place, a tenor of dis-ease, that Paul Giles in *Virtual Americas* calls a "dialectic of familiarity and alterity."[3] Campbell discerns a contradiction at the heart of the literary West—which includes the Great Plains: "This desire for rootedness in some essential tradition and authentic, communal narrative, such as the frontier or the Wild West, is, after all, so often seemingly at odds with another desire to articulate a 'routed' history of contact, cultural collision, and mobility."[4] Two decades earlier, Stegner was examining mobility and settlement—the complex cultural matrix of the West as living space—and concluded that "our migratoriness has hindered us from becoming a people of communities and traditions."[5] In space that has elevated the automobile, the motel, and the roadside attraction to iconic status, Stegner suggests that "the West is still primarily a series of brief visitations or a trail to somewhere else" (23).

The aftermath of World War II stirred a deeper restlessness, registered in contemporary nonfiction from the Plains, affecting in particular the youngest descendents of the first white settlers. Writing in 1987, Stegner surveys a western space that is emptying out. "The towns that are most western," he concludes, "have had to strike a balance between mobility and stability. . . . They are the places where the stickers stuck, and perhaps were stuck, the places where adaptation has gone furthest" (25). Still, adaptation to vast, arid spaces is difficult, leaving many towns on the verge of collapse, monuments to spiritual pellagra.

Three contemporary writers of the Great Plains, Julene Bair, Sharon Butala, and Linda Hasselstrom, examine Stegner's contention from three different Plains communities: the farming community of Goodland, Kansas, the ranching community of Eastend, Saskatchewan, and the ranching community of Hermosa, South Dakota. These communities ostensibly value the rootedness that comes with property and one's descent from settlement times; yet these writers address the environmental stresses (cultural and physical) that promote Stegner's "deficiency disease" and make adaptation to place difficult. Bair's *One Degree West: Reflections of a Plainsdaughter* (2000), Butala's *Wild Stone Heart: An Apprentice in the Fields* (2000), and Hasselstrom's *Feels Like Far: A Rancher's Life on the Great Plains* (1999; 2001) speak to the power of natural landscape to define the human community. Each approaches her home place cartographically; each measures out intimate domestic space against the backdrop of an altered biome. At times the deep map of place eludes each writer's survey as powerful fathers, economic necessity, and the forgetfulness of modernity eclipse the markings of previous worlds. At other times, these writers bend to the power and poetry of landscape, revealing spiritual dimensions that could offer healing and deeper insight, that tap into "the gods who make place holy."

Bair states, "Where you live becomes what you know, becomes who you are."[6] Bair's experience growing up on the High Plains has been equivocal. The patriarchal culture of Goodland in the 1950s and 1960s—a "narrowness" that seemed all the harder for dryland conditions—has left Bair maladapted: "Parts of me simply can't have existence here," she explains (129). Putting down roots, returning to Goodland, has proved impossible for Bair, though memory, dreams, and creativity pull her back to western Kansas and its formative landscape. She is torn between allegiance to the western Kansas High Plains and protection of self. Still, the inability to embrace this land pains her: "I can't uproot myself completely, nor reconcile myself to the fact that the land, once lost to me, then briefly reclaimed, is not our future" (7).

Butala, however, left an urban existence for a ranching life, seeking solace in the "austere beauty" of southwestern Saskatchewan.[7] In entering this landscape, she began an extended period of adaptation to an immense, lonely space. Yet she has learned to live here, indeed to relish the "presence" and "consciousness" of this landscape, despite its inhospitable nature.[8] Hasselstrom, though, loved the Badlands region of South Dakota from first sight, at age nine, when her stepfather, John Hasselstrom, moved his new wife and stepdaughter to Hermosa from Texas. Her connection to the land has become so visceral that Hasselstrom claims to have "a map carved into my flesh and bones, a pattern so deeply buried in my brain as to be nearly instinctual."[9] She has struggled against the conservative social environment of Hermosa, against the stubborn patriarchal dictates of her father and acquiescent mother. Hasselstrom's somatic connection to the land cannot withstand the assault of her father's discipline and irrational commands. She becomes, in her words, "a fugitive from my family, from my home, from my experience as a rancher, and from the future I had planned."[10] Bair, Butala, and Hasselstrom offer both confirmation and rebuttal to Stegner's diagnosis and offer literary case studies on the challenges and joys of living in a High Plains environment. Their deep maps give testament to the profound personal veins that tap into the landscape, bringing memoir to the forefront in their narratives.

Stegner's influence on these writers is considerable. As I have argued earlier, *Wolf Willow*, Stegner's deep map of his Great Plains childhood, has become the ur-text for much contemporary nonfiction writing about living in the West. In *One Degree West*, *Wild Stone Heart*, and *Feels Like Far*, Bair, Butala, and Hasselstrom give a choric nod to Stegner's multigenre experiment. The strata of cultural and personal, familial history in his story speak to the difficulties of working and living on the Plains. In underscoring the complexity of place and identity in place, Stegner subtitled his formative text "A History, a Story, and a Memory of the Last Plains Frontier." The story he was trying to unfold required attention on several fronts: his family's participation in settlement history; the recent assertion of Canadian national history; the displacement of Indigenous and métis cultures; and older than all of these, the geological imprints of deep time. But in *Wolf Willow*, Stegner's own memory provides the initial foundation for his extended essay. Such works with layers of memory and personal history interlocking self with place have proved fundamental in much Great Plains deep map writing.

Indeed, memoir writing in the last decade has emerged as a significant genre in American letters. Bair posits that the "unquenchable thirst for the untrammeled and real drives the current interest in place-centered memoirs."[11] Western American memoir writing, in particular, "is thriving," according to Richard Maxwell Brown, "giving us a new emotional history of the West."[12] Western landscapes, including Plains landscapes, have become narrative staging points, places where the personal intersects with national myth and political urgencies. As Kathleen Boardman and Gioia Woods argue, North American Western memoir writers must "perform identity through a trio of locations: *physical location, rhetorical location, and political location.*"[13] Stegner's writings demonstrate how unstable one's sense of self and place can be in the West, where physical and social conditions often defy personal dreams, economic plans, and political ideologies—facets of the imagined or mythic place. Bair, Butala, and Hasselstrom confirm the difficulty of defining one's "axis of identity" in the places that have helped shaped their lives.[14] It is not surprising, then, to discover such a strong imprint of self-writing in contemporary deep map narrative.

The latter half of the twentieth century ushered in enormous social and cultural changes in the American West: the rise of large-scale farming and ranching, divorce rates, education levels, and environmentalism; the migration to the urban West; the redefining of family structures; and the challenge to traditional gender alignments. Displacement and mobility stand in stark contrast to the mythos of settlement that Bair's father and mother struggle to preserve. In her intimate portrait of one family's adjustment to post–World War II America, Bair connects family history to larger historical developments. *One Degree West* bears witness to the aftermath of a half-century's upheaval. Bair carefully traces the fault lines within her family, divisions deepened by gender, colliding dreams, and death. Framing all is the intractable reality of western Kansas.[15]

She begins with an essay, "Disappearances," that eulogizes a "rock-hard farmyard, gnarly with implement tracks and bony bumps," a family farmhouse transformed into a figurative grave-yard of family stories, conflicts, and dreams.[16] In the present of the text, her older brother, Clark, is long dead, her formidable father is two years in the grave, her relations with her surviving brother, Bruce, are tense, and her mother is ailing. Looking at the old place that sheltered her young life, Bair imagines a new owner soaking rags in diesel and burning the farmhouse down. Yet during her early years, "[we] took life in this house our grandfather built for granted," as though the love and care of his carpentry could with-stand depopulation, hardscrabble economics, and death itself (15). The Bairs had made it, placing them in the farming elite of their community (15). That position cushioned them for a number of decades until disappearances began to erode their tenuous hold on the homestead, their ability to hang tough against climate and economic cycles.

The Bairs had been among the fortunate as industrial farming took hold on the Plains. Surveying her family's miles of cultivated and uncultivated acreage, Bair sees two competing narratives. On the one hand, "[o]ur way of life was dying" (4). On the other, Bair recognizes that

> ancestors only a couple generations before me had made their tenuous claim on the prairie, and now we were thundering over it in tractors bigger than their houses. But there were fewer of us. My parents, like so many farmers, had moved to town many years before, trading the farm I had grown up on for land closer to their other holdings. . . . Dad commuted to this farm as if it

were a factory, the land suited only for the mass production of crops, no longer a place to live. (4–5)

Her parents' move to town signifies their success as landholders and agricultural producers. But in Bair's assessment, a new paucity has taken hold in Goodland, making "life in Kansas . . . even lonelier than in childhood" (5). The enormous changes that have taken place in her lifetime disturb and pain her.

Bair places her family's story within the national narrative of pioneering. The Bairs and Carlsons—her mother's Swedish side—emigrated to western Kansas to stake claim in a better future. They struggled against the elements so that subsequent generations could live and profit off the land. Yet after World War II, the youngest family members began to abandon the founding patriarchs' dreams and to follow their own. Bair recalls that she and her brothers "fought and didn't know we loved each other and felt sorry for ourselves and longed to escape" (15). Goodland could not hold onto them, and like other young adults to this day on the Great Plains, they migrated away, alienated from home ground. In just a few generations, the pioneer story petered out, dissipated in reality while it gained a stronger toehold in the national imagination.

Looking back from middle age, Bair now recognizes that "our lives had a spiritual edge" (15). The spare, elemental landscape "nurtured a psychic dimension" (15). Bair sees herself and her family tangled in irony. The ancient buffalo grass had been turned over to support a growing nation. Settlement had been the solution to crowded cities and polluted industrial bases. Yet in the late twentieth century, the forces of depopulation were unraveling communities across the Plains, and the farms themselves were industrial sites. Bair's critique cuts:

Now, staring at the miles of wheat where the immense fan of buffalo grass had once opened onto the sky, I reflected on how ironic it was that our migration to the cities had not diminished our impact on the land. With the aid of machinery and chemicals, and with families a tenth of their former size, we conquered the Plains, not just out of greed, but out of failure to recognize what we loved and that love was reason enough not to destroy. Unable to fill the Plains with people, we settled for writing our name onto every inch of them, lest we forget ourselves and succumb to the spiritual vastness. (15)

Bair's opening essay establishes a keening tone as she examines the loss that has pervaded her deep map of Goodland.

The social world of the 1950s and 1960s crumbles as well. Her father, the family "star," led his brood with "substantial love and reliability," yet he could not protect his children from accidental forces, bad choices, and financial mishap (37). Twice married, now a single mother of a teenage boy, Bair recalls in the essay "Scattered Wheat" her "decades of missteps," capitulating at sixteen to a local James Dean wannabe, Mick, in his 1959 Chevy Impala, to running from an abusive second husband at thirty-five. While her parents' success "had seemed to confer dignity on me," Bair confesses, "I'd done nothing special to win my privileges then or now" (41). The world her parents' generation struggled to create seemingly topples under the feet of willful children who throw their love away, run off to the glamour of America's urban centers, or turn their backs on the farms that created them.

"It's as if we betrayed ourselves," Bair remarks in a later essay, "not appreciating our own past, unaware of how the vast, sweeping plains that surrounded our farmhouse provided the spiritual underpinning of our lives" (117). Even the parents sell or lease their land, settling into towns and suburban-style houses, "[evicting us] . . . from the place that birthed our stories" (116). The social fabric that appeared so strong on the farm, the world of "our light exchanges, our bedtime stories, our jokes and grudges," diminishes to "silence" when her parents move to Goodland (117). Bair connects her family's diminishment to a national diminishment: "The unraveling of our story corresponds with the predictable American denouement. We had this great open continent, this airy gift that filled so much more than our pragmatic needs, but we gave no credence to the nonmaterial things that derive from land and space, the things you can't really own" (117). Bair's tone is a familiar one among the late-settlement generations of children since the 1930s; memoirists from Stegner forward blend eulogy with demythologizing.

Yet this social world is also suffocating, and escape becomes a survival strategy. "Kansas values are male," Bair bluntly asserts (129). In the essay "Housewives, Fieldhusbands," Bair incisively maps the gender divide that pervades Goodland's cultural landscape. Her father, her brothers, and the hired men labor in the fields. She and her mother work in and near the house. Bair understands that this unspoken arrangement does offer her some protection. When stormy days threaten all that the men have been laboring to produce, Bair comments, she and her mother "were lucky not to be male" (48). The landscape reveals many sides, not all spiritual and benign: "The climate of western Kansas was harsh, the land huge and daunting. It fell to men to wage enterprise across that distance. A man had to keep spinning, like a gyroscope, the force of his energy keeping his family in balance" (48). Once a man lost this momentum, "the Plains got inside him, slowing his movement until he shuffled over the dirt" (48–49). Bair sees failed men all around in her family, uncles who have been unable to sear their will upon the landscape. When men fail and families teeter, Bair discerns the cost in depression and divorce that has weakened other familial branches. The social arrangement, where "mother's and father's realms seldom intermingled," is only as strong as the individuals in a family (51).

At the same time, American culture begins shifting away from proscribed marital relations, and Bair finds herself carried along in a new generational tide. As a girl, she relishes the safety of her mother's home space, where she lived "in the manner of a luxuriating house cat, normally free to wander the rooms and loll in any of them" (51). Maturing into her young adult years, however, she begins to balk at a culture in which "[it] would have been an honor for me to do my brother's work, but demeaning for him to lift a plate from the table or wield a broom" (54). She becomes aware that "we females were allowed the luxuries of the house and yard, but these comforts entailed a compromise in status" (54). While Goodland farm-wives dress up in heels, pearls, and gloves for their social clubs and other women-only activities, Bair notes that "the women rested in the lap of the men's world, not the other way around. Without husbands, quite simply, the women would have no food to serve, no home to demonstrate, no car to drive" (61). A disaffection begins to unsettle the teenage Bair, but she has no name to give this rebelliousness, no model on which to structure a different existence.

To be female in this place requires discretion, accommodation, and tongue-biting silence. Witnessing the "censure of the maternal" that quieted her mother, that "often drove my mother's hands to fist with tension and caused her mouth to clamp down in silent worry," Bair understands that her mother's world of acquiescence cannot be her own (128). Like many young women of the 1950s and 60s, she eludes her mother's choices through an early marriage and "[rides] the tidal wave out of Kansas," moving to San Francisco with a well-connected son of a wealthy Midwestern family (142).

Had Bair stayed in Goodland, she would have married one of the boys down the road, submitted to "a benevolent dictator" who would rule like her father ruled, "whose dominion no one thought to question" (147). Her mother had expected such a fate for her, had prepared her for it: "Life on land deluded us into believing in the generations. . . . My mother thought some neighbor boy would find me, the way Harold had found her. We would nest on land not far down the road. . . . We lived under the illusion we *had* gone on forever" (141). Ironically, Bair ends up back in Goodland when her own choices leave her flat on her back. Goodland culture, however, defines her as neither fish nor fowl, always a hybrid thing: "Native here, I am always trying to dispose of one side while keeping the other, an impossibility" (131). Whether she returns to Goodland or leaves it to pursue a new life in Laramie, Wyoming, she painfully feels "self-betrayal" (131). As "hired cartographer," Bair has become the map of this place despite herself, continually pulled back to its compass points, its values, and beliefs only to flee, gasping for life and release (131). Kansas, and the stories of homesteading Bairs and Carlsons, the paternal and maternal mix of heritage, remain the bedrock of this equivocal memoir. But the landscape so braided into her memory is no longer tenable, a home space turned toxic and cruel.

In her deep map of Goodland, Bair repeatedly turns to the image of buffalo grass. Beneath the surface layers of modern Plains history lie the roots of an ancient biome. It is part of the "Life in Space" (the title of one essay) that Bair surveys. All around them are the traces, the vestiges of an older earth, an earlier reality. The climatic conditions also speak to a deeper ecology than the domain of John Deere. Bair understands that her family's tenancy owes much to the contours of land, the presence of water, the vagaries of weather—all of the limitations of geography. In elevating human ingenuity and pioneer spirit above the luck of favorable circumstance, Plains settlers have found themselves paradoxically in charge of an intractable landscape, hedging their bets against drought, disease, and pests with machines, chemicals, irrigation, and science. Bair catalogues the Plains realities, harboring relics of alternative adaptations:

We found arrowheads on those pasture hills, where we also had to watch for rattlesnakes, for we lived on the High Plains side of that invisible rain curtain that meanders along the hundredth meridian and marks the beginning of the arid West. One degree, forty-two minutes beyond it, but beyond it just the same. Seldom more than fifteen inches of rain fell during a year. Rattlesnakes were among the kings of that dry country, as were the coyotes, who yelped, like mortally wounded children, just beyond our windbreak. These wild creatures gave the land its fangs, and despite all our taming influence, reminded us that our agenda, in staying alive, in raising sheep and wheat, was not uncontested. (112)

In reflecting upon her world, one degree West, Bair articulates a vision of Plains life often at odds with Plains space. Bair declares herself a "Plainsdaughter" in her title, but she admits how vexed this identity can be. In writing her deep map, Bair attempts what she calls the "miraculous": to re-create "the life of a place, of a family culture, in all its dimensions" (127). Late in the twentieth century, she tries to assess the effects of nineteenth-century desires, myths, and laws upon the western landscape. Family itself bears the imprint of lingering patriarchy. Bair has grown up in a house that her grandfather built, where the past continually edges into her present life. Even the land itself, "plotted and aligned," speaks to the formal designs of a now-dead century (64). All around her, Bair senses, in the silence of an empty homestead or the quiet of a Plains afternoon, the muted voices of a deeper history. Amid such powerful ghosts, Bair struggles to map this place and to embrace her part, her family's part, in its shaping.

Sharon Butala's *Wild Stone Heart* presents an inverse map of Bair's story: a woman brought to the Plains through marriage who must then adapt to the physical and social demands of place. Like Bair's, her adaptation is imperfect, leading to feelings of confusion, self-doubt, and at times deficiency. Butala desires to become the map of this place, yet much separates her from Eastend, including the history of settlement itself that has denied the presence of the native, human and otherwise. One of the deepest ironies of Butala's narrative is that the native has been staring at her all along, speaking to her, affecting her bodily health; she struggles to understand the instinctive response she has to her husband's land, a consciousness that runs deeper than the mere century that brought white settlement.

Literally running underneath her story is Stegner's literary cartography, for Butala's country is the landscape of *Wolf Willow*, Eastend. Like Stegner, Butala attempts to represent a landscape that demands submission to its idioverse, its particulars. In both writers' texts, memory fuses with place and fires one's bodily connection to the land—the feel of breeze, the stir of water, the motion of grass—sears remembrance. There is no story without the land itself stirring the traces of memory. The authors' own lives, pooled in memory, become intricate parts of the lived space. Living in the semiarid reaches of southern Saskatchewan, however, proves challenging and sometimes desperate. Haunting presences add complexity in Stegner's and Butala's stories, from the weathered bones of ancient sauropods to the tragic relics of genocide or climate. Memories not one's own, other histories independent of one's life, etch their tragic patterns into the land. Stegner and Butala turn keen ears and eyes to these markings, which provide clues to survival, Native practices, and adaptation—to life in less resistance to the land itself.

Butala's text, however, should not be read as an extension of *Wolf Willow*, a kind of deep map sequel. As much separates as connects these narratives: gender, political awareness (Butala is much more self-consciously postcolonial than Stegner), and era. The Butala family, unlike Stegner's, has not been dispossessed of the land. They are stickers. Eastend, in Stegner, is home lost; for Butala it is home found. What to do with this home, both literally and figuratively haunted (Butala's first chapter is "Hauntings"), and the land that has been in the Butala family for generations remains a central question of her story. Moreover, Butala's enigmatic physical malady—an inexplicable sapping of energy that defies diagnosis—seems somehow connected to her life in southern Saskatchewan, to her incomplete accommodation to rural culture and ranch life, and to misplaced desires to extract something from the land. In many ways, Butala is blind to the land and its history. Living in a place is not the same as being of the place. Spiritual pellagra has physically and emotionally invaded her.

All of us live in perpetual adaptation to the environments that surround us. Our bodies and spirits negotiate with place, whether in resistance, accommodation, or some other mode. When Sharon Butala accepted a new life in ranching country outside of Eastend, Saskatchewan, she entered an extended period of adaptation to the extreme, lonely, subtle, and windswept landscape of the northern Great Plains. In gauging such enormous space, Butala finds refuge in a barely used field within the Butala family's 13,000-acre ranch; this small, 100-acre field becomes her space for translation of and contact with the deep history of the Plains, a place of imaginative and spiritual transit. Her education in deep mapping this space gives her insight into concepts of wilderness, cultures of Amerindian tribes, and somatic contact with the uncanny. It also provides the title of the essay: *Wild Stone Heart*, each part receiving emphasis, a pause, a sense of difference connected ultimately to heart, body, and soul. Indeed, the body awakened transports her physically and imaginatively across time, cultures, and landscapes, making her "an apprentice in the fields" (her subtitle), a spiritual descendant of Henry David Thoreau. Indeed, her "field" echoes Thoreau's "bean field" chapter in *Walden*. With this book, Butala adds her important voice to the evolving deep map genre.

Butala first began chronicling her momentous life's change from the city to a ranch in southern Saskatchewan in her essay *The Perfection of the Morning: An Apprenticeship in Nature* (1994). Her most recent essay and my focus in this chapter is *Wild Stone Heart: An Apprentice in the Fields* (2000). Here, she continues her life's journey and her deepening appreciation of the northern Plains. In her earlier work, Butala admits, "I began to realize how life for all of us in the West is informed and shaped by Nature in ways we don't even realize, much less notice consciously."[17] Her desire to awaken to the land around her prompted Butala into experimenting formally: "In writing what the world will call autobiography, I am torn between the facts and history and the truth of the imagination, and it is to the latter, finally, in terms of my personal history, that I lean."[18] *Wild Stone Heart* continues this textual experimentation, placing personal history and memory within the context of what she calls "layers of presence."[19] But in this later text, these presences prove provocative, elusive, even perhaps hostile. How to unblock herself and become more receptive to them is a central challenge of her narrative.

Additionally, Butala's own blind hubris stunts her progress. Butala's keen, unrelenting self-reflection generates much of the story's tension. Early in the essay, she becomes aware of a snake, "the largest snake I have ever seen in the flesh, perhaps six feet long, four inches in diameter at its thickest part, and beautifully striped" (36). In all of her years walking the field, she has never noticed the many holes in a cliffside, marking the homes of bull snakes. "Now," Butala exclaims, "just when I was beginning to think I'd pretty much seen all there was to see in the field, the landscape had opened another crack to reveal one more of its secrets" (37). Triumphantly, she thinks, "now I *had* seen everything" (37). Yet triumph "dissipates" into immediate unease (37): the snake's sudden declaration of existence hints at other unknown layers of presence that have escaped her observation.

The field she has imagined as a social surrogate, a replacement for "friends who were far away . . . the teachers and counselors I didn't have . . . the family I had left behind," asserts its autonomy, and Butala understands that she must now "conceive of the field in an entirely new way" (35–36, 37). In reconceptualizing the field, Butala must critically examine herself and her placement in late settlement Canadian society. She must enter into the "geographics" of a new terrain, a space of "dynamic encounter" that repositions her and presents deeper knowledge of the field.[20] In this field space, Butala gains insight into Indigenous practices and history, into the dissonance of modern life, into the extractive mentality of the western Canadian economy (part of this dissonance), and into the difficulties of communicating a revised vision of one's existence to one's immediate community. The axes intersecting cultural, racial, sexual, spiritual, and personal worlds make the field a particularly rich, if conflicted and inflected site of encounter.[21] Butala's struggle endorses Wes Jackson's comment, in *Becoming Native to This Place*, that "cultural information like biological information is hard won."[22] "*What do you want of the field?*" an internal voice keeps prodding Butala (197). Knowledge, atonement, mourning, forgiveness, love are possible answers. Ultimately, muting the desire to want renews her energy, and in replacing the "want" with "give"—literally establishing, with her husband, Peter, the Old Man on His Back Prairie and Heritage Preserve—Butala finds, after twenty years, a sense of peace. The stones in the field hold the key to this transformation in the text.

The field at first appearance looks to be "simply grass with rocks protruding here and there" (54). Like so much of the Plains landscape, the field lacks definition—John Palliser, walking through this same landscape in the late 1850s called it an "immense waste."[23] The earliest settlers, Butala explains, "defined the field as barren and useless" (38). To uninitiated eyes, the field and the larger Plains region it represents appear empty, unyielding, barren. Closer inspection, however, reveals a stunning biodiversity of flora and fauna that sustained generations of Plains peoples before settlement.

One plant, *Juniperus horizontalis*, the creeping juniper, becomes an index species for Butala, demonstrating the abundance of the biome. From this one bush, Amerindians picked the berries for pemmican or soups; brewed the berries to alleviate stomach maladies; and brewed juniper root to make "a liniment for muscular pain, rheumatism, and arthritis" (44). Inhaling the steam of brewed berries or smoking them countered asthma. The oil in the berries served as an insect repellant and gave a horse a shiny coat. Butala continues:

> Once I decided to have a look at the uses Plains people put juniper to—boughs, berries, needles, roots—I laughed. To judge by my sources, everybody used various parts of it for more or less everything: to aid in childbirth and the expulsion of the afterbirth, to create a fumigant and antiseptic by burning the strongly scented boughs, to create a diuretic by chewing the berries . . . to control bleeding, to stop diarrhoea. The list goes on. Peigan women even boiled juniper berry pits till they were softened and then strung them to make necklaces. (44)

Junipers, along with indigenous grasses, "cactus, forbs, sedges, and shrubs" defy the idea of "waste," making the field increasingly a place of "growing reverence" and "devotion" for Butala (55, 58). "I have given myself over to it," she explains, "and it rewards me every trip I make out to it by showing me something new, something surprising, something beautiful" (57–58). Indeed, as Butala discovers in her *Oxford English Dictionary*, "waste" is a synonym for "wild," a concept she mulls over in depth in her chapter "The Wild." Though some might scoff at the idea of a one-hundred-acre field being wild, Butala argues otherwise. Wildness cannot be reduced to the undomesticated and uncultivated; wildness also suggests, for Butala, ineffable, "undescribable," possibly "unknowable" dimensions (94).

In her field, she encounters something she can only call "*presence*," some "quality of *consciousness*," a force that "[calls] on all my resources of concentration, energy, and devotion" (98). She feels compelled to be its supplicant. The field connects in vital ways to the original northern Great Plains grassland, a landscape "vanishing to such a degree," Butala explains, "that it has been said that few places on earth have been changed so much by human hands as southern Saskatchewan" (103). Part of the presence here in the field is ghostly, that of millions of acres of an evolved biome transformed by settlement agriculture.

Butala's position within this agricultural history makes her acutely aware of its contradictions. Settlement in western Canada, "*from the very beginning*," she emphasizes, was promoted as a purely business enterprise; "this imperative," she continues, "had a profound effect on how land itself was and is viewed by farmers and ranchers—as a commodity, and the more of it the better" (112). Yet connection to the land has inspired topophilia, a genuine love of the land and its beauties: "the clean air, the clear view of the rising of the sun and the moon, the return of the ducks and geese, the deer grazing under the window in the early morning, the coyote loping across the field, or the antelope racing up a hillside," she catalogues (114). Such aesthetic and spiritual appreciation counters material desires and complicates any understanding of settlement history. Butala fears that the generations of ranchers, fitted to the land, accommodating themselves to nature's cycles and demands, are like the grasslands that brought them to their enterprise, dying off. These concerns have provoked Peter and Sharon Butala into giving their ranch to the Nature Conservancy of Canada and preserving as much as possible of the native grasslands.

As noble as this gesture may seem, Butala's journey in the field and to recovery does not reach completion until she sees beyond the presence of stones and begins to understand them. She vaguely grasps that they are connected with the Amerindian people who lived on the land for millennia before the Butalas bought it and ranched it. In her regular walks in the field, she becomes familiar with stone features, clearly human made, arranged in circles and cairns. The stones are not tepee rings, as far as she can tell. Their arrangement suggests ceremonies, perhaps even burials.

Discovering the stones coincides with three uncanny happenings in Butala's life: the new house she and Peter have built is haunted, seemingly by capricious spirits who open and close things, create loud, thunderous noises in the walls and on the roof, and generally disturb the inhabitants. Second, Butala begins to suffer "a tide of illness," a "terrible exhaustion" that "was somehow connected to the field" (32–33). Finally, she experiences strange visions and dreams that give her cryptic glimpses into other, wilder dimensions in the field. The mystery of the stones suggests an axis of history that begs for disinterment.

Butala discovers that her field is a site of trauma: her map of the field must "refigure sorrow," to borrow Mark Allister's rich phrase.[24] Unconsciously she has grasped the presence of tragedy, but the full grip of its truth does not hold her until she has an epiphany in the field: many had died—from famine? from disease? from warfare?—and lay buried in the field. "Now I wondered," she muses, "if this disembodied presence or presences that I felt so strongly, that answered questions for me, that gave me help and advice . . . was not God . . . or even Nature . . . but the restless spirits of the many unhonoured dead of this field" (158). Butala hesitates to call in archaeologists, feeling that representatives of modern Plains Nations should be the ones to visit this field. Yet, like many white settlers in her community, her contact with First Nations peoples is limited, often vexed, and rife with miscommunication. With the dedication of the Old Man on His Back Prairie and Heritage Preserve, Peter and Sharon Butala invite Cree from the nearby reserve to perform ceremonies and to help mark the day. Yet Butala is unable to sit comfortably in the sweat lodge, fleeing it in shame. Somehow her good intentions are simply not enough, the cultural borderlands too stark.

The field, throughout *Wild Stone Heart*, has been a border space for Butala. Here she has felt the dynamic edge between dimensions that has opened her imagination to the past, to the land, and to nonmaterial, sacred reality. Cultural edges, however, remain fractious and difficult. "I've absorbed this North American Great Plains landscape into my blood and bones," she relates, "[but] I can't—I don't wish—to shake off my absorption in European culture" (183). This very European identity, though, connects to the dead in her field. She confesses,

> All those years I'd walked that field and seen the cairns, and not seen them, and then rediscovered them, and lost them again, only to see them once more, and I had felt no emotion other than surprise and sometimes pleasure at finding them, as if I were particularly perspicacious and vigilant and deserving.
>
> Now what I felt was what I should have felt all along, if had believed the bones of those beneath the cairns were once living and walking and breathing human beings: that they were *people.* . . . I wept for a moment, and my grieving was for once genuine. I felt ashamed that I had not felt this before, that I'd been so proud of myself, so possessive of what was not mine at all, of a place where I walked only on the sufferance of the ancestral spirits guarding it, and only because those to whom this field and those graves rightly belonged had been rendered powerless to stop me. (187)

At narrative's end, Butala comes to this recognition. Much of her deep map has expressed a reflexive need for hope and optimism, a need many of us understand, particularly those of us living on the Great Plains, a landscape so irretrievably lost in many ways. In establishing the weave of this history, Butala must face presences that are less benign, less comforting, even mournful.

Lived space must include layers of presence that discomfort as well. One reason the Butalas have given their land in trust is that "the farming economy . . . is in shambles," and "bad news" arrives "every day" that "with every passing year in economic terms we go farther backward" (198). In its own way, the path of settlers, the trajectory of people like the Butalas, may be leading to another kind of burial. This is profound knowledge for those experiencing such decline. Yet it is a truth that also helps heal Butala's body. Ultimately, she embraces a profound shift of consciousness. To map the land—"to walk on it with the respect born of real understanding of the traditional Amerindian, to see it as sacred"—one must submit, "to be terrified, shattered, humbled, and, in the end, joyous" (188). In that way, Butala argues, one can "come home at last" (188).

In her influential study, *Mappings: Feminism and the Cultural Geographies of Encounter* (1998), Susan Stanford Friedman proposes a locational approach to feminism, one that recognizes "the geopolitics of identity within differing communal spaces of being and becoming."[25] In a particularly insightful chapter, "Routes/Roots," she highlights the continual push and pull between movement or change and rootedness or stability. As Friedman puts it, "[a] geopolitical identity rooted in 'home' insists upon sameness within the home circle; one formed through leaving home base involves interaction with others, which fosters the formation of hybridic combinations."[26] Friedman's work at the intersections of feminist geography and literary studies advances Stegner's thinking on this cultural tension between rooted and routed histories and melds effectively with current studies of the American and Canadian West, which owe much to her and feminist theorists like Leigh Gilmore and Gerri Reaves.[27] This back-and-forth movement, an intrinsic feature of modern diasporic narrative, complicates an individual's need to set personal coordinates, but ironically helps the process of self-definition. Friedman asserts, "Identity often requires some form of displacement—literal or figurative—to come to consciousness."[28] Both Bair's and Butala's deep maps confirm Friedman's insights.

Linda Hasselstrom's string of personal narratives—*Windbreak: A Woman Rancher on the Northern Plains* (1987), *Land Circle: Writings Collected from the Land* (1993), *Going Over East: Reflections of a Woman Rancher* (2001), and *Between Grass and Sky: Where I Live and Work* (2002), among others—confirms the role of displacement in identity formation. In one of her most recent memoirs, *Feels Like Far: A Rancher's Life on the Great Plains*, Hasselstrom gives voice to a personal "geographics" that maps the contested terrain of a life divided: between Cheyenne, Wyoming, and Hermosa, South Dakota; between her beliefs and her father's will; between the past and present; between economic necessity and spiritual hungers. "Routes/Roots" are at the heart of this contest. In Cheyenne, Hasselstrom struggles with displacement: "I was without an anchor after four decades of knowing my location in every drop of my blood."[29] Life back home—Hermosa, South Dakota—is figuratively seared into her "flesh and bones," mapped into her DNA (9). Without an interior map of her new "home" place, Hasselstrom proceeds in confusion, "learning new ways home through the maze" (10). Her narrative chronicles the "near and far" of home, the mandates of love and duty, and the changing face of the American West, placing it among the significant "new western autobiographies" that Richard Maxwell Brown celebrates in his essay "Courage Without Illusion."[30]

As a narrative of "geographics," *Feels Like Far* bears testament to the complexities of "locational" identity in an age of "ceaseless change . . . nomadic wandering . . . [and] migratory cultures."[31] Aligned with this perspective, Kathleen Boardman and Gioia Woods have argued, in their introduction to *Western Subjects: Autobiographical Writing in the North American West*, that "one marker of autobiography produced in and about the North American West is a preoccupation with place, along with a focus on identity issues directly related to place: rootedness, anxiety, nostalgia, restlessness."[32] Hasselstrom's memoir registers all of these dimensions.

Hasselstrom begins her narrative with a conflation of life and geography. "*Looking back at the first fifty years of my life,*" she reflects, "*is a bit like flying over the great high plains prairie stretching from the Missouri River on the east to the Rocky Mountains on the west, from the southern tip of Texas to the Canadian border*" (1). These compass points connect the stages and facets of her life, from childhood in Texas, to graduate school at the University of Missouri, to ranch life in South Dakota, to her current urban existence in Cheyenne, Wyoming. The larger pattern of her memoir embraces this sweep, but each chapter takes us to ground level, to the immediacy of space and its intimate markings that make the map of life a deeply felt and deeply imagined thing.

As Hasselstrom has attested in her many books, her move from Texas to her stepfather's ranch in South Dakota was momentous. From age nine, she rooted herself so intrinsically, "*that I might be a stalk of grass myself, rooted in arid and meager soil*" (2). Until circumstances force her to relocate to eastern Wyoming, Hasselstrom explains that the land's coordinates have guided her instinctively, as though part and parcel of every pulse of blood (9). As a child, Hasselstrom rode her horse over the expanses of the family homestead, learning bit by bit "*the topographical map of the ranch*" (33). The map measures this space with its own standardized scale; Hasselstrom's experience fills in the two-dimensional cubes of space, imagining "*bluebells . . . a meadowlark singing on a mullein stalk, the Badlands wind smelling of clay*" (33). The familiarity of "*hills and ridges,*" the declension of "*rough limestone walls covered in grapevines,*" the somatic connection to the many pastures that stretched "*for four or five miles in all directions*" make the paper map into living tissue (33–34). In her memories of ranch life, Hasselstrom moves over the many facets of her home place, revising her interior map to reflect deeper intimacies and affiliations. This is country that inspires one rancher to have his cremated ashes buried in a badger hole (115). Hasselstrom admits to an inner ecology, gained through years of careful living on arid land, which has made her and others native to place.

Relocation has challenged her blood knowledge. In Cheyenne, Hasselstrom bemoans a new geography of the grid, a geometry "which allowed for the growth its founders predicted" (8). In Cheyenne, roads and railroad tracks align with the original surveyors' coordinates. Without the western profile of the Black Hills, a sure point of reference on the ranch, Hasselstrom must "nail down my personal compass" in new ways (8). Uneasy with street signs, she adapts her prairie methods to the city, tracking her directions through "natural landmarks": patches of "flax and blue fescue," sidewalks "lined with sagebrush," or yards "surrounded by unruly coneflowers, Shasta daisies, and blanketflowers" (8–9). She explains, "In trying to learn my way around Cheyenne, I was placing new information on top of a map of my native habitat"(9). In needing to create an urban map of her existence, Hasselstrom faces a profound disorientation akin to "drifting" or "levitation" (9). She literally becomes dizzy walking on city streets. Without the "calming" influence of recognizable flowers and grasses, Hasselstrom loses her sense of "where I belong" and suffers a form of spiritual pellagra (9).

To have her idea of self undermined in such a disturbing way places Hasselstrom in a transitional, in-between moment that requires readjusting, recalibrating, and realigning the coordinates of identity. As Friedman offers, "[in] terms of the roots/routes symbiosis, experiencing identity as roots requires some figurative or material engagement of routes through a contact zone of intercultural encounter. Conversely, identity developed through routes involves an experience of leaving roots, of moving beyond the boundaries of "home" (however that is defined or problematized)."[33] Much "feels like far" in Cheyenne: the home place, the past, the grasslands, the self. One of her strategies in "decoding" the city and feeling secure is to "[visualize] the center of my personal universe, my ranch home. I pictured myself standing on that hill in South Dakota, beside the home I now call Windbreak House" (9).

At the same time, none of these entities has ever stood still, unaffected by time's decay, life's contingencies, or the world's desires. Home has been a fragmented place ever since her parents' health began to fail. Ranching has become an increasingly difficult enterprise, particularly the kind of cow/calf operation that the Hasselstrom family has run over the years. Hasselstrom herself has changed, a divorcée, a widow, a rancher, a writer, and a partner of a man ten years her junior. On unstable ground, Hasselstrom declares, "I felt like a fugitive from my family, from my home, from my experiences as a rancher, and from the future I had planned" (5). She faces the tension that emplacement and mobility engender—"roots" and "routes"—and uses narrative to write herself into new territory. She must mediate between worlds and possibilities.

Mediation often feels like suspension, a kind of estrangement in time. Memories themselves at times materialize as alien landscapes or erupt into heightened, Technicolor snapshots. In the chapter "Looking for the Dark: Buffalo Winter," Hasselstrom examines family photos in her Cheyenne home and finds a picture from her first, failed marriage: "Staring at a picture from my first wedding, I feel I am looking at two strangers. The bride's face is bland above her long dress of ivory velvet; the freckled groom is smiling" (73). Holding these photos in her fingers, Hasselstrom enters a blizzard of memories that blows her to one pivotal moment a year after she divorces her first husband.

From a perch in the study of her Cheyenne home, pressed by summer heat, Hasselstrom enters something of a worm hole that transports her to a January chinook, a midnight hour, a boozy moment's impulse, an early morning's drive to Custer State Park where she unexpectedly encounters bison. In her mind's eye, Hasselstrom sees "[the] pointed horns . . . everywhere, glittering in the moonlight, aiming at the sky. I imagine my ears opening like flowers, becoming more sensitive. Grass mutters. I hear a coyote in the Badlands, an owl glide out of the tree beside my prairie house. The breath of fifty bison, a hundred, inhaling my scent makes the ground shake, trees quiver. I feel I am inside the earth's lungs" (78). Clearly, the bison connect her to deeper time, to the ancient grasslands stretching across eons, to the Lakota and earlier tribes who knew this land for many generations before settlement, before tourism, before Ted Turner's cultivation and purveyance of bison for his Montana Grill.

Hasselstrom ponders, "Living on the plains for ages, bison have forged deep connections to the grasslands while humans have survived only briefly on the prairie's surface, doing so much damage in our tenure" (85). This memory, born of displacement, returns Hasselstrom to "my soberest moment ever. My body remains in place, but I am not aware of it or of anything earthly for a long time" (80). She has encountered "a holiness I didn't understand," a mystery that "might deepen my own partnership with the plains" (85). In Cheyenne, years later, Hasselstrom draws this encounter into the present, melding two worlds into meaning, into a new map of being. Her "prairie eyes" allow her to negotiate the disturbances of new relationships and unknown streets (108).

Repeatedly, Hasselstrom's chapters return to the animal world: to owls, horses, steers, heifers, bison, bees, badgers, deer, young cows, elk, bulls, nighthawks, and hawks. She begins and ends with hawks. These animals run the gamut from vital and life-giving to ailing and dead. Through their stories, Hasselstrom runs the thread of her own. Some of these animals depend upon the labor of humans, others remain undomesticated, as their kind has for eons on the High Plains. These animals represent cartographic markers for Hasselstrom, part of the "natural landmarks" that help her map location and provide landscape lessons. Their lives run deep through time and space, both rubbing up on brief human time as well as standing separate as signifiers of a deeper ecology than evident in late-settlement economies.

When a hawk hits a window in the opening prologue, Hasselstrom reads this event symbolically: she, too, has "collided" in Cheyenne, felt the force of a monumental encounter with implacable reality (9). She has fled the disaster of home life and planted herself in a growing relationship with her lover, Jerry; she has left the rhythms and cycles of ranch life, so dependent upon nature's movements, to live in the grid. Her ranch world encompasses elemental dimensions: ground, sky, water, fire. Indeed, the one chapter that breaks from her bestiary is entitled "Looking for Life: Fire in the Wildlife Pasture." In this later chapter, Hasselstrom's father is five months dead, yet the impact of his personality remains strong. Her mother is wintering in Texas. In Cheyenne, Hasselstrom attempts to reconcile the pieces and places of her life. Family and friends are dying, the future of the family ranch is unclear, and legal papers, old receipts, and urgent responsibilities harass her. The emotional impact of life's changes and changed places presses in on her.

The threat of fire bristles in the air across the Great Plains that winter, when Hasselstrom receives word from her renter, Jill, that fire has erupted near Windbreak House, the home Linda and her second husband, George, built by hand. Fire represents an annual hazard on the Plains, made worse during drought conditions. It plays a crucial role in the ancient grasslands biome, one that nomadic Native inhabitants harnessed to their advantage. To the modern rancher, however, the grass feeds the livestock that provide money for living. The grass surrounds houses that archive family history, beloved possessions, and memories. The modern economy of the Plains is not mobile; it rests upon the acres of farmland and ranchland, upon the infrastructure of homes and towns and highways, upon the perishable bodies of animals and crops. This economy sits surrounded, as Hasselstrom's friend Margaret says, "by acres and acres of fuel" (202). On this December day, fire in the wildlife pasture threatens the livelihood of ranchers. From afar, Hasselstrom is unable to effect a rescue of her home or her parents' home. She can only hope that the winds, or rain, or the hard work of her renters and the Hermosa fire department will save her family's structures.

Internally, her geographies collide. With her dog, Frodo, as her sole companion that anxious day, Hasselstrom restlessly moves around Cheyenne, to the local park, to the grocery store and post office, and while standing in line to purchase or do business, she wants to scream, "Everyone I love is dead and my house is burning down!" (205). Doing an internal audit, she imagines all of the objects, mundane and meaningful, that will disappear in fire: the tablecloths, potholders, china, and handmade doilies, "like thin ancestral bones in a charnel house" (206). Worn-out toasters and irons will go, along with home movies, outgrown clothes, paper scraps, her father's diaries. Childhood books like *Ferdinand the Bull* and *The White Stag* will ignite and burn to white ashes. Steamer trunks full of family photos will face cremation. "Our whole family history may burn," Hasselstrom laments. She continues, "All my life I've felt responsible not only for each day's labor but for keeping track of the stories representing my past. I sense a tingle of relief: perhaps the obligation will vanish with no blame to me. Family pictures might turn to ash, fragile shadows as insubstantial as the solid bodies they represent" (208). This recognition serves as an epiphany in the text, even though the Hasselstroms' home escapes intact following this round of fire.

In the essay's prologue, the hawk that crashes into the window shakes its feathers and flies back into the sky. Hasselstrom must similarly right her coordinates to continue on course. The hawk remains a potent symbol throughout, and Hasselstrom's narrative ends with this totemic bird as well. In the spiral of a hawk, she reads the inner map of life, DNA, and the external swirls of life and destruction—water, tornadoes, the galaxies themselves. On rare occasions, hawks spiral together, creating a *"whirling shaft mounting the air,"* like a dust devil of birds (221). At this moment, the most fundamental coordinates of life intermix: ground, water, air, energy. Hasselstrom envisions *"torrents of air flowing outward from this center, covering the earth. The breath pouring into my lungs was power charged"* (221).

This vision is followed by a visit to the cemetery at Hermosa, to find another kind of ground truth. The dead and gumbo commingle in Hasselstrom's mind: "Flesh of our flesh mutates into sparse grass in these gumbo graveyards," she explains, "with little help from heavenly water and none from underground" (223–24). In the Hermosa cemetery lie her father, John Hasselstrom, and her beloved second husband, George, and Grandmother Ida. About an hour further south, at Edgemont Cemetery, lie Aunt Cora and her other maternal relatives. The hilltop burial ground in Hermosa was once part of the original grasslands, stretching back eons. With settlement came the first burials, then stagecoaches taking passengers between Cheyenne and Deadwood. A four-lane highway now marks one edge of the cemetery, and a new development rises from another direction. If the sight of spiraling hawks evokes one kind of deep, spinning history, the evolution of a community spawns another kind, the surface skin of modern change. Hasselstrom's position as writer bridges these movements across time and space, sometimes uncertainly, other times with "pinpoint" accuracy (227). She realizes that her words will outlast her, vestiges of an embodied history. "Like all stories, human and otherwise," she muses, "they will begin to spiral up and down, earth to sky, coyote to owl, to grass and rain" (227).

John T. Price, in his study *Not Just Any Land*, recalls Hasselstrom's struggle to write *Feels Like Far*, a book he read in draft after interviewing Hasselstrom about her identities as rancher and author. In her earlier works, Price attests, Hasselstrom's conflict with her overbearing, often paranoid father, who insisted that his daughter abandon writing and return as a hired hand to his ranch, "clarifies why her books reveal an increasing need to explain the depth of her commitment to the ranch, her need to stay there."[34] *Feels Like Far* chronicles her ultimate displacement from a life she loved. Still, Price argues, this book, born of rupture, "is ultimately a book about healing, where each negative is carefully balanced by a positive. It is a balance inspired by the land itself."[35] Hasselstrom brings her readers to the cemetery to suggest acceptance and grace, despite the incompletion, confusion, and imbalance that come with a life lived and ended.

With her friend Gail nearby, she weeds around her family's graves while Gail works at her daughter's grave, shoveling pink quartz into place as mulch for prickly pear cactus. Both women nurture native plants around these graves, connecting the bodies of their family members to the land that sustained them. At this moment, the deep past and the present align for these women, caring for the dead, caring for each other. The far and near come together. On the high prospect of the Hermosa cemetery hill, where sky and ground connect, Gail quotes Carl Sandburg: "I am the grass. Let me work" (229). With this final line, Hasselstrom paradoxically finds her true north in the ephemera of the yeoman grass blade, with roots working in eternity.

Space, in the deeply mapped narrative, archives many stories of existence, from present life all the way back to the Precambrian. The deep map has emerged in confluence with what Susan Stanford Friedman has called "the new geography of identity," sharing narrative interest in "a historically embedded site, a positionality, a location, a standpoint, a terrain, an intersection, a network, a crossroads of multiply situated knowledges."[36] Polyvocality is one of its hallmarks. In the deep maps of Julene Bair, Sharon Butala, and Linda Hasselstrom, one sees the interweaving of intergenerational stories integrated into the landscape itself. To tell such complicated stories, these authors must amplify the voices of other cultures, other Plains citizens and family members, in order to place themselves as autobiographical subjects within the coordinates of natural and human history. The knowledge that comes from such disparate connections can be painful and wrenching or, conversely, spiritually revelatory. In mapping their private geographies—scholar Gerri Reaves's metaphor—against the backdrop of the vast Plains earth and sky and their nations' histories, Bair, Butala, and Hasselstrom refigure and reshape their memories, textually and spatially.[37]

Place becomes, in their reconceptions, "the tangible or intangible, internal or external context for remembered experience," the necessary soil and grounding of narrative, even if that ground is shifting and uncertain.[38] In later middle age, these women understand that the narrative maps they present, while artfully conjectured, capture ephemeral essences and brief connections, that place can be as mortal and easily forgotten as any human life. Remembrance becomes that much more powerful, then, as an act, a gesture, and an antidote to loss, to rupture, and to the forces of crippling spiritual pellagra.

CODA

Spiritual Deep Mapping and Great Plains Vernacular

> When people give some of their allegiance to a place, they become
> more complex minds than they were before, more filled with
> contradictions, more unpredictable, more capable of learning.
> They may still persist in taking the wild risks of the uncommit-
> ted; on the other hand they may seek to discipline their desires
> and nurture that relationship. We have had both kinds of people
> in the West, as we have had elsewhere on the continent, though
> we have not always given those stickers and nurturers their due.
> Donald Worster, *Under Western Skies*

In his introduction to *Home Ground: Language for an American
Landscape*, Barry Lopez muses over the intimate relationship
between place-knowledge and "using a language so suited to the
place being described it fits against it like another kind of air."[1]
Arguing that language adapts to landscape, he notes that "[h]ow a
particular culture or subculture divides and names the features of
its homescape, and the way it perceives how one thing grades into
another . . . is in the end peculiar to that culture."[2] Lopez worries
that such local peculiarities are fading in America, dimming the
ability "to see deeply into a landscape."[3] Speaking for his generation of place-based writers, Lopez articulates a need "to gain—or
regain—a sense of allegiance with our chosen places, and along

with that a sense of affirmation with our neighbors that the place we've chosen is beautiful, subtle, profound, worthy of our lives."[4]

For writers from the Great Plains, this reclamation has been gaining momentum and urgency for two generations. On the heels of the farming crisis of the 1980s, a plethora of narratives limning the subtle beauties and enduring mysteries of Plains country appeared in bookstores, many of them reaching bestseller status. From Ian Frazier's *Great Plains* (1989) and William Least Heat-Moon's *PrairyErth* (1991) to Sharon Butala's *Wild Stone Heart* (2000) and Dan O'Brien's *Buffalo for the Broken Heart* (2001), the Great Plains enjoyed a decade of intense scrutiny that has only slightly abated in recent years. Grasslands that had been dismissed as mere flyover country, dusty burial grounds of dreams, generated deep interest from both sides of the forty-ninth parallel. The Great Plains mattered.

Writers as varied as Anne Matthews, Don Gayton, Kathleen Norris, Richard Manning, and Jonathan Raban, among others, turned their attention to the Plains, and concepts like buffalo commons, prairie restoration, and spiritual geography joined common speech. Peculiar local vernacular terms like buckbrush coulee, buffalo jump, woody draw, tallgrass, shortgrass, chop hills, badlands, bluffs, buttes, dugouts, and windbreaks propagated themselves within readers' imaginations. The singular realities of the Plains rebounded and focused attention on this vast, challenging biome.

In many ways, the Great Plains became ground zero for a reckoning. Over a century of settlement had left behind an ambivalent record, borne by extraction and diaspora, and where the Plains were headed seemed portentous to writers from two nations. As distinctive as these disparate American and Canadian authors are, they share a gestalt: they bend their ears to the Plains landscape, attempting to translate its vernacular into legible text, narrative that instructs, advocates, witnesses, and inspires. Richard Manning calls it an "effort to re-find the landscape, which is," he continues, "the same as the effort to re-attach our lives to the land."[5] This reattachment has a linguistic component that elevates spatial idiolect and projects a Plains-specific tongue.

Lawrence Buell has argued that reexamining the familiar drives much place-based writing. The environmentally attuned writer fights against complacency and the overfamiliarity that breeds neglect or worse, contempt. More urgent, he acknowledges, is the "delicate issue of how the sense of place can be kept alert and sensitive rather than left to lapse into dogmatic slumber in some cozy ethnocentric alcove."[6] In the 1980s, while residents of the Great Plains were facing economic and environmental challenges, most North Americans were gazing elsewhere. Once viewed as "the paradise of the agrarian democracy," the Plains during the 1980s and 1990s "[held] a quarter of one percent of [the U.S.] population."[7] Across the United States, intimacy with grasslands was unusual. Re-perceiving the Plains was difficult because this region, vast as it is, has held little cultural capital and captures little attention. This lapsed state induced the twilight slumbers of unfamiliarity and disinterest.

Writers of the Plains, however, were gearing up in their many locales to raise the alert level and open eyes. The outpouring of place-based writing spread and stirred the Zeitgeist to compel a reimagining and reinhabiting of the Plains. At the cusp of the 1990s, Frazier's *Great Plains* and Heat-Moon's *PrairyErth* appeared in excerpt in the *New Yorker* and *Atlantic Monthly*.[8] As noted, Heat-Moon invented a name for a particular kind of interwoven narrative—the deep map—that has proved to be especially durable for Plains writers. Frazier encouraged many kinds of writers to foray out onto the Plains, to examine how communities were adapting to environment late in the twentieth century and to report back to the larger culture on their findings. Frazier and Heat-Moon's successes opened up market space for other writers speaking Plains vernacular.

The literary annals are telling. Anne Matthews publishes *Where the Buffalo Roam* in 1992. Kathleen Norris follows a year later, with one of the widest-read books on the Plains, *Dakota: A Spiritual Geography*. Journalist Richard Manning reaches a huge readership with *Grassland* in 1995, and Jonathan Raban presents *Badland: An American Romance* in 1996. Both Dan O'Brien and Linda Hasselstrom, South Dakota writers like Norris, gain traction in their careers as well. Up in Canada, as we have seen, Don Gayton publishes his own deep map, *The Wheatgrass Mechanism* (1990), and Sharon Butala writes a series of nonfiction books, starting with *The Perfection of the Morning* in 1994, that gain an international readership and renew interest in the Canadian interior.

Something rhizomatic was going on, as wide-ranging nonfiction narratives about the Great Plains started popping nodelike up from Texas to Saskatchewan. Though journalists, scientists, ranchers, and poets, these writers were united through their topophilia, their love of a place many others found unlovable. Frazier explains, "A hundred years ago, it was not unusual to hear of single men and women and young couples with families moving out to start farms on the Great Plains. Today you hear of people my age being urban pioneers in some neglected neighborhood, or moving to the suburbs, or moving to Northern California or Washington or northwest Montana, like me. You never hear of us moving to the Great Plains."[9] Frazier, Heat-Moon, and their cohort present stories of rehabilitation, reclamation, and return. They give voice to the settlement communities that have endured on the Plains and channel the voice of the land itself. The accruing nonfiction books across a decade raise their voices to the big sky horizon, registering in concord and dissonance the many stories of success, failure, adaptation, destruction, epiphany, bankruptcy, and love. While Native writers and activists have reason to look askance at some of this production, questioning the motives and historical biases of deep map writers and journalists, as Elizabeth Cook-Lynn does in "Who Gets to Tell the Stories," an important cultural shift was beginning to take place that probed in profound, unsettling ways the received history of the American and Canadian Wests.[10]

Speaking at the Jefferson Lecture in the Humanities in spring 2012, Wendell Berry admonished his audience that "there is in fact no distinction between the fate of the land and the fate of the people."[11] From his home in Kentucky, Berry has witnessed wholesale destruction of the countryside to further the ambitions and demands of coal mining. Similarly, looking across the United States, he sees industrial agriculture that chokes the landscape in slow motion: "Corn and bean monocultures destroy the land more slowly . . . but down the way, down the line, the destruction will be as complete."[12] The Plains have been reorganized around monoculture, and while the geometric patterns of corn, soybeans, and wheat fields might pleasingly resemble modern abstract art from thirty-five thousand feet, the reality of median household incomes just above the national poverty threshold, shrinking and aging populations, and risk-averse town cultures pushes the young and ambitious out. The structural changes to the land and the fate of Plains people are intertwined.

Kathleen Norris provides a controversial anatomy of Lemmon, South Dakota, where "the fault line of suspicion and divisiveness exposed by the farm crisis in the mid-1980s has left wounds that have not healed."[13] The passing generations since early white settlement have left Lemmon and other Plains communities "filled with those who have come to idealize their isolation," Norris asserts.[14] In such a state, people do not adapt well to changes and view outsiders as a threat. While the agricultural landscape shifted into monocultural practices, so, too, did many Plains communities.

The agricultural system that sustains many of these communities largely destroyed the "perennial polyculture" that was the grasslands before disturbance.[15] Manning explains the system's organization:

> The central theme of agriculture is monoculture—that is, we raise early succession plants at the exclusion of all else. Early succession plants are evolved to move into a disturbed area and uniquely exploit the resources of the soil to pull from it maximum growth and energy in a single year. They are annuals, and the strategy of annuals is to put energy, literally its carbohydrates, into seeds. We and most other animals seek seeds, so our agriculture is simply a method to create disturbance. Put another way, agriculture is nothing but a determined effort to keep nature from taking its course.[16]

Nonfiction writers from the Great Plains stake many economic and political positions around the history of settlement disturbance. In the higher Plains, where ranching dominates, other issues negatively affect the grasslands, from overgrazing to degraded riparian areas to the decline and threatened extinction of native species of grasses and forbs. A 1980 survey of American rangeland, Manning summarizes, "concludes that 85 percent of the nation's grasslands have less than 60 percent of the potential vegetation, all as a result of overgrazing."[17] Dan O'Brien provides an acerbic look at the economics of modern cattle ranching:

> I worried about what could be done on this little Great Plains ranch to foot the bill for the land restoration and the bills of daily life. Cattle certainly wouldn't do it. From sad experience I knew that it cost at least $250 a year to produce a calf. The market for calves was around $300. If a guy had a thousand calves to sell, it might work. But this ranch can produce only a hundred without abusing the grass. That's $5,000 a year, about enough to pay the taxes. I might have been able to borrow money to buy the machinery to farm this place, but marginal farming is

the main cause of the trouble that the whole Great Plains has experienced. I knew I'd have to be subsidized, and even if I could bring myself to "farm the government," I'd be committing a kind of infanticide. I'd simply be pushing the restoration bill on to the next generation.[18]

When so much of a biome is restructured around high-yield crops and imported, nonnative cattle, when a landscape is altered in this way, what becomes of the people who live among the sparse remains of original grasslands? As O'Brien's depiction reveals, communities and individuals struggle and suffer as a result.

Those of us who travel frequently across the Plains and write from the modern Plains hear professions of love from dwellers in their particular locations. This love is complex and multifaceted. There is love that kills, love that fosters change, love that grasps for the past, love that propels activism, love that pushes back. Many families have prospered from modern agriculture, but far more struggle to remain on their home places.

The history of the modern Plains is a vexed one, and if the environmental degradation is not seriously addressed and attended to, the landscape will yield less and less. The enormous, ancient aquifers are already showing signs of stress and depletion under the relentless pressure of irrigation, especially west of the hundredth meridian. Ground and surface waters suffer contamination from the use of fertilizers to increase productivity and chemicals to stop weeds, insects, and fungal infections. Anne Matthews' journey across the Plains in the early 1990s, following geographers Frank and Deborah Popper as they were proposing their Buffalo Commons solution for the Plains biome, reveals the many flashpoints among dwellers of the grasslands. "All those now taking sides in the Buffalo Commons controversy," she explains, "academics, ranchers, developers, environmentalists, Native Americans, experts in prairie restoration—claim to love the land but passionately disagree on how to treat it. The idealism of a Buffalo Commons exhilarates many people but threatens even more."[19] When it comes to shaping the future, a Plains Tower of Babel exists, separating people who speak disparate tongues and implacable opinions.

When the Poppers published "The Great Plains: From Dust to Dust" in *Planning* (1987), they could not have anticipated the lively, often enraged public interest their ideas generated.[20] Matthews presents a verbal collage of editorials: "The Aberdeen, South Dakota, *American News*: 'New Jersey ethnocentrism . . . Leave us alone!' The Mandan, North Dakota, *News*: 'The Poppers cannot comprehend what we love about this wide-open and windy space, and you can't explain it to them'. . . A columnist in Wichita, Kansas: 'Let's turn New Jersey into a Dumping Commons.'"[21] Underlying such heated response was the effrontery of New Jersey speaking down to the Plains as provincial backwaters.

Frank Popper, standing before hostile Plains audiences, an academic Cassandra, gives a précis of the region's modern history from the Homestead Act of 1862 through the droughts and plagues of the 1920s and 1930s. Pushing into recent history, he presents the aftermath of "a heavy injection of federal subsidies":

> Through the 1970s there was energetic sodbusting, ten thousand acres at a time. Gas and oil boomtowns dotted the Northern Plains. But the eighties punctured it all, revealing the fragility of extractive (and quite possibly finite) economies. Now ghost towns are forming everywhere on the Plains, as the little settlements that once sustained the region lose doctor, bus stop, bank, stores, air service, clergy, young people. (49)

His is a message that a number of Plains people in the early 1990s did not want to hear. Matthews carefully records the plethora of opinions from McCook, Nebraska, Denver, Colorado, Oklahoma City, Oklahoma, and Billings, Montana. The stark maps and data of distressed, depopulated land that Deborah Popper shares with audiences often elicit "audible gasps, then a rising hum of defiance and dread," as they did in McCook (50). "Oh, my God," exclaim some people; "I ain't selling," a rancher shouts (50).

At the heart of these contentious encounters between academic geographers and Plains people lies an issue of language, of missed communication and tragi-comical translation. In embracing the metaphor of bison, the Poppers see themselves as reconnecting communities to idiolectical realities; many Plains people feel that, to use a Western metaphor of authenticity, they are the real McCoy, yet their idiom clings to the myth and cliché of Jeffersonian yeomanry and Hollywood, not of aridity, fragility, kinetic grasslands, and epic bird and quadruped migrations, the original flyovers.

In her afterword, Matthews updates her readers on events after the Poppers' barnstorming lecture tour. Preservationist groups, like the Nature Conservancy, have begun to purchase tracts of land to return to indigenous species. Private landowners are converting ranches and farms to buffalo herds and game habitat. In 1992, twenty-nine Plains tribes could claim buffalo herds. These individuals and communities believe that "curing the economic, social, and spiritual impoverishment of the Plains . . . cannot be done without reintroducing buffalo and the buffalo culture" (192). Dan O'Brien, who formed the Wild Idea Buffalo Company, has been part of this transformative return. Standing in his yard late in his narrative, O'Brien reflects, "There are no buffalo in sight today but I know that they are there. I'm confident that the matrix is being repaired, that the whole is being completed." Kneeling down to touch the grass, he "imagine[s] the vibration of hooves," bison energy that is "constant, enduring as bedrock, powerful as the prairie wind."[22]

Clearly, twenty years on, the Buffalo Commons idea or some revision of it is spreading rhizomatically across communities on the Plains. Perhaps with the advent of wind power, the potential of switch-grass biofuel, larger buffalo herds, including Ted

Turner's massive holdings, computer data centers staffed by rural people threaded out across the Plains, firmly established national and provincial grasslands parks, and community "feed and seed" events, Plains people are coming around to the idea that bioregional adaptation is not threatening but promising. Even urban gardens on the Plains now feature bluestem, butterfly milkweed, dotted gayfeather, Jerusalem artichoke, prairie coneflower, foxtail barley, and other grasses and forbs from the biome. Severe challenges persist: water remains scarce, boom-and-bust cycles linger, industrial agriculture and government subsidies feed inefficient or unsustainable production, factory animal farms pollute air and groundwater, topsoil still erodes, towns shrink, and the frontier widens its boundaries.[23]

As perceptions shift, many find resonance in the ideas that Barry Lopez presents in *Home Ground*: "We have named the things we've picked out on the land, and we've held on to the names to make ourselves abiding and real, to enable us to resist the appeal of make-believe lands, hawked daily as anodynes by opportunists, whose many schemes for wealth hinge on our loss of memory, the anxiety of our alienation, our hunger after substance," he writes from his home place on the McKenzie River in Oregon.[24]

Restoring a Plains idiolect, relearning the biome's syntax, echoes other language preservation and reintroduction efforts around the world. Wendell Berry's recent warning about unabated greed and heedless extractive practices suggests that monoculture denudes both our tongues and our hearts. "Pillage and indifference" damage us, he cautions. Lust erodes, love restores. To counter the dehumanizing effects of land grabs and shortsighted overproduction, he recommends "informed, practical, and practiced affection." His is a holistic diagnosis "because affection involves us entirely."[25] On the Great Plains, in the early twenty-first century, citizens are beginning to acknowledge the central power of place in defining us, shaping us, inspiriting us—and not the other way around. "The sense of place is unavoidable in western Dakota," Kathleen Norris muses, "and maybe that's our gift to the world. Maybe that's why most Americans choose to ignore us."[26] For over twenty years now, thanks to Norris and her peers, keeping the Plains landscape unspoken is no longer an option. The body of their work, which in so many ways ties to the body of the grasslands, has unlocked the indelible voice of the *genius loci*. This release of literary vernacular has been the true gift.

Norris's book, *Dakota: A Spiritual Geography*, remains among the most influential nonfiction books on the Great Plains. Part memoir, part literary cartography, part spiritual apologia, Norris's deep map, the final book in this study, has been widely anthologized, held up as a contemporary classic, and acclaimed as a definitive book on the late twentieth-century Great Plains. Thirteen sections, called "Weather Reports," help connect the writer's reflections from western South Dakota with contemplative essays on monastic life, particularly that of Benedictine monks. "Benedictines, male and female," Richard W. Etulain suggests, "willingly embrace change and clearly accept outsiders. Free from many of the myths of the past and local history," he concludes, "they are 'less likely to persist in thinking they can stand alone.'"[27]

Each "Weather Report" provides lyrical commentary on each month of a year's cycle, using a linear structure not unlike Henry David Thoreau's year at Walden Pond. Like Thoreau, however, Norris frequently veers from linearity in narrative that moves back and forth over her own life and plumbs deeply into spiritual traditions millennia old. Her chapter titles suggest a narrative mapping that connects present-day life on the Plains to ancient human worlds ("Status: Or, Should Farmers Read Plato?"), to deep time ("Star-Time"), and to global spiritual practices ("Deserts"). Norris understands that the details of life lived connect to older patterns and structures, to cycles of loss and return, to spiritual practices perfected through many generations. The present of her text is a continual touchstone to longer history not necessarily rooted in North America. Hers is a cosmically minded deep map.

When Norris declares "the Great Plains themselves have become my monastery, my place set apart," she sees an ancient calling at work in herself and in her world.[28] Her retreat from cosmopolitan life has also affected her linguistically. As she explains,

> On the Plains I have also drunk in the language of unschooled people, a language I was not much exposed to within the confines of the academic and literary worlds. Many farmers I know use language in a way that is as eloquent as it is grammatically unorthodox. Their speech often has great style; they never use the wrong word or make an error in phrasing. Magnificent old words like farrow, common English five hundred years ago, are still in use on the Plains. I even heard an old man use wain for wagon, a word that dates back to the Celts. Language here still clings to its local shading and is not yet totally corrupted by the bland usage of mass media. (19–20)

Norris sees a process of distillation and conservation at work on the Plains. Language "tends toward the concrete and personal: weather, the land, other people" (20). The landscape itself focuses and reduces while it frames all within huge skies and the wide horizon. Life on the Plains exists within a sharpened geometry that enhances clarity, what Norris calls "desert wisdom" (24).

In defining her spiritual geography, Norris exalts the paradoxical bounty of emptiness, the fertility of solitude (3). At the same time, she pulls no punches when speaking of her spiritual and emotional challenges, her ambivalent perceptions of "the tensions and contradictions I find in the Dakotas" (7). Contemporary nonfiction from the Plains actively resists sentimentality. In an era that celebrates the secular pleasures of city life, Norris takes a "countercultural" vow to remain on difficult soil, to seek continuity in a place "terrifying but beautiful" (8, 12). Norris's stance reflects what philosopher Henri Lefebvre lamented in postwar modernity: life "orchestrated by the logic of the commodity . . . lived according to the rhythm of capital."[29] Lefebvre examines critical "moments" that expose visionary possibilities, "a promise of the possibility of a different daily life."[30] Norris and her husband have planted themselves in South Dakota to seek such possibilities. But the quotidian continually challenges the vision.

In sizing up the Dakotas, Norris recognizes the signs of commodification even in "a land that rolls like the ocean floor it once was" (26). However, during the 1980s in the Dakotas, capital was withdrawing at the same time that "'Dakota chic' surfaced . . . in both tony urban restaurants and national advertising campaigns," from beer to pickup trucks (29–30). The Plains had symbolic cachet while Plains people faced degraded services and lowered expectations. "Since there is no market here, nothing that counts demographically," Norris reflects, "we don't exist" (31). Norris perceives a pernicious "colony" status for the Dakotas, "but," she adds, "the mystique has been there at least since 1876, when Custer rode out of Mandan to his doom, and Wild Bill Hickok was shot in a saloon in Deadwood" (33). The plethora of "starstruck Europeans" and tourists motoring "through Lemmon on their way to Montana or the Black Hills" complicates the Dakotas' perceived value (33). While incomes stagnate or shrink, public services dwindle, and national companies retrench, "Dakotans are in danger of becoming victims of their own mythology" (32). Rugged individualists, they appear to be falling—not rising—together.

In the much-cited chapter, "Gatsby on the Plains," Norris presents a scathing assessment of modern Lemmon. A young woman tells Norris, "You don't understand this town because you're an outsider. You don't know what it was like here twenty years ago. That's what we want; that's what we have to get back to" (45). Thinking back twenty years to war, civil unrest, assassinations, and Watergate,

Norris wonders how one could construct a remembered golden age from such turbulent times. How does larger, national history become detached from memory? When Main Streets empty out, people leave, and inertia sets in, some who remain turn to myth as a coping mechanism. "Change," Norris attests, "has not often been kind to the Dakotas" (47). Between the 1910 and 1980 census reports, "Perkins County, which includes Lemmon . . . has been slowly ebbing away" (47). The population has diminished from 11,348 to 3,932 in eighty years. Such a collapse makes the future look like certain death. Norris notices that "[even] the young here come to view the world as static" (51).

As curiosity withers, conspiracy theories grow and fear paralyzes townspeople. The farm crisis of the 1980s further erodes Lemmon's communal ties:

> When it became obvious that local farmers were indeed in trouble, and a county sheriff retired early rather than serve foreclosure papers on a relative, fears began to surface in town among businessmen worried for their livelihood and retired people worried about an eroding tax base. But no sense of community helped them face these fears honestly or directly. Instead, it seemed that the habit of insular thinking had become so deeply ingrained that many townspeople couldn't help but turn the farmers in trouble into a new class of outsiders from which the town had to be protected. (54)

In response to hard times, Lemmon's citizens turn against themselves and further threaten their future as a viable community. Circling their wagons against the forces of change, Lemmon's men and women "diminish their capacity for hope" (64).

Yet Norris stays. Hope, family roots, and spiritual need keep her in South Dakota. Choir singing, oblate work with the Benedictines, and the fierce beauty of the place water her soul in arid country. In the western Plains, she discovers moments of possibility: "But in all of these places that couldn't be more deprived by worldly standards I also find an expansiveness, a giddy openness that has allowed me to discover gifts in myself and others that most likely would have remained hidden in more busy, sophisticated, or luxuriant surroundings" (118). In these bare-bones surroundings, she has discovered the sacred.

Norris's own personal spiritual reframing assists in her revaluing of the Plains landscape. As Charles Mitchell explains, "meaning emerges only through a disciplined engagement with place, a thoroughgoing attention to where you are" (31). Indeed, now that she is becoming attuned to rural rhythms, Norris wonders if the "urban majority" have become today's "immigrants"; in "a world of asphalt and cement," she muses, "what they need more than anything is access to the old ways of being. Access to the spirits of land and of place" (168–69). Her spiritual acclimation on the Plains reaches deeper into the human past and into the older wisdoms of the biome. Norris embraces practices and attitudes that focus on diminutive things, encourage "a contemplative sense of fun," and distill a joyful freedom (215). Experiencing Lent at the Benedictine abbey, she feels an overwhelming contentment:

> As dark descended on our little ark, our feast of laughter became a remembered joy, a small bit of light and warmth that one could hope to return to. The silence of the present moment was awe-inspiring in its power, oceanic was the word that came to mind, as it carried away everything in its path. The flow of our liturgy had become one with nature's incessant movement from light to dark and back again. (214)

The conflation of space and spirit gives Norris tangible insight into a divine, intangible home, one's "own deepest commitments" (198).

In the chapter "Where I Am," Norris begins with the cartographical facts of Lemmon. "Where I am," she tells us, "is a marginal place that is at the very center of North America, roughly 1,500 miles from the Atlantic and Pacific Oceans, the Gulf of Mexico, and the Arctic Archipelago" (107). The climate is severe, with limited rainfall, temperature extremes, and powerful winter and summer storms. Other realities challenge her connection to place. "Where I am," she continues, "is a place where Native Americans and whites live along together. . . . Many small towns are Indian or white, and in general there is a deafening silence between the two worlds" (108). Geographical and cultural isolation cause "the human fabric" to "[wear] thin" (110). Pressure to accept "quiet conformity" increases one's sense of aloneness. Yet Norris, a professed "fledgling ascetic," is "learning to see loneliness as a seed that, when planted deep enough, can grow into writing that goes back out into the world" (111). Creativity, hospitality, and unexpected giddiness have reshaped Norris's connection to the Plains.

Her experiences with varied spiritual communities, from the Lakota traditions to Benedictine and Presbyterian practices, have brought her face-to-face with hard truths and stunning joys. "In Dakota," she muses, "death has an undeniable day-to-day reality" (120). The history of the place drives death's message home:

> The brutal massacres of Wounded Knee and the Killdeer Mountains (misnamed a "battle" to this day) are too recent to be comfortably relegated to history; they're still a living memory for the Native American community. And for white settlers, the period since the end of the "Indian Wars" has been marked by the slow death of their towns, churches, schools, and way of life. We learn to live with a hard reality: nothing lasts. (120–21)

There is grace in this knowledge, hard-won desert wisdom: "It is the desert's grimness, its stillness and isolation, that bring us back to love" (121).

In adjusting to prairie time and grasslands wisdom, Norris opens up to the deeper mysteries of the landscape. The Dakotas themselves are split between eastern and western realities. "The boundary,"

Norris explains, "is an ancient one" (150). Western space demands respect and disciplines with limitations. Norris notes that those residents of western Dakota who insist upon "watering a lawn to country club perfection" have not learned their landscape lesson yet (148). The division of land from the start of settlement days was predicated upon an illusion. "Encouraged by railroads and the government to pretend that the land could support families on homestead allotments of 160 acres," Norris argues, set the stage for ignoring the ancient voice of the place (148). The east and west division was established after the Wisconsin ice sheet receded and lay exposed in the "deep gorge of the Missouri" (150). When surveying this transition zone,

> Lewis and Clark marked this border by noting that the tallgrass to the east (bluestem, switch grass, Indian grass) grew six to eight feet high, while the shortgrass in the west (needle-and-thread, western wheat grass, blue grama grass, and upland sedges) topped at about four feet. You have left the glacial drift prairie for a land whose soil is the residue of prehistoric seas that have come and gone, weathered shale and limestone that is far less fertile than the land to the east but good for grazing sheep and cattle. Here you set your watch to Mountain time. (150)

Here, as well, one must also attune oneself to deep time, which has set the conditions of the modern landscape. It takes a "sea change," Norris professes, a "conversion," to embrace the conditions of such a place and to heed its idiom (145).

The Plains, as landscape, "are not forgiving," Norris asserts in one of her earlier sections. "Anything that is shallow—the easy optimism of a homesteader; the false hope that denies geography, climate, history; the trees whose roots don't reach ground water—will dry up and blow away" (38). At the end of her narrative, she stands outside in early December. A warm front chases bitter cold away. "The great vault of sky is painted with high, feathery clouds," she notes, "the ribs of a leviathan, or angels' wings" (220). At 3:00 a.m. in this spiritually charged setting, Norris contemplates a monk's wisdom: "You have only to let the place happen to you . . . the loneliness, the silence, the poverty, the futility, indeed the silliness of your life" (220). "Alone with the Alone," she drinks in a resplendent, illuminative emptiness (220).

Challenges, sufferings, hungers, deprivations, the abstemious blessings of Plains realities, paradoxically bring a deep, quiet joy. Norris's early morning reverie bespeaks reclamation, reinhabitation that has resonated with readers ever since *Dakota* was published. In connecting Plains vernacular to desert prophets, she has connected home-ground particularities to the sacred and embedded the concept of spiritual geography into the enduring layers of the Great Plains deep map.

Living near Norris in western South Dakota, Dan O'Brien has also watched with a mix of dismay and jubilation the efforts to relearn the spiritual vernacular of the Plains. "I live in a land," he explains, "suspended between the laws of nature and the laws of economics."[31] In his mind, the laws of nature are primary: "The North American grasslands are too fragile to be treated like a factory."[32] Examining the economic pressures that are reshaping Saskatchewan, north of the Dakotas, Candace Savage concurs with O'Brien. With each acre of grasslands ploughed under, indigenous species of the biome face habitat loss. The draining of wetlands to expand cropland has been equally devastating to native flora and fauna. "As for the surviving wild prairie," she tallies, "it is in declining health due to the incursions of invasive plants and the relentless, dendritic expansion of oil-and-gas exploration and other human demands."[33] What O'Brien, Savage, and Norris witness on the northern Plains is desecration no less pronounced than the loss M. Scott Momaday marks in *The Way to Rainy Mountain*. The forces of deicide continue.

Writing of the landscape, from the landscape, for the landscape, modern Plains essayists of place resist and counter those who refuse to honor this unique biome. The North American grasslands, as deep time shows us, will probably have the last word. Savage ardently pronounces, "[The] Great Plains grasslands are old, older than memory. For visitants like us, this ancient land offers a grounding in continuance."[34] The deep map writers I have surveyed all understand the primacy of this long view. They are creators of remembered earth, cartographers guided by Plains vernacular, translators of ground truths. In assembling the strata of their storytelling, Great Plains literary cartographers map the many worlds and eons that fold into the present. What these stories reveal is critical for the future of the North American grasslands, especially for those "stickers and nurturers" Donald Worster lauds in the chapter epigraph. These are the people who give allegiance to place, who "seek to discipline their desires and nurture that relationship."[35] They seek the spiritual discipline that comes with wise adaptation and bioregional awareness.

Deep map writing from the Plains engages fully with the material and spiritual contexts of this magnificent if stressed landscape, and in doing so gives voice to the accumulated lessons of place. "We will need to see both the splendor of the life that has faded away and the abundance that still extends across the whole wide world of the prairie in every direction," Savage argues, if Plains communities are to reap more than the aftermath of loss.[36] We will need to unfold and study the many maps of spiritual geography to avert further diminishment of the grasslands, to face facts, to regard the land's soil and soul, and to embrace the living matrices of the North American Plains.

PREFACE

1. Wishart, "Great Plains Region," *Encyclopedia of the Great Plains*, xvii.

2. Wishart, "Great Plains Region," xvii.

3. Wishart, "Great Plains Region," xvi.

4. Wishart, "Great Plains Region," xvi.

5. Another invaluable source for topographical information is Lavin, Shelley, and Archer, eds., *Atlas of the Great Plains*. Explaining the northern boundaries of the Great Plains, the editors explain that "on the north, the landscapes and cultures of the northern U.S. Great Plains states and the Canadian prairie provinces are too similar to use the international boundary along the forty-ninth parallel of latitude as a northern boundary for the Great Plains. Instead, the selected northern boundary more or less coincides with the northern range of American bison, whose past migrations extended into what Canadians call the Parkland Belt of mixed woodlands and grasslands, but rarely into the cooler coniferous zone of the taiga, or boreal forest" (11).

6. The concept of topophilia is explored in Yi-Fu Tuan's now classic study *Topophilia*.

7. Janovy, "Erma's Desire," *Back in Keith County*, 5.

8. Janovy, "Erma's Desire," *Back in Keith County*, 5.

9. Paul A. Johnsgard tell us, in *The Nature of Nebraska*, that "fossil remains of a sandhill crane dating back at least 8 million years have been found, suggesting the sandhill crane's love affair with Nebraska is a very long one indeed" (116).

10. Tuan, *Space and Place*, 54.

11. Tuan, *Space and Place*, 130.

12. Tuan, *Topophilia*, 97.

13. Tuan, *Topophilia*, 98.

14. Friedman, *Mappings*, 154.

15. Friedman, *Mappings*, 19.

16. Friedman, *Mappings*, 19.

17. Friedman, *Mappings*, 18.

18. Friedman, *Mappings*, 154.

19. Fleckenstein, "Writing Bodies," 282.

20. Fleckenstein, "Writing Bodies," 282.

21. Fleckenstein, "Writing Bodies," 281.

22. Fleckenstein, "Writing Bodies," 281.

23. Ryden, *Invisible Landscape*, 20.

24. Ryden, *Invisible Landscape*, 23.

25. Ryden, *Invisible Landscape*, 22.

26. Ryden, *Invisible Landscape*, 22.

27. Ryden, *Invisible Landscape*, 45.

28. Ryden, *Invisible Landscape*, 52.

29. Van Noy, *Surveying the Interior*, 3.

30. Van Noy, *Surveying the Interior*, 178.

31. See Maher, "Deep Mapping the Great Plains."

32. Roorda, "Deep Maps," 259.

33. Roorda, "Deep Maps," 259.

34. Roorda, "Deep Maps," 259.

35. This 2011 issue provides a reprint of an article from the online journal *eSharp* by Christopher C. Gregory-Guider entitled "'Deep Maps': William Least Heat-Moon's Psychogeographic Cartographies." Gregory-Guider states, "*PrairyErth* exchanges breadth for depth, concentrating entirely on a single relatively obscure county in Kansas. This shift from horizontal to vertical journeying is discernible in a subgenre of American travel-writing that seeks to discover the new directly beneath the feet rather than some-where over the horizon. Extending back at least to Thoreau, these works value the local as the preferred point of access to the infinite" (4). See the complete article in *eSharp* for Gregory-Guider's full argument.

36. Campbell, *Cultures*, 29.

37. Campbell, *Cultures*, 29.

38. Campbell, *Cultures*, 20.

39. Candace Savage, in *Prairie: A Natural History*, provides this useful descrip-tion of the rhizome: "Since most prairie grasses also produce lateral rootstocks, or rhizomes, that send down roots along their length, each plant—and each clump of root-bound earth—is connected to the next and the next. As plant intertwines with plant, and roots interweave with roots, the soil becomes tightly tied together in a thick, fibrous mat—the famous prairie sod, which the settlers used for building their first homes" (91). The metaphor of the rhizome and the idea of a rhizomatic West are particularly well suited for studies of the North American Plains.

40. Campbell, *Rhizomatic West*, 26, 37.

41. Campbell, *Rhizomatic West*, 38.

42. Campbell, *Rhizomatic West*, 38.

43. Thacker, *Great Prairie Fact*, 9.

1. DEEP MAPPING THE GREAT PLAINS

1. Momaday, *Way to Rainy Mountain*, 83.
2. Momaday, *Way to Rainy Mountain*, 83.
3. Momaday, *Way to Rainy Mountain*, 4.
4. Momaday, *Way to Rainy Mountain*, 10.
5. Momaday, *Way to Rainy Mountain*, 10.
6. Momaday, *Way to Rainy Mountain*, 10.
7. Momaday, *Way to Rainy Mountain*, 10.
8. Momaday, *Way to Rainy Mountain*, 7, 10.
9. Momaday, *Way to Rainy Mountain*, 11.
10. Momaday tells us in *The Way to Rainy Mountain*, "A single knoll rises out of the plain of Oklahoma, north and west of the Wichita Range. For my people, the Kiowas, it is an old landmark, and they gave it the name Rainy Mountain" (5).
11. Worster, *A River Running West*, 40–42.
12. Campbell, *Rhizomatic West*, 9–10.
13. Campbell, *Rhizomatic West*, 9.
14. Candace Savage, in *Prairie*, provides a useful précis of Plains Indigenous agricultural settlements. "Sometime around the beginning of the current era, circa AD 1," she states, "[Plains Woodland] people began tending small plots of corn and sometimes beans, along the tree-lined river valleys of the tall-grass region, from western Missouri to Nebraska" (225). Severe drought approximately a millennium later appears to have caused the collapse of these people. Plains Village Culture people "established themselves in small, scattered clusters of earth lodges along rivers and creeks from the upper Missouri River south to the Republican River and its tributaries, in present-day Nebraska and Kansas," she continues (225). The Plains Village Culture dates from AD 1000 and included "peoples such as the Pawnees, Mandans, and Hidatsas for more than eight hundred years" (225). These villages collapsed "after the introduction of smallpox" (225).
15. Momaday, *Way to Rainy Mountain*, 85.
16. Momaday, *Way to Rainy Mountain*, 85.
17. Momaday, *Way to Rainy Mountain*, 85–86.
18. Momaday, *Way to Rainy Mountain*, 4.
19. Simpson, "Listening to Our Ancestors," 125.
20. West, *Way to the West*, 166.
21. West, *Contested Plains*, xxiv.
22. West, *Way to the West*, 166.
23. Campbell, *Cultures of the American New West*, 18.
24. Campbell, *Cultures of the American New West*, 20.
25. Campbell, *Rhizomatic West*, 6–7.

26. Campbell, *Rhizomatic West*, 37.

27. West, *Way to the West*, 166.

28. Worster, *Under Western Skies*, 253.

29. Jackson, "Living Nets in a New Prairie Sea," 77–78.

30. Savage, *Prairie*, 226–28.

31. Kunstler, *Geography of Nowhere*, 185.

32. Bevis, "Region, Power, Place," 21.

33. Manning, *Grassland*, 105.

34. Manning, *Grassland*, 105.

35. Quantic, *Nature of the Place*, 14.

36. Butala, *Perfection of the Morning*, 88.

37. In *The Great Prairie Fact and Literary Imagination*, Robert Thacker states, "Historically ill-equipped to view and to understand the prairie landscape, Europeans did not foresee and often misunderstood the practical and epistemological problems posed by prairie topography, which had to be reckoned with as the region was explored, traveled through, and ultimately settled between the sixteenth and nineteenth centuries" (2).

38. Stafford, *Having Everything Right*. This collection popularized the phrase "essays of place."

39. Roorda, "Deep Maps," 259.

40. Roorda, "Deep Maps," 259.

41. Gregory-Guider, "'Deep Maps,'" 7.

42. West, *Way to the West*, 166.

43. Bakhtin, *Dialogic Imagination*, 84.

44. McDowell, "Bakhtinian Road to Ecological Insight," 372.

45. Fleckenstein, "Writing Bodies," 281.

46. Fleckenstein, "Writing Bodies," 301.

47. Buell, *Environmental Imagination*, 3.

48. Thayer, *LifePlace*, 3.

49. Martone, "The Flatness," 29.

50. Heat-Moon, *PrairyErth*, 10.

51. Gayton, "Cycles of Fire," 61–62.

52. Lynch, Glotfelty, and Armbruster, *Bioregional Imagination*, 4.

53. Buell, *Environmental Imagination*, 109.

54. Johnsgard, *Nature of Nebraska*, 127.

55. Candace Savage, in *Prairie: A Natural History*, notes that "little of this land has been formally protected by law. In fact, across the Great Plains as a whole only about 1 percent of the countryside has been set aside in parks or conservation reserves, less than in any other biome in North America" (260).

56. Gayton, "Tallgrass Dream," 100.

57. West, *Way to the West*, 166.
58. Weltzien, "Topographical Map of Words," *Great Plains Quarterly*, 121.
59. Ryden, *Mapping the Invisible Landscape*, 247.
60. Eiseley, "The Slit," 4. Subsequent quotations from this text.
61. Eiseley, "Flow of the River," 16. Subsequent quotations from this text.
62. Janovy, "Swallows," 66. Subsequent quotations from this text.
63. Norris, *Dakota*, 10.
64. McPhee, *Annals of the Former World*, 628.
65. Savage, *Prairie*, 29.
66. David Quammen, "Rocks of Ages," *New York Times Book Review*, July 5, 1998, 9–10.
67. McPhee, "Gravel Page," 82.
68. Gayton, "Tallgrass Dream," 96.
69. Jackson, "Living Nets," 78.
70. Matthews, *Where the Buffalo Roam*, 128.
71. Manning, *Grassland*, 263.
72. Butala, *Perfection of the Morning*, 178.
73. Butala, *Perfection of the Morning*, 180.
74. Hasselstrom, *Going Over East*, 94.
75. Hasselstrom, *Going Over East*, 66.
76. Hasselstrom, *Going Over East*, 180.
77. Hasselstrom, *Going Over East*, 153.
78. Thacker, *Great Prairie Fact*, 224.
79. Frazier, *Great Plains*, 7.
80. Frazier, *Great Plains*, 7–8.
81. Heat-Moon, *PrairyErth*, 82.
82. Leopold, *Sand County Almanac*, 189.
83. Leopold, *Sand County Almanac*, 189.
84. Heat-Moon, *PrairyErth*, 82.
85. Heat-Moon, *PrairyErth*, 268; and Price, "What This Prairie Will Awaken," 26, 36.
86. Heat-Moon, *PrairyErth*, 269.
87. Manning, *Grassland*, 206.
88. Savage presents a map of the ecoregions of the Great Plains in her study *Prairie: A Natural History*. The central and northern Plains are complex and run the gamut from tallgrass to mixed-grass to shortgrass prairies. Included in these sections of the Plains are the Flint Hills and High Plains of Kansas, the Sand Hills and Wildcat Hills of Nebraska, the Black Hills of South Dakota, the transitional foothill grasslands of the Rockies, and the Saskatchewan Plain—areas focused on in this study. See Savage's chapter "Where Is Here?"

89. Prairyerth is a soil type noted for its rich organic composition. Savage tells us, in *Prairie: A Natural History*, that the "surplus resources have collected in thick layers of dark, crumbly, humus-rich earth. . . . To an earlier generation of soil scientists, these remarkable grasslands soils were known as 'prairyerths,' simply and profoundly because that is what they were" (92).

90. Heat-Moon, *PrairyErth*, 27. Subsequent quotations from this text.

91. Christianson, introduction to *The Night Country*, by Loren Eiseley, xi. Christianson explains, "Never deeply committed to fieldwork, Eiseley began composing what he termed the 'concealed essay,' cloaking his vision of the world in the raiment of science" (xi).

92. Gayton, *Wheatgrass Mechanism*, 13. Subsequent quotations from this text.

93. Jackson, *Becoming Native to This Place*, 2.

94. Jackson, *Becoming Native to This Place*, 3.

95. Janovy, *Dunwoody Pond*, 6.

96. Jackson, *Becoming Native to This Place*, 4.

97. Jackson, *Becoming Native to This Place*, 60.

98. Janovy, *Dunwoody Pond*, 277.

99. Janovy, *Dunwoody Pond*, 277.

100. Gayton, *Wheatgrass Mechanism*, 146.

101. See Krall, *Ecotone*. Krall writes, "In the natural world, edges where differences come together are the richest of habitats. . . . Transitional species, plants and animals such as those found in tidal zones, have become highly adapted for life 'on the edge'" (4). These edges or boundaries are ecotones.

102. Krall, *Ecotone*, 4.

103. Omhovère, "Female Body as Garrison in Three Prairie Biotexts," 179.

104. J. Bair, *One Degree West*, 123.

105. Hasselstrom, *Feels Like Far*, 3.

106. Calder, "Who's from the Prairie?" 96.

107. Butala, *Wild Stone Heart*, 1. Subsequent quotations from this text.

108. Lynch, Glotfelty, and Armbruster, *Bioregional Imagination*, 6.

109. Norris, *Dakota*, 161. Subsequent quotations from this text.

110. Eiseley, "Secret of Life," from *Immense Journey*, 210.

111. Gayton, *Wheatgrass Mechanism*, 148.

2. DEEP MAPPING HISTORY

1. Jameson and Mouat, "Telling Differences," 205.

2. Van Noy, *Surveying the Interior*, 146.

3. Stegner, *Wolf Willow*, 13. Subsequent quotations from this text.

4. Moul, *National Grassland*, 2–3.

5. Van Noy, *Surveying the Interior*, 146.

6. Kroetsch, "Disunity as Unity," 24–25.

7. Daniel, "Stegner's Hunger," 35.

8. Van Noy, *Surveying the Interior*, 151.

9. Daniel, "Stegner's Hunger," 36.

10. Cook-Lynn, *Why I Can't Read Wallace Stegner*, 37.

11. Cook-Lynn, *Why I Can't Read Wallace Stegner*, 37. Moreover, Candace Savage's recent book, *A Geography of Blood*, reexamines Stegner's portrayal of history in *Wolf Willow* and critiques "the confidant assertion of white European superiority and the unquestioned value of European 'civilization'" (63–64).

12. See Groening, *Listening to Old Woman Speak*, 24. Groening states, "Based on the record of our literary history . . . I am less optimistic about a true and equal merging of Native and non-Native cultures. Before hybridity can become a life-affirming alternative for Natives as well as non-Native writers, the cultural baggage associated with the Manichean allegory must be unpacked."

13. Stegner, "Sense of Place," *Where the Bluebird Sings to the Lemonade Springs*, 201, 204.

14. Stegner, "Sense of Place," *Where the Bluebird Sings to the Lemonade Springs*, 202–3.

15. Van Noy, *Surveying the Interior*, 153.

16. Van Noy, *Surveying the Interior*, 153.

17. Harlow, "Whitemud Revisited," 26.

18. Van Noy, *Surveying the Interior*, 157.

19. Van Noy, *Surveying the Interior*, 167.

20. Van Noy, *Surveying the Interior*, 170.

21. Olsen, "Wallace Stegner and the Environmental Ethic," 126.

22. Olsen, "Wallace Stegner and the Environmental Ethic," 125.

23. Daniel, "Stegner's Hunger," 136–37.

24. West, "Stegner, Storytelling, and Western Identity," 64.

25. West, "Stegner, Storytelling, and Western Identity," 64.

26. Kittredge, "Good Rain and the Wild," 41.

27. Dillon, "Time's Prisoners," 47.

28. Stegner and Etulain, *Stegner*, 5.

29. Van Noy, *Surveying the Interior*, 148.

30. Van Noy, *Surveying the Interior*, 148.

31. Weltzien, "Topographical Map of Words," 120.

32. Averill, "Essays on Place," 125.

33. Weltzien, "Topographical Map of Words," 120.

34. Ronda, "'A Chart in His Way,'" 84.

35. Lewis, "Maps, Mapmaking, and Map Use by Native Americans," 51.

36. Walker, "Necessity of Narrative in William Least Heat-Moon's *Blue Highways* and *PrairyErth*," 294.
37. Van Noy, *Surveying the Interior*, 4.
38. Wood, *Power of Maps*, 1.
39. Wood, *Power of Maps*, 1.
40. Wood, *Power of Maps*, 1.
41. Wood, *Power of Maps*, 5.
42. Weltzien, "Topographical Map of Words, 110.
43. Weltzien, "Topographical Map of Words," 111.
44. Gregory-Guider, "'Deep Maps,'" 6.
45. Heat-Moon, *PrairyErth*, 15.
46. Wall, "Walking," 70.
47. The Emma Chase Café in Cottonwood Falls has proven more durable than Heat-Moon had anticipated. It remains a viable operation in Chase County. In the present of Heat-Moon's text, he tells us in *PrairyErth*, "the Emma Chase Café has just closed, reopened, and closed again, and the only place on Broadway now for a cup of coffee is at the Senior Citizen's Center" (53). The Emma Chase has its own web page now: http://www.emmachasecafe .com.
48. Price, *Not Just Any Land*, 112.
49. Grim, "Mapping Kansas and Nebraska," 127.
50. *Terra nullius*, according to geographers Daniel Dorling and David Fairbairn in *Mapping*, is a legal concept emerging from explorations and colonization; to justify occupation, colonial agents would declare land *terra nullius* ("empty land") (82). Dorling and Fairbairn further argue, "[the] concept of *terra nullius*. . . was used to justify the westward expansion of the United States of America, the settlement of Australia, and the colonization of Africa" (88). In 1973, the International Court of Justice ended this legal practice.
51. Dorling and Fairbairn, *Mapping*, 82.
52. See Weltzien for an extended discussion of this metaphor, coined by Weltzien.
53. Weltzien, "Topographical Map of Words," 122.
54. MacEachren, *How Maps Work*, 14.
55. MacEachren, *How Maps Work*, 14.
56. Duncan and Ley, *Place/Culture/Representation*, 3.
57. Cosgrove and Domosh, "Author and Authority," 30–31.
58. Ronald, *Ghost West*, 6.
59. Ronald, *Ghost West*, 6.
60. Buell, *Environmental Imagination*, 274.
61. Wall, "Digging Into the West," 142.

62. Ryden, *Mapping the Invisible Landscape*, 243.

63. Ryden, *Mapping the Invisible Landscape*, 249.

64. Kowalewski, "Writing in Place," 181.

65. Comer, *Landscapes of the New West*, 13.

66. Worster, *Under Western Skies*, viii.

67. Worster, *Under Western Skies*, 253.

68. Robertson, "Henry Adams, Wallace Stegner, and the Search for a Sense of Place in the West," 96.

3. DEEP MAPPING THE BIOME

1. Tuan, *Space and Place*, 83.

2. Nickerson's *Disappearance* maps an Alaskan landscape; Marshall's *Story Line* details the eighteen-hundred-mile trail up the spine of the Appalachian Mountain range; and White's *Prairie Time* presents a deeply mapped depiction of grasslands in Texas that run from San Antonio up to the Red River.

3. Buell, *Environmental Imagination*, 261.

4. Ricou, "Imprinting Landscapes," *Canadian Literature* 157 (1998), 187.

5. Jackson, *Becoming Native to This Place*, 78.

6. See Nabhan, *Cross-Pollinations*.

7. Flores, *Natural West*, 15.

8. Buell, *Environmental Imagination*, 101.

9. Price, *Not Just Any Land*, 9.

10. Gayton, *Wheatgrass Mechanism*, 42.

11. Corner, "Agency of Mapping," 214.

12. Fleckenstein, "Writing Bodies," 281–82.

13. Jackson, *Becoming Native to This Place*, 44.

14. Janovy, *Keith County Journal*, 92.

15. Janovy, *Keith County Journal*, 92.

16. Fleckenstein, "Writing Bodies," 286, and Gayton, *Wheatgrass Mechanism*, 18.

17. Jackson, *Becoming Native to This Place*, 98.

18. Gayton, *Wheatgrass Mechanism*, 23.

19. Corner, "Agency of Mapping," 224–25.

20. Corner, "Agency of Mapping," 226.

21. Corner, "Agency of Mapping," 214.

22. Flores, *Natural West*, 91.

23. Tuan, *Space and Place*, 179.

24. Gayton, *Wheatgrass Mechanism*, 22. Subsequent quotations from this text.

25. Worster, *Dust Bowl*, 231.

26. Manning, *Grassland*, 40.

27. Manning, *Grassland*, 40.

28. West, *Way to the West*, 39.

29. Pringle, "Landscapes of the Interior," 86.

30. Manning, *Grassland*, 55.

31. According to Bamforth's essay, "Bison," in *The Encyclopedia of the Great Plains*, the bison "populations now total some 70,000, thanks to efforts by government agencies and private groups like the National Bison Association and the InterTribal Bison Cooperative" (622). He also notes that "herds on the Plains today live in limited areas, including national, state, and local parks and private ranches. Most herds are also managed, to some degree, through selective slaughter and provision of winterfeed" (621). However, Lavin, Shelley, and Archer, in *Atlas of the Great Plains*, put the current bison population "at about 350,000 animals" (54). They note, however, that "many have interbred with domestic cattle, and biologists estimate that the purebred population of wild bison in the United States and Canada numbers less than 20,000 animals" (54).

32. West, *Way to the West*, 52.

33. Gayton, "Tallgrass Dream," 99.

34. Gayton, "Tallgrass Dream," 98.

35. Buell, *Environmental Imagination*, 262.

36. Janovy, *Keith County Journal*, 157. Subsequent quotations from this text.

37. Buell, *Writing for an Endangered World*, 55.

38. Buell, *Writing for an Endangered World*, 55.

39. Fleckenstein, "Writing Bodies," 295.

40. Flores, *Natural West*, 173.

41. Janovy, *Dunwoody Pond*, 282. Subsequent quotations from this text.

42. Ryden, *Mapping the Invisible Landscape*, 513.

43. Johnsgard, *Nature of Nebraska*, 23.

44. Johnsgard, *Nature of Nebraska*, 23–24.

45. Johnsgard, *Nature of Nebraska*, 20.

46. Johnsgard, *Nature of Nebraska*, 189.

47. Johnsgard, *Nature of Nebraska*, 191.

48. Tuan, *Space and Place*, 197.

49. Flores, *Natural West*, 92.

50. Jackson, *Becoming Native to This Place*, 2. Subsequent quotations from this text.

51. Heat-Moon, *PrairyErth*, 504.

52. Heat-Moon, *PrairyErth*, 497.

53. Price, *Not Just Any Land*, 112.

54. Jackson, *Becoming Native to This Place*, 12.

55. The "What's New" section of the Land Institute's website announced on September 4, 2008, that "[the] Land Institute is selling its real estate holdings in Matfield Green, Kansas—in the region of the Flint Hills tallgrass prairie." This announcement also states, "The Matfield Green Grade School will also soon be listed for sale." Available online at http://www.land institute.org.

56. Gayton, *Wheatgrass Mechanism*, 15.

57. Buell, *Environmental Imagination*, 266.

58. See Tuan, *Topophilia*, 129.

4. DEEP MAPPING DIMENSIONS

1. McPhee, "The Gravel Page," in *Irons in the Fire*, 81. Subsequent quotations from this text.

2. MacEachren, *How Maps Work*, 10.

3. MacEachren, *How Maps Work*, 12.

4. Eiseley, *Immense Journey*, 150.

5. Eiseley, *Immense Journey*, 150.

6. Stevens, "John McPhee's *Annals of the Former World*," 229.

7. Stevens, "John McPhee's *Annals of the Former World*," 230.

8. Stevens, "John McPhee's *Annals of the Former World*," 238.

9. Eiseley, *All the Strange Hours*, 238.

10. Eiseley, *All the Strange Hours*, 91.

11. Christianson, introduction to *Night Country*, xi.

12. Christianson is quoting a letter in the University of Pennsylvania Archives from Fisher to Eiseley dated July 14, 1953. See Christianson, *Fox at the Wood's Edge*, 282.

13. Breschinsky, "Reaching Beyond the Bridge," 78.

14. Breschinsky, "Reaching Beyond the Bridge," 78.

15. Eiseley, *All the Strange Hours*, 23.

16. Eiseley, *Night Country*, 21.

17. Eiseley, *All the Strange Hours*, 82–83.

18. Eiseley, *All the Strange Hours*, 83.

19. "The Great Deeps" is the third essay in *The Immense Journey*. In it, Eiseley investigates the concept of the abyss, Darwinian theory, and oceanic science.

20. Eiseley, *Immense Journey*, 59.

21. Eiseley, *Immense Journey*, 120.

22. From Eiseley's essay "The Chresmologue," *Night Country*, 75.

23. Eiseley, *Immense Journey*, 4.

24. Eiseley, *Immense Journey*, 6.

25. Eiseley, *Immense Journey*, 19. Subsequent quotations from "The Flow of the River" from this text.

26. Soja, *Thirdspace*, 11, 56–57.

27. Ryden, *Mapping the Invisible Landscape*, 250–51.

28. Ryden, *Mapping the Invisible Landscape*, 251.

29. Ryden, *Mapping the Invisible Landscape*, 266.

30. Eiseley, "The Slit," *Immense Journey*, 3. Subsequent quotations from this text.

31. Soja, *Thirdspace*, 57.

32. Heidtmann, *Loren Eiseley*, 50.

33. Heidtmann, *Loren Eiseley*, 50.

34. Eiseley, "The Flow of the River," *Immense Journey*, 15. Subsequent quotations from this text.

35. Bachelard, *Poetics of Space*, 183.

36. Bachelard, *Poetics of Space*, 188.

37. Tilden, "Stratigraphies," 25.

38. Tilden, "Stratigraphies," 33.

39. McPhee, *Basin and Range*, 79.

40. Van Noy, "Plate Tectonics of Language," 211.

41. Stevens, "John McPhee's *Annals of the Former World*," 229.

42. Stevens, "John McPhee's *Annals of the Former World*," 239.

43. Gregory, *Geographical Imaginations*, 73.

44. McPhee, *Annals of the Former World*, 625.

45. McPhee, *Annals of the Former World*, 626.

46. Tilden, "Stratigraphies," 29.

47. McPhee, *Annals of the Former World*, 628. Subsequent quotations from this text.

48. McPhee, *Annals of the Former World*, 13.

49. Geographer David J. Wishart, in *Encyclopedia of the Great Plains*, explains Wyoming's unique position as a Plains state, where the clarity of the western boundary along the Rockies blurs: "in the Wyoming basin, for example, where the Great Plains rise to more than 7,000 feet and merge less perceptibly with the Rocky Mountains" one sees places where mountains "interpenetrate with the Plains" (xvi). One of Wishart's maps of the Great Plains, showing "fifty published versions of the Great Plains regional boundary" (xvii), brings the western boundary of the Plains within the Love ranch as described by McPhee in *Rising from the Plains*, "just under the forty-third parallel and west of the hundred-and-seventh meridian—coordinates that place it twelve miles from the geographic center of Wyoming" (77–78). The ranch site is north of present-day Rawlins, Wyoming.

50. McPhee, *Rising From the Plains*, 43. Subsequent quotations from this text.
51. Chief Washakie was a renowned leader among the Eastern Shoshone people of Wyoming. He participated in the Battle of Crowheart Butte, when Shoshone and Bannock warriors faced off against the Crow. Chief Washakie took on Chief Big Robber, man to man, and defeated him. He famously cut out his opponent's heart in tribute to the defeated man's bravery. Crowheart Butte was named to commemorate this victory. Crowheart Butte lies east of present-day Dubois, Wyoming, along the Chief Washakie Trail. See Stamm's *People of the Wind River* for the context for this struggle among tribes.
52. Stevens, "John McPhee's *Annals of the Former World*," 230.
53. For direct access to her writings, see Waxham, *Lady's Choice*.
54. Tilden, "Stratigraphies," 28.
55. Tilden, "Stratigraphies," 28–29.
56. Tilden, "Stratigraphies," 32.
57. Molly Wood is the Virginian's love interest in Owen Wister's novel *The Virginian, a Horseman of the Plains* (1902).
58. Howarth, "Itinerant Passages," 636.
59. Howarth, "Itinerant Passages," 636.
60. McPhee, *Annals of the Former World*, 627. Subsequent quotations from this text.
61. Bryson, "Nature, Narrative, and the Scientific Writer," 381.

5. DEEP MAPPING LIVED SPACE
1. Stegner, *American West as Living Space*, 22.
2. Campbell, *Rhizomatic West*, 26.
3. Giles, *Virtual Americas*, 5.
4. Campbell, *Rhizomatic West*, 46.
5. Stegner, *American West as Living Space*, 22. Subsequent quotations from this text.
6. J. Bair, *One Degree West*, 134. Subsequent quotations from this text.
7. Butala, *Wild Stone Heart*, 16.
8. Butala, *Wild Stone Heart*, 98.
9. Hasselstrom, *Feels Like Far*, 9.
10. Hasselstrom, *Feels Like Far*, 10.
11. J. Bair, *One Degree West*, 131.
12. Brown, "Courage Without Illusion," 56.
13. Boardman and Woods, eds., introduction to *Western Subjects*, 19.
14. Gilmore, *Autobiographics*, 184.
15. For another perspective on the Bair family's farming world in Goodland, Kansas, see Bruce Bair's book, *Good Land*. He provides a compelling narrative of the same years, examining the commodification of sons in a

patriarchal system and giving insight into a young man's difficult maturation in western Kansas.

16. J. Bair, *One Degree West*, 1. Subsequent quotations from this text.
17. Butala, *Perfection of the Morning*, xiii.
18. Butala, *Perfection of the Morning*, xiv.
19. Butala, *Wild Stone Heart*, 37. Subsequent quotations from this text.
20. Friedman, *Mappings*, 18–19. Friedman connects geographics to an emerging interest in "the centrality of space—the rhetoric of spatiality" that focuses on "the locations of identity within the mappings and remappings of ever changing cultural formations" (19).
21. Friedman, *Mappings*, 109–110.
22. Jackson, *Becoming Native to This Place*, 106.
23. Palliser, *Rambles and Adventures of a Hunter in the Prairies*, 88. Thacker in *The Great Prairie Fact* notes that Palliser's descriptions present an affective response to an alien landscape: "The prairie, according to Palliser, is a primordial landscape—it makes him feel small and insignificant. Unlike the earliest commentators, therefore, Palliser does not describe the prairie mainly in terms of comparison with known things—his strange feelings of insignificance seem to require the unknown, so he alters his allusions accordingly. Similarly, so overpowering is the impact of the prairie that it overrides any conventional landscape notions Palliser may have had before he ventured into it" (37).
24. See Allister, *Refiguring the Map of Sorrow*. Allister notes at the beginning of his study that a number of life-writings follow writers as they "reframe and work through their grief by focusing on external subjects that absorbed each writer as a replacement for their loss" (1). "By writing of a subject that moves them deeply," he continues, "by working to understand themselves primarily in relation to the non-human world around them, they learn ways of responding that teach them how to reenvision their own pasts" (1).
25. Friedman, *Mappings*, 3.
26. Friedman, *Mappings*, 154.
27. See Gilmore's *Autobiographics* and Reaves, *Mapping the Private Geograph*.
28. Friedman, *Mappings*, 151.
29. Hasselstrom, *Feels Like Far*, 9. Subsequent quotations from this text.
30. Brown, "Courage Without Illusion," 56.
31. Friedman, *Mappings*, 19.
32. Boardman and Woods, *Western Subjects*, 3.
33. Friedman, *Mappings*, 154.
34. Price, *Not Just Any Land*, 79.
35. Price, *Not Just Any Land*, 79.
36. Friedman, *Mappings*, 19.

37. Reaves, in *Mapping the Private Geography*, states, "A better understanding of the roles of spatial metaphors in the autobiographer's sense of self is crucial, given the extent to which *America* and *Americanism* are inevitably bound up with the right to consume space, to move freely, to set and cross boundaries at will, to command and own space—ultimately, to mark space, to inscribe the landscape; the extent to which textual metaphors overlap with geographical ones; and the extent to which the autobiographical act is a seizing of territory, a taking of textual space. What does one's spatial or geographical existence have to do with identity boundaries, difference, identity formation, separation, and anxiety—i.e., with autobiography itself?" (14). The answer is everything.

38. Reaves, *Mapping the Private Geography*, 15.

CODA

1. Lopez, *Home Ground*, xvi.
2. Lopez, *Home Ground*, xxii.
3. Lopez, *Home Ground*, xxi.
4. Lopez, *Home Ground*, xvi.
5. Manning, *Grassland*, 259.
6. Buell, *Environmental Imagination*, 261.
7. Manning, *Grassland*, 144.
8. Frazier's *Great Plains* appeared in a three-part "Reporter at Large" series in the *New Yorker* in 1989. Heat-Moon's *PrairyErth* appeared in excerpt in the *Atlantic Monthly* in the fall of 1989.
9. Frazier, *Great Plains*, 12.
10. See Cook-Lynn, "Who Gets to Tell the Stories."
11. Serena Golden, "Wendell Berry delivers the annual Jefferson Lecture in the Humanities," *Inside Higher Ed*, 24 April 24, 2012, http://www.insiderhighered.com.
12. Golden, "Wendell Berry," *Inside Higher Ed.*
13. Norris, *Dakota*, 50.
14. Norris, *Dakota*, 50.
15. Manning, *Grassland*, 268.
16. Manning, *Grassland*, 268.
17. Manning, *Grassland*, 133.
18. O'Brien, *Buffalo for the Broken Heart*, 75–76.
19. Matthews, *Where the Buffalo Roam*, xii.
20. See Deborah Epstein Popper and Frank J. Popper, "The Great Plains: From Dust to Dust," *Planning* 53 (December 1987) 12–18.
21. Matthews, *Where the Buffalo Roam*, 25. Subsequent quotations from this text.

22. O'Brien, *Buffalo for the Broken Heart*, 254.
23. Recent headlines across the United States have highlighted a number of economic activities that have divided Plains communities. The proposed Keystone XL pipeline, a $7 billion, 1,700-mile-long project slated to cross the fragile Nebraska Sand Hills, instigated protests across the Plains and in Washington DC. When TransCanada announced that it would reroute the pipeline, the *Omaha World-Herald* reported that the "majority of landowners, in face- to-face conversations with state and pipeline officials, said the new route was no better and still crossed areas with high water tables and fragile, sandy soils like those in the Sand Hills" (*Omaha World-Herald* online edition, May 10, 2012). National Public Radio aired a segment on *Morning Edition* that was printed online declaring "Roosevelt's Badlands Ranch Faces Potential Threat" (August 7, 2012, online). Reporter John McChesney explains that Theodore Roosevelt's famous Elkhorn Ranch, close to the North Dakota oil boom and potential mining claims, may lose the very quality that Roosevelt cherished—"a place for recovery, reverie and reflection about the future of the West." The Bakken Oil Fields of North Dakota are bringing money and headaches. This new boom event, like past boom times, attracts thousands of workers seeking steady employment. The result is a deficit in decent housing options. Moreover, local landowners receive one-time compensation from oil companies and then watch their grasslands properties become industrial sites. Meanwhile, prices rise and long-term residents struggle with inflationary pressures that extractive industries can bring. In August 2012, the *Minneapolis Star Tribune* sounded the alarm on "open land falling to the plow" (August 6, 2012,online). Many farmers across the Plains are abandoning conservation practices to cash in on "record high commodity prices, demand for ethanol, and . . . crop insurance programs that guarantee profits for farmers, even on marginal land." In the prairie pothole region of North and South Dakota, as Sam Cook reported in the *Duluth News Tribune,* "grasslands, including native prairies, are disappearing at alarming rates, and wetlands are disappearing, too"(August 26, 2012, online). Farmers are plowing to the maximum to take advantage of the high commodities prices, putting short-term gain ahead of long-term environmental sustainability. All of these news reports remind us that Plains communities continue to grapple with priorities that may have detrimental impacts in the future.
24. Lopez, *Home Ground*, xxiv.
25. Golden, "Wendell Berry," *Inside Higher Ed.*
26. Norris, *Dakota*, 169.
27. Etulain, "Western Stories for the Next Generation," 16.
28. Norris, *Dakota*, 17. Subsequent quotations from this text.

29. Translated and quoted in Highmore, *Everyday Life and Cultural Theory*, 113.

30. Highmore, *Everyday Life*, 116.

31. O'Brien, *Buffalo for the Broken Heart*, 256.

32. O'Brien, *Buffalo for the Broken Heart*, 256.

33. Savage, *Prairie*, xi.

34. Savage, *Prairie*, x.

35. Worster, *Under Western Skies*, 253.

36. Savage, *Prairie*, 25.

Allister, Mark. *Refiguring the Map of Sorrow: Nature Writing and Autobiography.* Charlottesville: University of Virginia Press, 2001.

Angyal, Andrew J. "Loren Eiseley's *Immense Journey*: The Making of a Literary Naturalist." In *The Literature of Science: Perspectives on Popular Science Writing*, edited by Murdo William McRae, 54–72. Athens: University of Georgia Press, 1993.

Averill, Thomas Fox. "Essays on Place: The Map as Big as the World." *Great Plains Quarterly* 19, no. 2 (1999): 123–26.

Bachelard, Gaston. *The Poetics of Space: The Classic Look at How We Experience Intimate Places.* Translated by Maria Jolas. Boston: Beacon, 1994.

Bakhtin, M. M. *The Dialogic Imagination: Four Essays.* Edited by Michael Holquist. Translated by Caryl Emerson and Michael Holquist. Austin: University of Texas Press, 1981.

Bair, Bruce. *Good Land: Or, My Life as a Farm Boy.* South Royalton VT: Steerforth Press, 1997.

Bair, Julene. *One Degree West: Reflections of a Plainsdaughter.* Minneapolis: Mid-List, 2000.

Bamforth, Douglas B. "Bison." In *Encyclopedia of the Great Plains*, edited by David J. Wishart, 621–22. Lincoln: University of Nebraska Press.

Bevis, William W. "Region, Power, Place." In *Reading the West: New Essays on the Literature of the American West*, edited by Michael Kowalewski, 21–43. Cambridge MA: Cambridge University Press, 1996.

Boardman, Kathleen A., and Gioia Woods, eds. Introduction to *Western Subjects: Autobiographical Writing in the North American West*, 1–37. Salt Lake City: University of Utah Press, 2004.

Breschinsky, Dimitri N. "Reaching Beyond the Bridge: Time's Arrow in the Works of Loren Eiseley." ISLE (*Interdisciplinary Studies in Literature and Environment*) 9, no.2 (2002): 75–99.

Brown, Richard Maxwell. "Courage Without Illusion." In *A New Significance: Re-Envisioning the History of the American West*, edited by Clyde A. Milner, 56–61. New York: Oxford University Press, 1996.

Bryson, Michael A. "Nature, Narrative, and the Scientist Writer: Rachel Carson and Loren Eiseley's Critique of Science." *Technical Communication Quarterly* 12, no.4 (2003): 369–87.

Buell, Lawrence. *The Environmental Imagination: Thoreau, Nature Writing, and the Formation of American Culture.* Cambridge MA: Belknap, 1995.

———. *Writing for an Endangered World: Literature, Culture, and Environment in the U.S. and Beyond.* Cambridge MA: Belknap, 2001.

Butala, Sharon. *The Perfection of the Morning: An Apprenticeship in Nature.* Toronto: HarperCollins, 1994.

———. *Wild Stone Heart: An Apprentice in the Fields.* Toronto: HarperCollins, 2000.

Calder, Alison. "Who's from the Prairie? Some Prairie Self-Representations in Popular Culture." In *Toward Defining the Prairies: Region, Culture, and History,* edited by Robert Wardhaugh, 91–100. Winnipeg: University of Manitoba Press, 2001.

Campbell, Neil. *The Cultures of the American New West.* Edinburgh: Edinburgh University Press, 2000.

———. *The Rhizomatic West: Representing the American West in a Transnational, Global, Media Age.* Lincoln: University of Nebraska Press, 2008.

Christianson, Gale E. *Fox at the Wood's Edge: A Biography of Loren Eiseley.* Lincoln: University of Nebraska Press, 1990.

———. Introduction to *The Night Country,* by Loren Eiseley, vii–xiii. Lincoln: University of Nebraska Press, 1971.

Comer, Krista. *Landscapes of the New West: Gender and Geography in Contemporary Women's Writing.* Chapel Hill: University of North Carolina Press, 1999.

Cook-Lynn, Elizabeth. "Who Gets to Tell the Stories?" *Wicazo Sa Review* 9, no. 1 (1993): 60–64.

———. *Why I Can't Read Wallace Stegner and Other Essays.* Madison: University of Wisconsin Press, 1996.

Corner, James. "The Agency of Mapping: Speculation, Critique and Invention." In *Mappings,* edited by Denis Cosgrove, 213–52. London: Reaktion Books, 1999.

Cosgrove, Denis, ed. *Mappings.* London: Reaktion Books, 1999.

Cosgrove, Denis, and Mona Domosh. "Author and Authority: Writing the New Cultural Geography." In *Place/Culture/Representation,* edited by James Duncan and David Ley, 25–38. London: Routledge, 1993.

Daniel, John. "Wallace Stegner's Hunger for Wholeness." In *Wallace Stegner and the Continental Vision: Essays on Literature, History, and Landscape,* edited by Curt Meine, 31–42. Washington DC: Island Press, 1997.

Dillon, Dave. "Time's Prisoners: An Interview with Wallace Stegner." In *Critical Essays on Wallace Stegner,* edited by Anthony Arthur, 47–59. Boston: G. K. Hall, 1982.

Dorling, Daniel, and David Fairbairn. *Mapping: Ways of Representing the World.* Harlow, Essex, England: Addison Wesley Longman, 1997.

Duncan, James, and David Ley, eds. *Place/Culture/Representation*. London: Routledge, 1993.

Eiseley, Loren. *All the Strange Hours: The Excavation of a Life*. Lincoln: University of Nebraska Press, 2000. First published 1975 by Charles Scribner's Sons.

——. *The Immense Journey: An Imaginative Naturalist Explores the Mysteries of Man and Nature*. New York: Vintage, 1959.

——. *The Night Country*. Lincoln: University of Nebraska Press, 1971.

Etulain, Richard W. "Western Stories for the Next Generation." *Western Historical Quarterly* 31 (2000): 4–23.

Fleckenstein, Kristie S. "Writing Bodies: Somatic Mind in Composition Studies." *College English* 61, no. 3 (1999): 281–306.

Flores, Dan. *The Natural West: Environmental History in the Great Plains and Rocky Mountains*. Norman: University of Oklahoma Press, 2001.

Frazier, Ian. *Great Plains*. New York: Penguin, 1989.

Friedman, Susan Stanford. *Mappings: Feminism and the Cultural Geographies of Encounter*. Princeton: Princeton University Press, 1998.

Gayton, Don. *Landscapes of the Interior: Re-Explorations of Nature and the Human Spirit*. Gabriola Island BC: New Society, 1996.

——. *The Wheatgrass Mechanism: Science and Imagination in the Western Canadian Landscape*. Saskatoon: Fifth House, 1990.

Giles, Paul. *Virtual Americas: Transnational Fictions and the Transatlantic Imaginary*. Durham NC: Duke University Press, 2002.

Gilmore, Leigh. *Autobiographics: A Feminist Theory of Women's Self-Representation*. Ithaca NY: Cornell University Press, 1994.

Gregory, Derek. *Geographical Imaginations*. Oxford: Blackwell, 1994.

Gregory-Guider, Christopher C. "'Deep Maps': William Least Heat-Moon's Psychogeographic Cartographies." *eSharp* 4 (2007): 1–17.

Grim, Ronald. "Mapping Kansas and Nebraska." In *Mapping the North American Plains*, edited by Frederick C. Luebke, Francis W. Kaye, and Gary E. Moulton, 127–44. Norman: University of Oklahoma Press, 1987.

Groening, Laura Smyth. *Listening to Old Woman Speak: Natives and AlterNatives in Canadian Literature*. Montreal: McGill-Queen's University Press, 2005.

Harlow, Robert. "Whitemud Revisited." In *Critical Essays on Wallace Stegner*, edited by Anthony Arthur, 23–26. Boston: G. K. Hall, 1982.

Hasselstrom, Linda. *Feels Like Far: A Rancher's Life on the Great Plains*. Boston: Mariner Books, 2001.

——. *Going Over East: Reflections of a Woman Rancher*. Golden CO: Fulcrum, 1987.

Heat-Moon, William Least. *PrairyErth: (a deep map)*. Boston: Houghton Mifflin, 1991.

Heidtmann, Peter. *Loren Eiseley: A Modern Ishmael*. Hamden CT: Archon Books, 1991.

Highmore, Ben. *Everyday Life and Cultural Theory: An Introduction*. London: Routledge, 2002.

Howarth, William. "Itinerant Passages: Recent American Essays." *Sewanee Review* 96 (1988): 633–43.

Jackson, Wes. *Becoming Native to This Place*. Washington DC: Counterpoint, 1996.

———. "Living Nets in a New Prairie Sea." In *Altars of Unhewn Stone: Science and the Earth*, 77–82. New York: North Point, 1987.

Jameson, Elizabeth, and Jeremy Mouat. "Telling Differences: The 49th Parallel and Historiographies of the West and Nation." *Pacific Historical Review* 75, no. 2 (2006): 183–230.

Janovy, John. *Back in Keith County*. Lincoln: University of Nebraska Press, 1981.

———. *Dunwoody Pond: Reflections on the High Plains Wetlands and the Cultivation of Naturalists*. 1994. Reprint, Lincoln: University of Nebraska Press, 2001.

———. *Keith County Journal*. 1978. Reprint, Lincoln: University of Nebraska Press, 1996.

Johnsgard, Paul A. *The Nature of Nebraska: Ecology and Biodiversity*. Lincoln: University of Nebraska Press, 2001.

Kittredge, William. "The Good Rain and the Wild." In *Wallace Stegner: Man and Writer*, edited by Charles E. Rankin, 39–42. Albuquerque: University of New Mexico Press, 1996.

Kowalewski, Michael. "Bioregional Perspectives in American Literature." In *Regionalism Reconsidered: New Approaches to the Field*, edited by David Jordan, 29–46. New York: Gale, 1994.

———. "Writing in Place: The New American Regionalism." *American Literary History* 6, no. 1 (1994): 171–83.

Krall, Florence R. *Ecotone: Wayfaring on the Margins*. Albany: State University of New York Press, 1994.

Kroetsch, Robert. "Disunity as Unity." In *The Lovely Treachery of Words: Essays New and Selected*, 21–33. Oxford: Oxford University Press, 1989.

Kunstler, James Howard. *The Geography of Nowhere: The Rise and Decline of America's Man-Made Landscape*. New York: Touchstone, 1993.

Lavin, Stephen J., Fred M. Shelley, and J. Clark Archer, eds. *Atlas of the Great Plains*. Lincoln: University of Nebraska Press, 2011.

Lefebvre, Henri. *The Production of Space*. Translated by Donald Nicholson-Smith. Oxford: Blackwell, 1991.

Leopold, Aldo. *A Sand County Almanac: And Sketches Here and There*. 1949. Reprinted, Oxford: Oxford University Press, 1989.

Lewis, G. Malcolm. "Maps, Mapmaking, and Map Use by Native North Americans." *The History of Cartography*. Vol. 2, bk. 3, of *Cartography in the Traditional African, American, Arctic, Australian, and Pacific Societies*, edited by David Woodward and G. Malcolm Lewis, 51–133. Chicago: University of Chicago Press, 1998.

Lopez, Barry, ed. *Home Ground: Language for an American Landscape*. San Antonio: Trinity University Press, 2006.

Lynch, Tom, Cheryll Glotfelty, and Karla Armbruster, eds. *The Bioregional Imagination: Literature, Ecology, and Place*. Athens: University of Georgia Press, 2012.

MacEachren, Alan. *How Maps Work: Representation, Visualization, and Design*. New York: Guilford, 1995.

Manning, Richard. *Grassland: The History, Biology, Politics, and Promise of the American Prairie*. New York: Penguin, 1995.

Marshall, Ian. *Storyline: Exploring the Literature of the Appalachian Trail*. Charlottesville: University of Virginia Press, 1998.

Martone, Michael. "The Flatness." In *A Sense of Place: Essays in Search of the Midwest*, edited by Michael Martone, 29–33. Iowa: University of Iowa Press, 1988.

Matthews, Anne. *Where the Buffalo Roam: The Storm Over the Revolutionary Plan to Restore America's Great Plains*. New York: Grove, 1992.

McDowell, Michael J. "The Bakhtinian Road to Ecological Insight." In *The Ecocriticism Reader: Landmarks in Literary Ecology*, edited by Cheryll Glotfelty and Harold Fromm, 371–91. Athens: University of Georgia Press, 1996.

McPhee, John. *Annals of the Former World*. New York: Farrar, Straus and Giroux, 1998.

———. *Basin and Range*. New York: Farrar, Straus and Giroux, 1981.

———. *Crossing the Craton*. Bk. 5 of *Annals of the Former World*. New York: Farrar, Straus and Giroux, 2000.

———. "The Gravel Page." In *Irons in the Fire*, 81–147. New York: Farrar, Straus and Giroux, 1997.

———. *Rising from the Plains*. New York: Farrar, Straus and Giroux, 1986.

Mitchell, Charles. "Reclaiming the Sacred Landscape: Terry Tempest Williams, Kathleen Norris, and the Other Nature Writing." *Women's Studies* 32, no. 2 (2003): 165–82.

Momaday, N. Scott. *The Way to Rainy Mountain*. Illustrated by Al Momaday. Albuquerque: University of New Mexico Press, 1969.

Moul, Francis. *The National Grasslands: A Guide to America's Undiscovered Treasures*. Lincoln: University Of Nebraska Press, 2006.

Nabhan, Gary. *Cross-Pollinations: The Marriage of Science and Poetry*. Minneapolis: Milkweed, 2004.

Naramore Maher, Susan. "Deep Mapping the Great Plains: Surveying the Literary Cartography of Place." *Western American Literature* 36, no. 1 (2001): 4–24.

Nickerson, Sheila. *Disappearance: A Map: A Meditation on Death and Loss in the High Latitudes*. New York: Doubleday, 1996.

Norris, Kathleen. *Dakota: A Spiritual Geography*. Boston: Houghton Mifflin, 1993.

O'Brien, Dan. *Buffalo for the Broken Heart: Restoring Life to a Black Hills Ranch*. New York: Random House, 2001.

Olsen, Brett J. "Wallace Stegner and the Environmental Ethic: Environmentalism as a Rejection of Western Myth." *Western American Literature* 29, no. 2 (1994): 123–42.

Omhovère, Claire. "The Female Body as Garrison in Three Prairie Biotexts." In *Toward Defining the Prairies: Region, Culture, and History*, edited by Robert Wardhaugh, 179–94. Winnipeg: University of Manitoba Press, 2001.

Palliser, John. *Rambles and Adventures of a Hunter in the Prairies*. 1853. Reprinted, Rutland VT: Charles E. Tuttle, 1969.

Price, John T. *Not Just Any Land: A Personal and Literary Journey into the American Grasslands*. Lincoln: University of Nebraska Press, 2004.

———. "What This Prairie Will Awaken." *Organization and Environment* 11, no. 3 (1998): 356–62.

Pringle, Heather. "Landscapes of the Interior." *Canadian Geographic* 116, no. 6 (1996): 86.

Quantic, Diane Dufva. *The Nature of the Place: A Study of Great Plains Fiction*. Lincoln: University of Nebraska Press, 1995.

Reaves, Gerri. *Mapping the Private Geography: Autobiography, Identity, and America*. Jefferson NC: McFarland, 2001.

Ricou, Laurie. "Imprinting Landscapes." *Canadian Literature* 157 (1998): 185–89.

Robertson, Jamie. "Henry Adams, Wallace Stegner, and the Search for a Sense of Place in the West." In *Critical Essays on Wallace Stegner*, edited by Anthony Arthur, 90–97. Boston: G. K. Hall, 1982.

Ronald, Ann. *Ghost West: Reflections Past and Present*. Norman: University of Oklahoma Press, 2002.

Ronda, James P. "'A Chart in His Way': Indian Cartography and the Lewis and Clark Expedition." In *Mapping the North American Plains*, edited by Frederick C. Luebke, Frances W. Kaye, and Gary E. Moulton, 81–91. Norman: University of Oklahoma Press, 1987.

Roorda, Randall. "Deep Maps in Eco-Literature." *Michigan Quarterly Review* 40, no. 1 (2001): 257–72.

Ryden, Kent. *Mapping the Invisible Landscape: Folklore, Writing, and the Sense of Place*. Iowa City: University of Iowa Press, 1993.

Savage, Candace. *A Geography of Blood: Unearthing Memory from a Prairie Landscape*. Vancouver BC: Greystone Books, 2012.

———. *Prairie: A Natural History*. Vancouver BC: Greystone Books, 2011.

Simpson, Leanne. "Listening to Our Ancestors: Re-Building Indigenous Nations in the Face of Environmental Destruction." In *Every Grain of Sand: Canadian Perspectives on Ecology and Environment*, edited by J. A. Wainwright, 121–34. Waterloo: Wilfred Laurier University Press, 2004.

Soja, Edward W. *Thirdspace: Journeys to Los Angeles and Other Real-and-Imagined Places*. Oxford: Blackwell, 1996.

Stafford, Kim R. *Having Everything Right: Essays of Place*. New York: Penguin, 1987.

Stamm, Henry E., IV. *People of the Wind River: The Eastern Shoshones, 1825–1900*. Norman: University of Oklahoma Press, 1999.

Stegner, Wallace. *The American West as Living Space*. Ann Arbor: University of Michigan Press, 1987.

———. *Where the Bluebird Sings to the Lemonade Springs*. New York: Penguin, 1992.

———. *Wolf Willow: A History, a Story, and a Memory of the Last Plains Frontier*. 1962. Reprint, New York: Penguin, 1990.

Stegner, Wallace, and Richard W. Etulain. "Biography." In *Stegner: Conversations on History and Literature*, 1–19. 1983. Reprint, Reno: University of Nevada Press, 1996.

Stevens, Barbara. "John McPhee's *Annals of the Former World*: Geology, Culture, and a Fountain of Metaphor." In *Coming into McPhee Country: John McPhee and the Art of Literary Nonfiction*, edited by O. Alan Weltzien and Susan N. Maher, 226–41. Salt Lake City: University of Utah Press, 2003.

Thacker, Robert. *The Great Prairie Fact and Literary Imagination*. Albuquerque: University of New Mexico Press, 1989.

Thayer, Robert L., Jr. *LifePlace: Bioregional Thought and Practice*. Berkeley: University of California Press, 2003.

Tilden, Norma. "Stratigraphies: Writing a Suspect Terrain." *Biography* 25, no. 1 (2002): 25–45.

Tuan, Yi-Fu. *Space and Place: The Perspective of Experience* Minneapolis: University of Minnesota Press, 1977.

———. *Topophilia: A Study of Environmental Perception, Attitudes, and Values*. New York: Prentice-Hall, 1974. Reprint, New York: Columbia University Press, 1990.

Van Noy, Rick. "A Plate Tectonics of Language: Geology as a Vernacular Science." In *Coming into McPhee Country: John McPhee and the Art of Literary Nonfiction*, edited by O. Alan Weltzien and Susan N. Maher, 209–25. Salt Lake City: University of Utah Press, 2003.

———. *Surveying the Interior: Literary Cartographers and the Sense of Place.* Reno: University of Nevada Press, 2003.

Walker, Pamela. "The Necessity of Narrative in William Least Heat-Moon's *Blue Highways* and *PrairyErth*." *Great Plains Quarterly* 14, no. 4 (1994): 287–97.

Wall, Eamonn. "Digging Into the West: Tim Robinson's Deep Landscapes." *Reflective Landscapes of the Anglophone Countries*, edited by Pascale Guibert, 133–46. Amsterdam: Rodopi, 2009.

———. "Walking: Tim Robinson's *Stones of Aran*." *New Hibernian Review* 12, no. 3 (2008): 66–79.

Waxham, Ethel. *Lady's Choice: Ethel Waxham's Journals and Letters, 1905–1910*, edited by Barbara Love and Frances Love Friodevaux. Albuquerque: University of New Mexico Press, 1997.

Webb, Walter Prescott. *The Great Plains.* 1931. Reprint, Lincoln: Bison Press, 1981.

Weltzien, O. Alan. "A Topographical Map of Words: Parables of Cartography in William Least Heat-Moon's *PrairyErth*." *Great Plains Quarterly* 19, no. 2 (Spring 1999): 107–22.

West, Elliott. *The Contested Plains: Indians, Goldseekers, and the Rush to Colorado.* Lawrence: University Press of Kansas, 1998.

———. "Stegner, Storytelling, and Western Identity." In *Wallace Stegner: Man and Writer*, edited by Charles E. Rankin, 61–71. Albuquerque: University of New Mexico Press, 1996.

———. *The Way to the West: Essays on the Central Plains.* Albuquerque: University of New Mexico Press, 1995.

White, Matt. *Prairie Time: A Blackland Portrait.* College Station: Texas A&M University Press, 2006.

Wilson, Edward O. *Consilience: The Unity of Knowledge.* New York: Vintage, 1998.

Wishart, David J., ed. *Encyclopedia of the Great Plains.* Lincoln: University of Nebraska Press, 2004.

Wisner, William H. "The Perilous Self: Loren Eiseley and the Reticence of Autobiography." *Sewanee Review*: 113, no. 1 (2005): 84–95.

Wood, Denis. *The Power of Maps.* New York: Guilford, 1992.

Worster, Donald. *A River Running West: The Life of John Wesley Powell.* Oxford: Oxford University Press, 2001.

———. *Dust Bowl: The Southern Plains in the 1930s.* Oxford: Oxford University Press, 1979.

———. *Under Western Skies: Nature and History in the American West.* New York: Oxford University Press, 1992.

INDEX

adaptation, 16, 34, 139, 140, 151, 171; communal, 27, 78–79, 99–100, 102, 104, 178; evolutionary, 26, 67, 74, 83, 85–86, 90, 91, 93, 113–14; as heroic, 7–8; individual, 126, 149–50, 151; of language, 169; resistance to, 173; as spiritual discipline, 187; stories and, 6, 7–8

affection for land, 178

aftermath, definition of, 14

agriculture: economy and, 63, 158, 173–75; extractive, 8, 27, 67, 77, 78, 134, 143–45, 155, 204n23; and farm crisis, 170, 171, 173, 182; maladaptive, 9, 102, 174; monocultures and, 173, 174; sustainable practices of, 27, 67, 99, 100–104

Allister, Mark, 156; *Refiguring the Map of Sorrow*, 202n24

All the Strange Hours (Eiseley), 108, 109

America and Americanism, 203n37

The American West as Living Space (Stegner), 138

animalized water, 111

animals. *See* fauna

Annals of the Former World (McPhee), 18, 28, 120, 122

Appadurai, Arjun, xvi

aquifers, 175

archaeology, 41–42, 148, 155–56

Assembling California (McPhee), 122, 135–37

Atlas of the Great Plains (Lavin, Shelley, and Archer), 189n5, 198n31

Averill, Thomas Fox, 56–57

axis of identity, 142

Bachelard, Gaston, xii, 116; *La poétique de l'espace*, x

Back in Keith County (Janovy), viii, 88

Bair, Bruce: *Good Land*, 201–2n15

Bair, Julene, 29, 30, 139; *One Degree West*, 140, 141, 142–49

Bair family, 201–2n15

Bakhtin, M. M., 11, 12, 58

Bakken oil fields, 204n23

Bamforth, Douglas B.: "Bison," 198n31

Basin and Range (McPhee), 122

Becoming Native to This Place (Jackson), 74, 100–104, 153

belonging, 161

Berry, Wendell, 173, 178

Between Grass and Sky (Hasselstrom), 159

Bevis, William, 8

biodiversity, 153; loss, 91–92

biology, 16–17

biomass, 14, 79

biome, Great Plains, 26, 71–104; alteration of, 3–4, 7, 37, 44, 74, 76, 77, 98, 155, 173–78; fire and, 164; humans as part of, 6, 78, 91–92, 99–100, 104, 155, 183, 186;

Dirty Thirties, 53
Disappearance (Nickerson), 197n2
"discontinuous" place, 53, 54
displacement: of the descendents of colonizers, 47, 142–43, 158, 159, 167; identity and, 29–30, 158, 159, 167; of Native Americans, 2–3, 4, 37, 44–45, 46–47, 65, 82, 101, 102. *See also* roots and routes
Dodge, Grenville, 124
Dorling, Daniel: *Mapping*, 196n50
drought, 53, 78
dump, town, 41–42, 53
Duncan, James, 62
Dunwoody, Duane, 99
Dunwoody Pond (Janovy), 73, 88, 91–98

"earth-bonding," 27, 33–34, 78, 88, 99, 163, 169–71
earthworm, 78
Eastend SK, 35–56, 149–58
ecological illiteracy, 101
ecology, 43, 64, 71–104; in deep maps, 12, 16, 72, 73, 91; disruption of, 8, 37, 44; historical, 78; restoration, 84, 86, 99, 103; tools for studying, 96–97. *See also* adaptation
economic inequality, 133, 173
economy: extractive, 102, 103, 176, 178, 204n23; greed and, 178; history of, 129; hubris and, 33; *vs.* laws of nature, 186; loss of humanity and, 92, 153; maps and, 58; Wyoming and, 28–29, 129, 132–34
Ecotone (Krall), 194n101
"ecotone," metaphor of, 27–28, 194n101
education: about Great Plains, 40–41, 46; and field research, 27, 97–98
Eiseley, Loren, 15–16, 24–25, 28, 108–19, 137

—Works: *All the Strange Hours*, 108, 109; "The Flow of the River," 111, 115, 116; *The Immense Journey*, 25, 33, 107, 110–19, 137, 199n19; *The Night Country*, 194n91; "The Slit," 15–16, 110–11, 112–15
Elkhorn Ranch, 204n23
Elmdale KS, 65
embodied narrative. *See* somatic discourse
Emma Chase Café, 60, 196n47
empire. *See* colonization; settlement
encountering place, 16, 17, 36, 75, 87, 90–91, 96, 108, 115, 120, 153
Encyclopedia of the Great Plains (Wishart), vii, 123, 198n31, 200n49
"energy colonization," 129, 133
energy extraction, 103, 126–27, 129, 132–33, 134
entrada, 100–101, 102
environmental consciousness, 12, 50, 55, 72, 88, 171. *See also* Buell, Lawrence
environmental degradation, 19–20, 98–99, 102–3, 173–78, 186, 204n23; bison and, 81, 82–83; empire and, 36–37, 101; energy and, 132–33; farming and, 78, 82, 144–45, 173–75; loss of humanity and, 92
environmentalism, xviii; aesthetics and, 12; deep map genre and, xv, 12, 34; frontier myths and, 53–54
Erma's Desire (Raimondi), viii, ix–x, xviii–xix
ethics, 55
ethics and writing, 12
Etulain, Richard W., 55, 179
Europeans: history and culture of, 41, 46, 49, 57, 157, 192n37, 195n11; prairie misunderstood by, 192n37

www.ingramcontent.com/pod-product-compliance
Lightning Source LLC
Chambersburg PA
CBHW030357100426
42812CB00028B/2748/J